Bawdy Ballads

Bawdy Ballads
Compiled and Edited by Ed Cray

Omnibus Press
London/Sydney/Cologne

First published in Great Britain 1970 by
Anthony Blond Limited, 56 Doughty Street, London WC1

This edition © Copyright 1989 Omnibus Press
(A Division of Book Sales Limited)

Cover designed by Carroll, Dempsey and Thirkell

ISBN 0.7119.1805.8
Order No. OP 45343

Exclusive distributors:

Book Sales Limited
8/9 Frith Street,
London W1V 5TZ, UK.

Music Sales Corporation
225 Park Avenue South,
New York, NY 10003, USA.

Music Sales Pty. Limited
120 Rothschild Avenue,
Rosebery, NSW 2018, Australia.

To the Music Trade only:
Music Sales Limited
8/9 Frith Street,
London W1V 5TZ, UK.

Printed in England by
St. Edmundsbury Press,
Bury St. Edmunds, Suffolk.

Contents

One may cover over secret actions,
but to be silent on what all the world
knows, and things which have had effects
which are public and of so much consequence
is an inexcusable defect.

—Montaigne, *On the Duty of Historians*

For two teachers,
Sara N. Shaffer,
my mother,
and
Wayland D. Hand,
my friend

Introduction

Until recently, the open publication of a collection of bawdy songs would have been impossible. The guardians of public morality, self-appointed or legally constituted, would have seen that that would be prevented. But a new found maturity in matters sexual, reflected in court decisions, New Wave films and best-seller lists, has in recent years changed that sorry situation.

Yet even during the great age of the censor in England and America —roughly 200 years —the self-righteous could not completely suppress bawdry. However much they bowdlerized, banned and even denied the very existence of erotica, out of sight was certainly not out of mind.

While the pillars of society, the "good" people, turned Pecksniffian noses skyward, bawdry flourished, and even crept into parlor-polite circles.

There are dozens of stories told of noted people who have known and sung some of the ballads and songs in this collection. In his definitive study of *The Limerick,* Gershon Legman notes that Learned Hand, one of the more influential jurists of the twentieth century, sang a version of "The Wayward Boy" for Oliver Wendell Holmes and Felix Frankfurter, those equally eminent figures in American law. While Legman's report is not first hand, it is true that Judge Hand recorded other, less randy ballads for the Archive of American Folk Song in the Library of Congress, and it is a rare folk singer who does not know at least one song he considers to be "off-color."

In his widely noted, reluctantly concurring opinion in the case of *Roth* v. *United States,* Judge Jerome Frank made discretely anonymous reference to other learned bearers of bawdy oral tradition:

> Those whose views most judges know best are other lawyers. Judges can and should take judicial notice that, at many gatherings of lawyers at bar association or of alumni of our leading law schools, tales are told fully as "obscene" as many of those distributed by men, like defendant, convicted for violation of the obscenity statute.

Judge Frank added in a footnote this observation from an earlier opinion:

> One thinks of the lyrics sung at many such gatherings by a certain respected and conservative member of the faculty of a great law school which considers itself the most distinguished and which is the Alma Mater of many judges sitting on upper courts.[1]

Not only is the bawdy song found in such good company, but frequently it is said to be sired by equally prominent poets. Rudyard Kipling, the team of Gilbert and Sullivan, Robert Service, Gene Fowler, Ogden Nash, James Joyce, even

Alfred Lord Tennyson have all been so honored—in some cases, deservedly. Indeed, Eugene Field turned out so many of these underground ballads that friends privately published an anthology of his "secret" poems.

Still, the bawdy song needs no apologetic introduction as the consort of those in high places. It can stand or fall on its own merits—as song. If it is rarely great poetry, in the commonly accepted sense of what may or may not be great poetry, it *is* humorous. If the melodies are only a notch or two above the ditty class, they are, for all that, the borrowed melodies of popular songs or the same oft-praised tunes used for "clean" folk songs.

This borrowing, in fact, rather vexed one scholar who wrote with undisguised distaste:

> In general, the rule has been that a good traditional tune is good enough to put to spiritual uses. In fact, folk-music, morally speaking, is virtually incorruptible. Folk-tunes have within them as their inalienable birthright such a gift of purity that they are a standing contradiction of the axiom, "Evil communications corrupt good manners." They associate unhesitatingly with the dirtiest companions, and come away unsoiled. In spite of Falstaff's allusion to "filthy tunes," there never has been such a phenomenon in folk-music, apart from momentary nonce-associations.[2]

Some of those nonce-associations in the body of ribald songlore, no less than in folk song generally, are happy accidents: an occasional doggerel lyric and pedestrian tune will unite in that particular alchemy of folk song to create a song so appealing that it may persist in popularity literally for centuries.

For two hundred years, One-Eyed or One-Balled Reilly (his infirmity varies) has been melodically reamed in the following:

"Kathusalem" boasts no such age, yet it, too, contains one of those seemingly classic lines and tunes well met:

In the even younger "Fuck 'Em All," a merry-go-round tune is coupled with a sprightly internal rhyme to fashion another of those particularly effective amalgams:

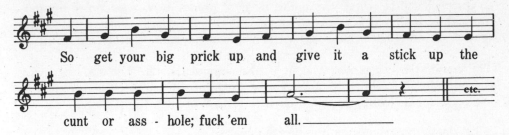

So get your big prick up and give it a stick up the cunt or ass - hole; fuck 'em all._____ etc.

Regardless of the peculiar merit, or lack of it, of an individual scrap, bawdy songs have survived when other folk songs have died, victims of urbanization and the blight of the mass media. The staying power of the bawdy song, this ability to charm or entertain successive generations of singers, is the single most important point of this collection.

The reason for this staying power is easily found: bawdy songs are funny.[3] Their appeal is elemental, more constant than most matters of public fancy; consequently, collecting bawdy lore, especially jokes and songs, is not at all difficult. The "dirty" joke is ubiquitous, a staple of cocktail parties and lunch hours, stag smokers and business conventions.

Similarly hundreds of indelicate ditties, some hoary with age, others as new as yesterday's parody, are sung in barracks and fraternity houses, in men's clubs and college dormitories, in neighborhood bars or their backrooms, anywhere the masculine atmosphere is conducive or the feminine companionship friendly.

At other times and in other places, many of the songs in this collection would not have been considered to be obscene. Some of the older have, in fact, survived cycles of both public approval and public censure. Times change and peoples' attitudes change with them.

Prior to the sixteenth century, the word "fuck" carried no opprobrium. Sometime after 1571, when it appeared in a poem satirizing the clergy, the word fell into disrepute, to appear only in learned dictionaries and underground literature.

As early as 1300, "shit" appears in print as a verb; "piss" is equally as old. An unexpurgated Chaucer is peppered with them; until perhaps the middle of the eighteenth century, their use was perfectly proper. Up to the fifteenth century, "cunt" meant "cunt" and there was no attempt to find new euphemism or dysphemism for this integral contributor to female fecundity.

Although it was considered to be correct from 1000 A.D. on, the word "breast" fell into disrepute with the Victorians, and was replaced by the more ambiguous "bosom." A hundred years later, "breast" was again in use, "bosom" being relegated to flowery valentines and women's clothing patterns.

According to Peter Fryer's *Mrs. Grundy, Studies in English Prudery*, the word "cock," even when it did not refer to the penis, was banned well before the Age of Queen Victoria, whose very name, irony of ironies, is now a term of opprobrium. The male chicken was a rooster after 1772. Cockroaches became just roaches in the 1820's. Haycocks were renamed haystacks at the same time.

The censorable being mercurial, it is also temperamental. The scrivener who compiled for J. Walthoe *A Collection of Epigrams* in 1735, felt constrained to apologize for including this quatrain within his "complete" anthology:

> If death must come, as oft as breath departs,
> Then he must often die, who often farts;
> And if to die be but to lose one's breath,
> Then death's a fart; and so a fart for death.

Added the chagrined editor in a footnote, "We think the coarseness and indelicacy of this epigram abundantly aton'd for by its poignancy of thought, and pleasantness of conceit, which justly entitle it to a place in this collection."

At the same time, without so much as a by-your-leave, the editor included the following epigrams:

Saving Advice to E[dmund] C[url]l, on His Advertising a Third Volume of Letters

> C——l, let me advise you, whatever betides,
> To let this third volume alone;
> The second's sufficient for all our backsides,
> So pray keep the third for your own.

Epitaph on Sally Salisbury

> Here flat on her back, but inactive at last,
> Poor Sally lies under grim death;
> Thro' the course of her vices she gallop'd so fast,
> No wonder she's now out of breath.
> To the goal of her pleasures she drove very hard,
> But was tripp'd up ere half way she ran,
> And tho' everyone fancied her life was a yard,
> Yet it prov'd to be less than a span.

And, finally:

> Storm not, brave friend, that thou hadst never yet
> Mistress, nor wife, that others did not swive;
> But, like a Christian, pardon and forget,
> For thy own pox will thy revenge contrive.[4]

If poets and parsons cannot agree upon a single measure of the obscene, lawyers can hardly do better; obscenity remains a legal as well as literary and social variable.

By 1792, each of the fourteen states ratifying the Constitution of the United States, had adopted laws providing for the prosecution of either blasphemy or profanity.[5] As early as 1712, Massachusetts made it a crime to publish "any filthy, obscene, or profane song, pamphlet, libel or mock sermon" which mimicked a religious service. Apparently, "filthy," "obscene" and "profane" referred to the anti-clerical; that which is now considered to be "obscene" little troubled the legal profession of the colony, however much it may have agitated the clergy. (It might be added, too, that even the anti-clerical might be tolerated, so long as it was not directed at the predominant Protestant faith.)

Nor were the colonists alone in their cherished conceits; the same was true in the mother country. Although there were prosecutions under various acts which made it a crime to publish "obscene" works, "obscene" was limited directly and specifically to that which offended established institutions. Great Britain did not formulate a legal test for sexual obscenity until 1868.

Not until erstwhile postal inspector Anthony Comstock mounted his crusade in the 1870's did the United States Congress get around to passing laws against mailing obscene matter, simply because that matter was sexually graphic. Paradoxically, the United States does not now find legally censorable those speeches and pronouncements which in defaming a particular religion were once felt to be criminally actionable.

Clearly, the definition of "obscene" or "prurient," the pivotal word in legal circles, is warped by subjective interpretation and shifting cultural norms. The "folk" then, as creatures of a culture which permits no little accommodation or adaptive behavior, can hardly be more certain of the meaning of the word.

Folk song collectors have reported, for example, that informants were reluctant to sing "Little Musgrave and Lady Barnard" (Child 81) because it deals in modest terms with the pair's concupiscence. The most explicit stanzas are these:

> "Lie down, lie down, little Matthy Groves,
> And keep my back from the cold;
> It is my father's shepherd boys
> A-blowing up the sheep from the fold."

> From that they fell to hugging and kissing
> And from that they fell to sleep;
> And next morning when they woke at break of day
> Lord Arnold stood at their feet.

> "And it's how do you like my fine feather-bed,
> And it's how do you like my sheets?
> And it's how do you like my gay ladie
> That lies in your arms and sleeps?"

"Very well do I like your fine feather-bed.
Very well do I like your sheets
But much better do I like your gay ladie
That lies in my arms and sleeps."

"Now get you up, little Matthy Groves,
And all your clothes put on;
For it never shall be said in Old England
That I slew a naked man."[6]

The very unwillingness of the cuckolded lord to kill the naked lover bespeaks its own prudery, too.

However much a sweet mountain singer might have been reluctant to offend what he imagined were the sensibilities of the well-dressed gentleman from the university in the early part of this century, the song has little which would be considered offensive fifty years later.

Were this not vagary enough, to the temporal and temperamental nature of obscenity must be added what would appear to be levels or gradations of the obscene, reflected in an inordinate number of adjectives which describe all that might be called bawdy: improper, coarse, risque, ribald, blue, basic, dirty, gross, prurient, indelicate, rakish, smutty, roguish, indecent, lewd, loose, racy, randy, crude, and, of course, obscene. Except to the most puritanical, these are not synonyms; their specific meaning varies—from word to word and from individual to individual.

Still, in the third quarter of the twentieth century, a folk song is considered censorable in some quarters if it is more or less specific in dealing with matters amorous, if it discusses excretory functions and products, if it uses such tabooed words as "fuck," "shit," "piss," "cunt," or the more indelicate euphemisms for these.

Even if a song does not concern itself with biological functions, a sprinkling of currently prohibited words (especially when they are involved in hard-to-edit rhymes) is enough to ban a song. In "The Lehigh Valley," for example, the triple rhyme of the last line—"I'll hunt the runt who stole my cunt"—simply cannot be edited in a fashion suitable for presentation to polite company. Into locked files went this hobo classic.

Worse still, the bowdlerization which might permit publication can be debilitating. The first stanza of "The Lehigh Valley," with chip on shoulder, runs:

"Don't look at me that way, mister;
I didn't shit in your seat.
I just came down from the Lehigh Valley
With my balls all covered with sleet."

Edited, this has appeared as:

> "Don't look at me that way, mister;
> I didn't sit in your seat.
> I've just come down from the Lehigh Valley
> With my beard all covered with sleet."

The redacted text leaves all the rhymes in the right place, but the rewrite lacks the virility of the original—a virility which the mock lament demands. After all, the narrator *is* a former pimp hunting the city slicker who stole his true love and meal ticket away.

Until recently, the collector who gathered a bawdy song or tale was permitted three alternatives: he could make no mention of the text at all (a hard choice); he could merely insert ellipses for the forbidden words or lines; or he could re-write the offensive portions.

At best, whatever the course elected, the result was uncomfortable. One editor who elected to bowdlerize his texts—carefully telling the reader he was doing so—was forced to concede that he could not print *en clair* a rare find in "Put Your Shoulder Next to Mine and Pump Away":

> The pumping song we now give is in print for the first time. Owing to its ribald theme, much "blue-pencilling" has been done. It was popular in British ships only. It may have given rise to the popular war-song "Roll Me Over in the Clover!"[7]

The irony is inescapable. The editor felt constrained to edit a forebearer of an equally ribald ditty which is one of the most popular of bawdy songs in the United States, known and sung by literally thousands.

Those who were unwilling to edit the songs into grotesque self-parodies filed away some of their choicest finds. Arthur Kyle Davis, Jr., surveyed the reports of "Our Goodman," the expurgated version of "Five Nights Drunk," noted its occurrence in fifteen states and added, "If ribald versions were collected and printed, no doubt every state would be represented."[8] The same could be said for most of the songs in this collection.

This censorship has created far more problems than publication would have raised. Students of American culture, whatever their particular specialty, have much to learn from unexpurgated folklore in general, and the bawdy song in particular. So obvious a notion is hardly new. Ninety years ago, Henry Spencer Ashbee, the pseudonymous herald of English erotic studies, argued:

> I hold that for the historian, or the psychologist, these [erotic] books, whether in accordance with, or contrary to the prejudices and tendencies of the age, must be taken into account as well as, if not in preference to those in many other and better cultivated fields of literature. . . . I main-

,tain that no production of the human brain should be ignored, entirely disregarded, or allowed to become utterly lost; for every writing, however trifling or insignificant it may seem, has a value for the *true* student, in estimating the individual who wrote it, or the period in which it was produced.[9]

Whether the timid bibliographer knew it or not, a good number of cherished beliefs and scholarly shibboleths are questioned by bawdy lore, trifling or insignificant as it may seem.

Anthropologists are aware of this; a few, such as Westermarck, Boas and Malinowski, early dealt with the bawdy—as long as it came from so-called "primitive" or non-literate people. With few exceptions—one most notably—similar lore from the "primitives" and non-literates, let alone the educated, in American society has yet to receive the same serious study.[10]

The long and growing shelf of American folk song collections barely hints at the wealth of bawdy song still in oral tradition. This is ironic, for even as folklorists lament the passing of traditional folk song, the bawdy song flourishes. Indeed, bawdy song may be the only form of folk song—with the possible exception of children's street songs—invigorated by the same mass media which have all but destroyed the familiar patterns of oral transmission.[11]

The very variety of the tradition has only been suggested by the publications of earlier scholars, especially F. J. Furnivall and John S. Farmer.[12] Their work was presented in privately printed, subscribed and limited runs as if to insure their books would have little impact and that only upon presumably older pedants immune to priapic compulsion.

There are still other hints that bawdy song is not the exception which published collections would suggest it is.

The foremost collector of Scots folk song prior to this century was Robbie Burns who had more than 360 songs published for public consumption. Some Burns noted down from the folk singers and instrumentalists he happened to meet, sending the songs on to his publisher with little or no changes. Others he either edited heavily or dressed with new lyrics. According to Sidney Goodsir Smith's introduction to *The Merry Muses of Caledonia*, many of the songs Burns heard on his travels in the countryside, if not most, were indecorous.

In addition to the 360 songs Burns handled which were published, another 100 were too basic for publication, and remained in his special notebook for bawdy songs. Some saw print in a skimpy book published for a group of Burns' fellow roisterers, the Crochallan Fencibles; the great majority did not. As Burns wrote in a letter, "If that species of Compisition be the Sin against the Haly Ghaist, 'I am the most offending soul alive.' "

Discount if you must the statement that *most* of the songs Burns heard on his rambles were somewhat bawdy, the fact remains that some 20 percent of Burns' surviving songs are ribald. This proportion alone suggests that perhaps one in five Scots songs is censorable, a proportion too large to be overlooked, as most folklorists have done in the past. Furthermore, what is true of Scots folk song may be true of Anglo-American balladry in general. We simply do not know.[13]

There would be no need for a collection of bawdy songs such as this had these ballads and verses been treated in the same forthright fashion accorded other —the uncontaminated—folk songs. The resultant gap in the literature has even served to discolor the scholarship itself.

Francis James Child, whose lifetime effort produced the misnamed *THE English and Scottish Popular Ballads* (emphasis added to that singular article), deliberately omitted from his scholarly monument such classic bawdy songs as "The Sea Crab," the many ribald versions of "Our Goodman" and "Get Up and Bar the Door." "The Darby Ram," similarly bawdy and similarly excluded, also failed to meet Child's unstated criteria for a ballad because of its episodic, unconnected narrative—technically termed a quatrain ballad—and because its main character, like those in the equally worthy "The Marriage of the Frog and the Mouse," is a quadruped. For all that, "The Darby Ram" is older by far than any of the Child ballads which were still circulating in oral tradition when that son of a Boston sailmaker completed his work.

Similarly, in detailing the contents of his mammoth motif index of folk narrative, Stith Thompson candidly admits, "Many [jests] have been omitted, particularly those whose only point is obscenity . . ." The fabliaux—satiric tales, hardly longer than jokes, which lampoon or burlesque societal institutions—are handled in similar fashion. Those "with obscenity as the only point have been excluded, though good jests with risqué elements are retained." Thompson thus must make two value judgments: He must first consider a story as more than merely obscene; and then he must consider them "good" tales. No such subjective evaluation is settled upon the non-bawdy, of course; all that available or accessible is indexed.[14]

One can understand Thompson's uneasy compromise between what he considers to be good scholarship and good citizenship. Risqué stories with some redeeming elements are indexed, for apparently the redeeming social significance of the material may be studied without reference to the bawdry. That the very pruriency of the lore, in and of itself, is worth consideration he seems to overlook, or tacitly ignore.

Nor are these scholars exceptionally modest. To judge from the published collections, one could well assume that folk singers in the English-speaking world were a curious lot, arch-Victorians all, blue-noses who sang in aching tones of unrequited love and lovers' trysts, with nary a thought to what the idealized romanticism was all about. Except for an occasional mention of babies, one might conclude that the heroes and heroines of folk song lacked sexual organs. Yet any collection of bawdy songs will indicate that this is a distorted picture, and as more of these omnibuses are put into print, the warp will be even more apparent.[15]

Nowhere is this dim-sighted humbuggery more obvious than in collections of children's lore. Trusting the collectanea in print—the exceptions are very few—one could only conclude that the youngsters are quite as sexless as their elders. But as much as parents may wish this were the case, the fact is that children learn a good deal about sex and excretion quite early in life.

A close personal friend of the editor, just six years old, recited, "A," pointing to her head, "B," pointing to her buttocks, "C," to her eyes, and then progressing from her nose to her pudenda in inch-long steps, "D, E, F, G, H, I, J, K, L, M, N, O," to end triumphantly at "P."

Moments later, she chanted what may fairly be called her first bawdy song, pointing out as she sang, her breasts, genitals and buttocks:

> Milk, milk, lemonade,
> Around the corner where fudge is made.

Material such as this is rampant among youngsters. That it has so rarely seen print may, in part, be laid to the infirmities of field workers. Kenneth S. Goldstein has warned:

> Because children's materials are so in-group oriented, there is a real challenge to the collector to obtain anything more than simply those materials which the children are willing to permit him to hear and observe. But children have a whole world of private beliefs, rhymes, and erotica which only a few sensitive and understanding adults are ever allowed to penetrate.[16]

Yet this is only half of the explanation for the miserable representation of scatological and erotic lore in children's collections. The fact is that many workers have simply refused to collect this material, fearing a loss of supporting stipends, social standing or rapport in the community.

Nonetheless, there is a sexual content to children's lore, some of it of respectable age and surprising geographical dispersal. About 1944, the editor was singing to the tune of "My Bonnie Lies Over the Ocean":

> My bonnie lies over the ocean.
> My bonnie lies over the sea.
> My father lies over my mother,
> And that's how I came to be.

That the editor was not unduly precocious is substantiated by the fact that twenty years later, Mrs. Jacqueline Brunke garnered the same rhyme from her ten-year-old daughter in West Los Angeles.

The twice-told tale of Johnny Fuckerfaster and Mary Holdstill is yet another example of the continuity of this lore:

> Once there was a boy named John Fuckerfaster and a girl named Mary Holdstill. One day, Mary was walking past John's house and John came out and said, "Mary, I will give you two bags of candy if you will come in my house, and four more if you will come in my bedroom and take off your dress. She did and she laid down and he began fucking her. His mother came in and said, "John Fuckerfaster and Mary Holdstill!"[17]

This joke was a favorite twenty years earlier when the editor first heard it in the schoolyard. Roger Abrahams had it from Philadelphia Negroes, describing it as one of "the first kind of joke a child learns and remembers . . ."[18]

To the historicity of such children's lore, one can add a geographical dimension little appreciated. Afanasyev's *Stories from the Folk-lore of Russia* reprints a tale purportedly told by Ukrainians sometime about the middle of the nineteenth century:

> A louse met a flea. "Where are you going?"
>
> "I am going to pass the night in a woman's slit."
>
> "And I am going into a woman's backside."
>
> They part. The next day they met again. "Well, how did you sleep?" asked the louse.
>
> "Oh, don't talk about it. I was so frightened. A kind of bald head came to me and hunted me about. I jumped here and there, but he continued to pursue me. At last he spat on me and went away."
>
> "Well, gossip, there were two persons knocking about outside the hole I was in. I hid myself, and they continued to push about, but at last they went away."[19]

A similar story narrating the adventures of three fleas who spend the night upon and within the body of a famous movie actress—one imagines the identity of the hostess changes with the fortunes of film popularity—currently circulates among school children in Los Angeles. One flea nestles between her breasts but finds the heaving landscape to be unsettling. Another beds down in her navel, but complains of the rumbling beneath him which disturbs his sleep. The third finds "a cave," enjoys the deep warmth, but is routed by "some bald-headed bastard who kept spitting at me."

The very popularity of such lore and its persistence in oral tradition over time and space is another reason for the study of bawdy song. While collectors beat ever more remote bushes, bringing to light ever fewer folk songs, the bawdy song flourishes.

Urbanization and the mass media have made self-entertainment less a necessity of life in recent years. Television in the living room has replaced the family musicale in the parlor. Motion pictures have pre-empted the play-party, the square dance, the house-raising, the corn-shucking. The phonograph record has supplanted the homemade music of local, self-taught musicians and singers.

With the passing of the need for local or community musicians, so have passed the songs, ballads and instrumental tunes these musicians carried. The recovery of a good text of one of the 305 English and Scottish ballads raised to peerhood by Francis James Child—during the first part of this century reports of Child ballads were commonplace—is now comparatively rare. Old-Timey Fiddlers' Contests are staged to artificially inseminate a lagging enthusiasm; the winners frequently turn out to be professional or semi-professional instrumentalists. Creatures, or victims, of this mass culture, younger singers are not learning the songs their grandparents cherished. The old order passeth.

Or almost passeth. Two types of folk song are stubborn exceptions to this general rule: children's rhymes and bawdy songs. These have flourished, each for good reason.

Children's lore is the product of a very special social group. For all the imposed activities which teachers, recreation leaders and parents hope will mold the youngsters of America, there remains a vast body of lore which children stubbornly use among themselves. It provides an in-group form of communication, a code, or a password to cross the boundaries between the adult's and the child's domains. This lore is sometimes disrespectful, frequently fanciful, often antagonistic; it is the jargon of throttled rebellion. It flourishes because all of the organized recreational activities in the world cannot supplant the temporary independence offered by a game of stickball or kick-the-can played in a vacant lot or busy street.

The great bearers of children's verbal lore, the five- through ten-year-olds, have only partially learned the art of conformity. They do conform to parental standards, far more than parents sometimes think; they have early on learned the taboos; they know the ways to adult, that is, societal approval. Yet within their games, rituals and rhymes—as "cute" as they may seem—are the seeds of the rebellion, the outraged protest against cultural discipline, and the means to provide the temporary security of identification with a group of similarly afflicted children. The rebellion is masked now, as it will be later, when as adults they will confront and struggle with ill-defined, compelling desires to reject responsibility, to rebel, however briefly.[20]

As they grow older, these five- to ten-year-olds are more and more pressured into adaptive conformity. In direct proportion to the growing force of this inevitability, they forget the songs and folksay of their childhood, replacing this with similar lore and rituals deemed acceptable adult behavior. In the meantime, however, there are always other children to learn the "right" way to play hopscotch, or jump double dutch, or choose up sides on a playground.

Bawdy songs are remembered and sung by adults because they, too, feel a need to "rebel." The prevailing public opinion, or what the singers feel is the prevailing public opinion, that somehow bawdy songs are "dirty" or not fit for polite society permits the bawdy songster to thumb his nose at convention even as he relieves his own fears and guilt with laughter. Further, he must confine his songs to the stag smoker or the fraternity party, far from prying ears. The very locale of the presentation lends a covert, "underground" sense of group identification—a (usually) masculine camaraderie or "we-feeling" so necessary for the emotionally mature male.[21]

Freudian-oriented psychiatrists have probed for the social significance of obscenity, following the lead of the master's *Wit and Its Relation to the Unconscious*. According to Freud and his followers, the function of bawdy lore is to permit people to air or momentarily to relieve their fears of matters which are ordinarily taboo in polite society. By laughing at a joke about castration, the listener is coping with the massive fear most American males have of losing their own manhood. By laughing at the antic bedding of One-Eyed Reilly's daughter and the subsequent sodomy perpetrated upon that lady's irate father, the listener is responding to his own desires to knock off the pubescent girl living across the street. The deed is done, One-Eyed Reilly violated as well, the listener has vicariously participated, and escaped punishment—all because the wit of the song makes the unmentionable momentarily acceptable.

Because the story is funny and "O'Reilly's Daughter" an indecorous delight, the listener laughs. The wit, as Freud had it, is the license to thumb his nose at convention; without wit, as singer and audience define it, the song or the story has no point, no saving grace, and no social function.

Commenting on the "smutty" joke (his term), the analogue in prose to the bawdy songs in this collection, Martin Grotjahn asserts that off-color stories

> pretend convincingly to be aimed at sexual satisfaction. Actually they serve, like wit, as the outlet of disguised aggression and for the satisfaction of infantile pleasures. While doing so, they continue to work on residual anxieties and conflicts which began in the time before the oedipal phase of our development.[22]

Grotjahn sees the "smutty" joke as something other than wit, or the "wit" of Freud's essay. Freud makes no such distinction. For him laughter is the result of the sudden unleashing of the forbidden as the result of wit. Suppressed or repressed, this forbidden thought is triggered by the aggression of the witticism. The listeners disguise their own vicarious aggression unconsciously; that aggression emerges in the conscious as harmless play, and in the company of others as laughter.

There are some exceptions to the Freudian argument that the public function of bawdy song is to entertain. One is the work song "Sound Off," which may amuse, but also sets the cadence of the march. Another is the couplet sung to the opening bars of "The Billboard March," and used as a form of social control of those who become too friendly with people in authority:

> There's a brown ring around his nose,
> And every day it grows and grows.

These exceptions notwithstanding, laughter remains crucial to the bawdy song. If the song is not humorous, the listener is left with fear and guilt unassuaged by amusement. The loss of laughter is disastrous not only to the quality of the song, but to the individual, too; the humorless fellow who cannot chuckle at the dirty joke or bawdy song is frequently the most sexually guilt-ridden.

Despite the shared *raison d'être* of bawdy songs and so-called "dirty" jokes, their content is not the same. As Gershon Legman has pointed out in his article, "The Rationale of the Dirty Joke," that form of humorous folk-tale falls largely into two classes: those with sexual themes involving castration or pseudo-castration, and the scatological. The sexual jokes dealing with castration, says Legman, have one purpose: to reassure the listener with laughter; the scatological joke's function is to shock.[23]

Unlike the dirty joke, the bawdy folk song, humorous though it may be, is rarely devoted in its entirety to either the subject of castration or to matters scatological. These themes may appear, as incidental details in ballads or as occasional verses inserted into portmanteau songs like "I-Yi-Yi-Yi" (limericks in that case), but they are rarely the focus of such songs.

Castration—in the form of contracting venereal disease—appears frequently in songs with a strong occupational currency. "The Chisholm Trail," "The Fire Ship," "Lee's Hoochie," "The Sewing Machine," among others, have an occupational circulation and deal with the problem. Similarly, "The Gay Caballero," lacking the occupational currency, is also a diseased whoremaster's complaint.

While there are some bawdy songs which may be considered to be homosexual—a psychoanalytic form of castration—none has achieved wide currency in oral tradition. What few mimeographed smirks which have turned up are of dubious currency *as songs* and bear the heavy hand of literary creation. Sodomy, buggery, and related acts usually take place, as in "The Tinker" or "Christopher Columbo," only after the horny hero has run through the available women. In effect, he is reasserting his super-masculinity by a homosexual act.

The most explicit example of this occurs in the song, "Sam MacColl":

> If the girls want no more, want no more,
> Or they say they're very sore, very sore,
> If the girls moan and weep,
> Or they say they want to sleep,
> I try horses, cows, and sheep, cows and sheep.

xxiv

Bawdy songs are concerned with heterosexual matters. Their viewpoint is masculine. Sexual intercourse, often in heroic bouts; penes of equally heroic proportions; cunts worthy of such cocks; seduction of the innocent but agreeable maiden—this is the stuff of bawdry.

It is also the stock material of that which, for lack of a better definition, is labelled "hard-core" pornography, though there is a major difference in the handling of these between the two media.

Pornography is rarely humorous. Indeed, if it has any distinguishing characteristic, it is this lack of humor. Pornography is grim in its determination, its single-minded insistence upon clinical detail.

Not so the bawdy song. There is little time for erotic detail; situations are boldly sketched in a line or two. The bawdy song rushes to climax the scene in laughter; the pornographer grinds relentlessly for an erection.

It is probably no accident that rape rarely figures in bawdy song. Seemingly, the social—and sexual—stigma attached to forcible entry makes such a subject, by its very nature, beyond the bounds of true masculinity. The rapist uses force; the hero of bawdry uses wit. He may be as much a scoundrel as the rapist, but by wit, or guile, or sexual attractiveness, by deceit or straightforward seduction, he achieves his heterosexual ends.

At the same time, rape is a staple of "hard-core" pornography, a reflection of the medium's abiding interest in sadism. That particular aberration, and its mirror image, masochism, may be rationalized in bawdy song; they do not serve as the basis for erotic episodes, openly dealt with. The brutality—genteel, to be sure—of flagellational fiction is obvious; one must read into bawdy song such sadistic satisfaction.

The pornographic world is pre-eminently a sexual *Schlauraffenland*, the erotic pervading the fantasy, fantasy pervading the erotic. The people of Pornographia are capable of unending sexual bouts, only now and again fortified by aphrodisiacs. (Their use by the characters in such fiction is a nod towards reality; the fact remains that the potions prescribed are more effective in fiction than in life.) The men ejaculate in super-human streams, again and again, past all limits of reported capability. The women are ever-willing, cardboard receptacles whose response—how different from the real world—is invariable, predictable, oriented to the gratification of their partners, male or female. Sexual intercourse results in no untoward effects. The female is rarely impregnated despite the interminable coitus. Venereal disease goes unmentioned. Nothing, not even a stray menstrual period, is permitted to intrude upon paradise.

Above all, pornography is a male-oriented art form. It is loveless, mechanistic, centered upon the act itself, not upon the emotive aspects which women in Western European cultures demand of sex.[24] Its concern apparently is to reassure the reader of his own potency.

"Hard-core" pornography—there seems to be no better phrase current—is not unlike the songs in this collection in certain fashions. Both pornography and bawdy song are all but devoid of character development, of narrative detail, of descriptive setting. Pornography eschews this material as unimportant to its main purpose: sexual titillation. Bawdy song has no time for it; the lack of characterization, of detail, of setting is a trait shared with the rest of folk balladry. As part of the larger corpus, there is every reason for bawdy song to reflect the characteristics of the whole. That folk balladry and pornography share that trait is accidental.

To some extent, a handful of the songs in this collection would seem to be closer to "hard-core" pornography than others. Like "Casey Jones," these are the exception, and even these have the requisite leavening of wit lacking in "hard-core" literature.

Most of the songs here, and most bawdy songs in oral tradition, make it clear that even the "loose" sorts who sing bawdy songs retain some form of self-restraint or cultural censorship. "Hard-core" pornography has no such limitations; sexual taboos are openly flouted, their violation explicit and glorified. (The incest taboo is particularly assaulted, perhaps because it is the most deeply held.)

This cultural censorship is reflected in a number of songs still in oral tradition. Avoiding the basic Anglo-Saxon, relying instead on the wit of the poetry, they might be fairly, if imprecisely, termed more "clever" or "naughty" than "dirty." Except by implication, they are not obscene.

"The Whang Song" is one of these "clever" efforts:

> I'll tell you a little story,
> Just a story I have heard,
> And you'll swear it's all a fable,
> But it's Gospel, every word.
> When the Lord made Father Adam,
> He danced, He laughed and sang,
> And then sewed up his belly
> With a little piece of whang.
>
> But when the Lord was finished,
> He found He'd measured wrong,
> For when the whang was knotted,
> It was several inches long.
> He said, "It's just eight inches long,
> So I think I'll let it hang,"
> And He left on Adam's belly
> That little piece of whang.
>
> But when the Lord made Mother Eve,
> I imagine He did snort,
> For He found the whang He sewed her with

Was just eight inches short.
"Twill leave an awful gap," He said,
"But I don't give a hang.
She can fight it out with Adam
For that little piece of whang."

So ever since that far-off day
When human life began,
There's been a constant struggle
'Tween the woman and the man,
But if you asked the women
And the men, they would agree,
They'd rather go on struggling
Through all eternity.[25]

In some gradation determined by the ratio of humor to the overtly shocking, the bawdy song becomes increasingly pornographic.

Thus "Aimee McPherson" appears to be more waggish than "Five Nights Drunk"; "The Ball of Kirriemuir" is more to the obscene end of the spectrum than the crapulous "Four Old Whores."

Short of some mathematical formula which allowed an absolute value to each humorous element and each "dirty" word, there can be no absolute rating of "filth"; the matter is a subjective one.

To some, or perhaps most, all of the songs in this collection are beyond the pale. Without making that value judgment, the singers themselves class the songs together for, when bawdy songs are sung, the actual "obscenity" will vary from number to number. Apparently, once beyond the singers' estimate of the contemporary community consensus—whatever that is—a song, however bawdy, is "dirty." It goes underground, to emerge only at the improper time when momentarily that consensus is waived or ignored.

This is not to suggest that the singers do not recognize that one song is less "offensive" than another, or more suitable for a mixed audience. They do. The singer's awareness of the bawdry is, though, less important than his appreciation and value of the humor within the song. After all, the function of bawdy song is to amuse the audience, be that audience only the singer, or 100 men crowded into a men's club smoker.

The forms of humor within the songs vary from the play-upon-words to the satirical, from the witty to the sly. Generally, one may suspect the hand of better-educated authors in those songs such as "Caviar Comes from Virgin Sturgeon" or "I Used to Work in Chicago" or "Roll Your Leg Over" which depend upon special knowledge or plays upon words for their humor.

A significant proportion of the songs in this collection, perhaps as high as one-half, bears these marks of a literate author at work, and the freight of a literate group of carriers. (This is especially true of parodies, a form of humor which requires something more than an ability to rhyme "moon" with "June.") While this surprisingly high proportion may be inflated by a biased sample—a majority of the informants who contributed to this collection were themselves college-educated—nonetheless, a good share of bawdy songlore still in oral tradition is the apparent product of literature creators.

There is precedent for this "literate" as opposed to "folk" origin. George Pullen Jackson spent a lifetime winnowing the traditional sources of shapenote hymns, incidentally underscoring the role of the singing school masters and hymn writers as stimulators of oral currency. Legman has flatly identified the limerick as almost exclusively the work of educated authors and the property largely of educated narrators or singers. Similarly, these same people seem to preserve graffitti.

This "literate" authorship and currency of bawdy songlore is reflected most clearly in the great number of parodies which are to be collected. Parodies of more recent origin are almost invariably set to the borrowed melodies of popular —and familiar—songs. The tune comes first; the words are written to fit the melody. This new text is patterned, to some degree, after the old, and usually there is some attempt to imitate in the first line(s) of the bawdy parody at least the first line(s) of the song vehicle.[26]

This deliberate copying immediately provides a humorous shock, in and of itself. The unexpected lyrics may be so effective as humor that nothing more than the first lines of the new song will ever be written. So it is that a parody of "The Anniversary Waltz" (actually, Ivanovichi's "Danube Waves") is set only to the tune's opening musical phrases:

Oh, how we danced on the night we were wed;
We danced and we danced 'cause the room had no bed.

On the other hand, when a bawdy song's melody is drawn from the entire stock of Anglo-American folk tunes, it would seem that the words come first and are then set to an appropriate tune, the two fitted together as seems most effective. This would be the only possible explanation for the fact that textual variants of bawdy songs set to traditional tunes may be carried by completely unrelated melodies.

The parody, of course, cannot lose its tune and still retain its identity as a parody. In that extra-musical sense, the parody is far more intimately related to its melody than is the non-parodic folk song.

Published collections of American folk song do not indicate the prevalence of parody, bawdy or otherwise, in oral tradition. Few parodies, at least those recognized as such, have been included in the various regional collections of American folk song, and only a handful have been published in the academic journals.

xxviii

But parody is common, both in popular and folk musics. In their introduction to *The Songs of the Gold Rush,* Richard A. Dwyer and Richard E. Lingenfelter note that the forty-niner ". . . mended his tunes to suit his life, and, as that life was hard, the songs were rough. Parody was the chief result. . . . It seems not too improbable that prospectors sang the same parodies they heard in the saloons, for the miners' taste for the familiar-with-a-difference may have been more basic than has hitherto been suspected. . . . Apparently, along with their diet of imported Eastern ballads and plays, the forty-niners relished a saltier draught of their own making. The parodic note seems to have been pervasive in their entertainment, and not restricted to song."

Earlier, Duncan Emrich had noted the same prevalence of parody in the songlore of Western miners. Hugh Anderson divined the hand "of itinerant professional ballad-monger(s)" in Australian balladry. John Greenway's survey of *American Folk Songs of Protest,* the Carawan compilation of the recently composed songs from the Freedom Movement throughout the South, and Reuss' overview of campus songlore all reflect this same dependence on a second-hand muse.[27] Judging from the available, though scattered, evidence and from this collection, it would appear that the role of parody in folk song must be more seriously considered and studied.

If, as the present editor believes, parody is predominantly the product of the better-educated or the professional entertainer, then a major re-evaluation of the process of oral tradition must be considered. Folklorists can no longer tacitly accept the stereotyped image of the "folk" as a relatively isolated group, homogenous within the community, largely uninterested in the world about itself, insular if not isolationist.

Parody, bawdy or otherwise, is not apparently the way of the folk, if "folk" is to be defined in traditional terms. It is a borrowed technique, or, more properly, the products of that technique are borrowed. This borrowing implies contact with, and interest in, a world beyond the local or regional "community."

In another manner, too, the analysis of bawdy song texts reveals a variance from generally accepted definitions of folklore and song.

It is axiomatic in the study of folklore that there is no one, single "correct" version of a song or story as there is of the latest popular tune to make the best-seller lists. There is an accepted score for a Beethoven symphony and, within narrow limits, a generally accepted manner of performing that symphony. This is not true in folk song. A folk song has no single melody or set of words; every singer has his own version. One may be better than another in an aesthetic sense, but none is the *right* way to sing the song. Beethoven's symphony is not performed with the movements scrambled or with an *adagio* from a Haydn symphony dropped in because the conductor thought it appropriate, but many folk songs are sung with stanzas interposed, transposed, dropped or borrowed from entirely different songs because the singer felt like it at the moment.

Quite atypically, those folk songs with bawdy lyrics seem to change at a rate much slower than do non-bawdy songs. This lack of change, completely unexpected if one is familiar only with classic ballad studies, cannot in this case be attributed to that enemy of oral tradition, the printed word. Normally, when a song gets into print, even a folk song, that particular version acquires a certain sanctity; it becomes the "correct" version in the mind of the singing public, and it is this which is likely to survive, driving out of oral tradition equally good texts and tunes.[28]

In more recent years, the great enemy of oral tradition has been the phonograph record, not the printed page. The Andrews Sisters' recording of "Down in the Valley" during the Second World War, and the Weavers' rendition of "On Top of Old Smoky" a few years later, to cite just two examples, gained wide circulation, and the songs long dormant in oral tradition were again widely known. But they were known only in the versions recorded by those groups. Parodies quickly popped up, but these were completely new songs, not rewrites ground piecemeal as oral tradition refashions a song.

The bawdy song, for the obvious reason, has not been favored with such attention. Such prints and records of these songs have been generally peddled furtively, the limited editions quickly exhausted. Only twice have bawdy songs been extensively recorded in all their inglory, and neither recording is likely to be found in neighborhood record shops. Their influence on oral tradition cannot be considered to be very great.

Yet despite the lack of "correctives" applied by print or phonograph records, there appear to be "correct" versions of bawdy songs, or what seem to be closely-adhered-to standards of what "Ball of Yarn," "The Fucking Machine," or "No Balls at All" should contain. The ballads do not appear to change in oral tradition as much as do their "clean" relatives. The lyric or non-narrative songs generally contain a core of verses common to most texts, and to these additional stanzas are added; that core is rarely as extensive in the "clean" lyric songs in oral tradition—"The Cuckoo," "Asheville Junction," "The Wagoner's Lad," or their peers.

This anomaly can only be explained by the suggestion that the people who sing bawdy songs take some pains first to learn and then to remember them. They do so because of the wit or humor of the piece; the comic element serves as both the *raison d'être* of the song and the mnemonic device preserving the integrity of the text.

The slow rate of change, or, viewed another way, the ability of generations of singers to accurately remember a song strongly supports those scholars who credit the folk with a collective ability to well-remember a historical fact, if it is worth remembering or accurately recounting. Thus Robert Lowie's assertion that folk history is mere fancy, or Lord Raglan's argument that the peasant mind is virtually incapable of accurately retaining anything past the third generation, are seriously questioned. If generations of folk singers can hew so closely to a single standard in singing "The Sea Crab" for 350 years, cannot these same generations accurately recount historical occurrences?[29]

So much for problems raised, unsettled or unsettling.

It is expected that the editor of a work such as this state the ground rules of his collection, including a definition of folk song if he has folly enough or nerve. If he has either, and does, there will inevitably be controversy, for no two folk song scholars have quite the same definition of what a folk song is, or, perhaps more importantly, what it is not.

This editor believes a folk song to be any song—no matter its origin, no matter if the composer is known, no matter how rudimentary text and tune may be—which has passed from a first generation to a second. Generation is defined not in the demographer's 25 years, or the biblical 33, but in terms of occupational or sub-group limits.

If a college freshman writes a song lampooning a rival institution, and, if four years later, after the author has graduated, the song is still sung, that song is a folk song. A college generation lasts but four years; at the end of that period, a new student body is on campus.

Similarly, a generation of miners is six, or eight, or ten years long, depending upon whose estimate of the job longevity in the mines one accepts.

A generation of elementary school children is seven years, and in highly transient communities, may well be less. As long as the great majority of the first generation has passed, consider a generation to have passed.

Should a song persist for only one generation, then it is considered a topical or local song, of great interest, in and of itself, since this is the stuff from which folk song comes.

One last qualification to this definition: The singers must remain unconcerned with changes in the song. Change is not mandatory, only permissible.

All of the songs in this collection are, by the definition above, folk songs. Dubious pieces have been excluded unless a second version has come to hand. At times, the exclusions have been painful: A version of "Van Amburgh's Show" was omitted in spite of the fact that the piece, usually found as a recitation called "Larry, Turn the Crank," had a tune; there was no corroborative text to indicate that this single find was anything more than one informant's creative effort.

In fashioning a collection such as this, the prudent editor will avoid some criticism if he sketches the parameters of his work.

This is not, it should be clear, a compendium of all the bawdy songs in the English language. It does not include material unique to the American Negro.

("Frankie and Johnny" and "Stagolee" have passed from Negro provenience to general currency; it is the white tradition which is sampled here.) The omission of Negro material is deliberate; the editor's collection in this area is small, his understanding correspondingly limited. Negro bawdy song needs, and merits, its own study, not the incidental attention which Negro tradition is generally afforded in folk song collections.

This anthology samples a white, largely urban tradition as it is currently carried by largely middle-class, educated informants. There is some reason to believe that class distinctions make little difference in the songs which will be collected from an informant—"Charlotte the Harlot" and "The Ring-Dang-Doo" are common to all; "Bang Away, Lulu" is seemingly ubiquitous; hardly a soldier or marine who served in Korea during the police action failed to learn "Movin' On."

It may be that in our eroticism we share a common humanity after all, but for the moment, the editor is not prepared to proffer bawdy song as proof of an essentially classless society. This collection will permit no such generalizations since it but sparingly samples the bawdy song repertoires of either rural or less-well-educated urban dwellers.

Finally, there is the matter of the great name-calling debate 'twixt purists and popularizers. Shall texts be cobbled together to print a full version of a song if none is at hand? Shall a defective text be repaired with spare parts cannibalized from other versions? After a good deal of thought, this editor has decided to conflate where necessary so as to present full versions of rare songs, provide the non-academic reader full value, and offer scholars as complete a set of jury texts as possible.

The latter reason weighed heavily in favor of this decision. This is, to the editor's knowledge, the first annotated collection of English-language bawdy songs offered for public sale without asterisk, dash, or similar emendation of words considered offensive. As such, it can serve as a guide to collectors yet to come, suggesting what more or less constitutes a full text of any given song.

If this places the editor in that clever company of catch-penny compilers—those whom Richard Dorson has dubbed fakelorists—so it must be.

Whenever texts have been conflated, this is end-noted stanza by stanza. Thus the scholar is forewarned and can make use of the text as he will; meanwhile, the more casual reader is offered full measure. Those who wish to cavil at conflations and editorial judgment will find there the wherewithal to do so.

The skeletal melodies notated here are reasonable approximations of what the singers actually sang. Folk song is a free art, the singers take liberties which would be considered indecent in art song. In times past, the range of variation, the idiosyncratic and regional performance styles have been as multifarious as the singers themselves. Apparently, this absolute freedom—within little understood cultural limits—has been narrowed in recent years. Singers now hew much more closely to the skeletal melodies.

This lessening of variation is apparently the result of a number of factors: a near universal, if incomplete, musical education in the public schools which places a premium upon *pro forma* performance; the all-pervasive influence of popular music, which may be more free than art song but does not permit the variety of folk song; and the inculcated stress upon "excellence" in performance which serves as an inhibiting factor (even in bawdy song), whereby the singer consciously attempts to produce an aesthetically pleasing performance. Since one of the accepted criteria of the aesthetic of music is accurate performance, the variation of the vocal line traditional in folk music is much lessened.

In earlier collections of folk song, the skeletal melodies were suggestions of the framework upon which singers embroidered interpolations, glissandos, grace notes, and a dozen other stylistic devices. In this collection, the skeletal tunes are far more close to actual performance. In that sense, these notations are examples of what Charles Seeger has termed prescriptive music writing rather than descriptive.[30]

There are other reasons, too, for this shift in traditional performance standards. Above all else, bawdy song is *speech-oriented* music, more so certainly than other forms of traditional singing.[31] In contemporary bawdy song sessions, the performance is geared to delivery of the words; music is secondary. Beyond some gesture in the direction of popular music's performance standards, the vehicle for the text is little considered.

If accompanied—and in recent years more and more singers have considered accompaniment mandatory when singing in company, that is, *performing*—the arrangements tend to fall into two distinct categories. One includes the simplest of ump-pa-pa, ump-pa-pa harmonic supports for the text, usually on the guitar, sometimes on a piano. The second is more elaborate, delivered by a performer with sufficient talent or skill to embellish the melody with simple melodic figures or haphazard counterpoint. Even with this second group of singer-instrumentalists, the performance is likely to be simple and direct; again, one geared to the presentation of the words. (The editor has heard any number of guitar accompaniments to bawdy song, but never one which suggested the performer had consciously prepared an "arrangement." Either bawdy songs are unrehearsed— probably true—by casual singers, or there is some feeling that complex musical arrangements would detract from the text.)

Viewed as a body of music, bawdy song is apparently an audience-oriented music, and there is no question but that the reactions of the listener affected the performance to a great extent. Short of documentary motion pictures—a collecting technique first proposed to the editor by the creative, if impractical, Kenneth S. Goldstein—there is no accurate way to report this interplay. Bawdy song, again thought of as a body of music, is fundamentally a social experience, one dependent for full appreciation upon this x-factor the audience provides. (Lest the reader think all this very simple, consider the range of permissable audience response to church music as sung in a High Mass and a Pentecostal Holiness service.)

The editor has seen singers stop in lame confusion when they realized that a favorite song has somehow alienated the listeners; has seen other singers erupt in laughter, their song suddenly interrupted; has seen performers stopped by the laughter of the audience which drowned out the song. Incidents such as these—more could be added—strongly underscore the immediate social function of the performance.[32]

This collection of American bawdy songs, or, more properly, bawdy songs sung in America, was gathered by a number of the editor's former students who deserve special credit. The collection made by Dean Burson at UCLA during 1960 was especially rich and so systematically gathered as to provide a "table of contents" of the most popular songs then circulating on that campus.

A quartet of colleagues was generous to the point of collaboration. Mrs. Bess Lomax Hawes permitted the use of songs collected by her students at San Fernando Valley State College, Northridge, California, between 1961 and 1963. J. Barre Toelken searched the holdings of the Robert W. Gordon Collection of American Folk Song at the University of Oregon, then forwarded more than 50 songs and fragments of critical historical value. D. K. Wilgus of UCLA furnished a farrago of notes, texts and tunes from both his own sturdy repertoire and the Western Kentucky Folklore Archive at UCLA.

Roger D. Abrahams of the University of Texas contributed numerous items gathered by his former students, frequently with helpful notes, then spent hours critically reading the manuscript. His friendship greater than his disagreements, Abrahams saved the present editor from many an embarrassing error of interpretation. Those remaining must be charged to my stubbornness, not to his lack of zeal.

Whenever possible, both collectors and informants are credited, though a number thought anonymity the better part of valor for the while. Their wishes are respected.

Ed Cray
Los Angeles
March, 1969

When I travelled, I took a particular delight in hearing the songs and fables that are come from father to son and are most in vogue among the common people of the countries through which I passed; for it is impossible that anything should be universally tasted and approved by a multitude, tho they are only the rabble of a nation, which hath not in it some peculiar aptness to please and gratify the mind of man. Human nature is the same in all reasonable creatures, and whatever falls in with it will meet with admirers amongst readers of all qualities and conditions.

—Joseph Addison, *The Spectator*

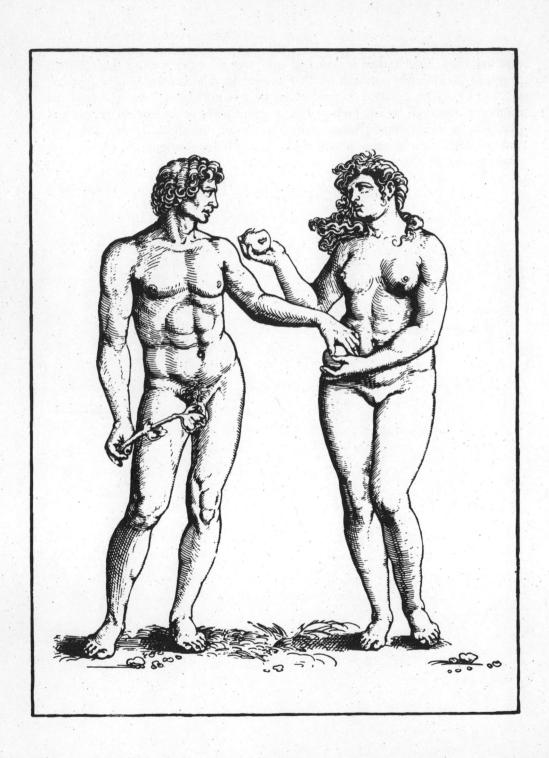

OLD, NEW, BORROWED, BLUE

The songs and ballads in this section have not been awarded their just deserts since most collections of Anglo-Irish ballads and songs have omitted texts or references for bawdy songs. Consequently, songs as ancient as those frequently anthologized, as worthy of consideration as those frequently praised, have been overlooked.

The bawdy song is simply one form of folk song. It is subject to the same process of change as every other folk song. Entirely new lines, or even whole stanzas, are inserted in old songs; snips and fragments are revised; verses from other songs are added— all at the singer's discretion.

The constant change and smoothing of rough-hewn lyrics has produced these Anglo-American favorites.

1

The Sea Crab

"The Sea Crab" is one of those living artifacts of another era which has been passed down in oral tradition for more than 300 years. As a song it can be dated to 1620, and in tale form, it was first printed ten years before that. Well known in Elizabethan England, it was apparently recognized as an old song even then.

Three centuries and more have hardly dimmed its popularity, nor has the usual wearing-down process of oral tradition changed it much. In spite of the vast differences between Elizabethan and contemporary society, the humor underlying "The Sea Crab" continues to appeal to singers. How else can its long currency and wide popularity be explained?

"Good morning, mister fisherman, I wish you well.
Good morning, mister fisherman, I wish you well.
Please tell me have you any sea crabs to sell?"
    Mush a ding eye, mush a toodle eye day.

"Yes, I have got sea crabs, one, two and three.
Yes, I have got sea crabs, one, two and three.
Take any you want; it makes no matter to me."
    Mush a ding eye, mush a toodle eye day.

He grabbed one old sea crab by his back bone. (2x)
He hustled and tussled 'til he got that crab home.
    Mush a ding eye, etc.

When the old man got home, the old wife was asleep, (2x)
So he put him in the pisspot just for to keep.
    Mush a ding eye, etc.

2

The old wife got up for to take a long shit. (2x)
The God damned old sea crab grabbed her by the slit.
    Mush a ding eye, etc.

"Husband, oh, husband, now what shall I do? (2x)
The devil's in the pisspot and he's got me by the flue."
    Mush a ding eye, etc.

The old man ran over and lifted her clothes, (2x)
And he took his other pincher and he grabbed at his nose.
    Mush a ding eye, etc.

"Now Johnny, have the doctor hitch his horse and cart, (2x)
Come get your father's nose and your mother's cunt apart."
    Mush a ding eye, etc.

It tickled the children right down to their soul (2x)
To see their pa's nose in their mother's peehole.
    Mush a ding eye, etc.

Cod Fish Song

The crab of old has become a cod fish, that poor fellow is beaten to death with brush and broom, and the song has acquired a moral, of sorts, yet it is still "The Sea Crab." The melody for this version is "The Chisholm Trail."

Chorus:

Singing ti yi yipee, yipee ya, yipee ya,
Singing ti yi yipee, yipee ya.

There was a man who had a little horse.
He saddled it, bridled it, and threw his leg across.

He rode and rode until he came to a brook,
And there sat a fisherman baiting his hook.

"Oh, fisherman, fisherman," said he,
"Have you a codfish for my tea?"

"Oh, yes," said he. "There's two:
One for me and one for you."

Well, he took that codfish by [the] leg bone
And mounted on his horse and galloped back home.

But when he got home he couldn't find a dish,
So in the chamberpot he put the little fish.

All night he could hear his woman cry,
"There's a devil down below; I can see his beady eyes."

Well, in the morning, she sat down to squat,
And the codfish jumped up her you-know-what.

She yelled bloody murder; "Well," cried she,
"There's a bloody big something getting up me."

Well, she hopped and she jumped and she gave a roar.
There went the codfish a-skating 'round the floor.

They chased that codfish all around the room.
They hit him with a brush and banged him with a broom.

First they hit him on the belly and they hit him on the side.
They hit him on his arse until the poor fellow died.

Well, the moral of the song is easy for to define:
None of us has got an eye on our behind.

So better be sure before you squat
There's nothing swimming in the chamberpot.

Four Old Whores

One of the most persistent notions in folklore is the mistaken belief that the greater the size of the sexual organ, the greater the sexual pleasure. The idea appears again and again in folk song, sometimes as an incidental line, and sometimes, as in this sea song, as a series of outlandish lies.

The number of girls who match wits and physical endowments varies from version to version; there are sometimes three, sometimes four. Just why they generally call Baltimore home is impossible to say, except "Baltimore" neatly fits the meter.

4

There were four old whores from Baltimore
Drinking beer and wine.
The topic of conversation was
"Mine is bigger than thine."

Chorus:

Roly, poly, tickle my hole-y,
Smell of my slimey slough.
Then drag your nuts across my guts,
I'm one of the whorey crew.

The first old whore from Baltimore said,
"Mine's as big as the air.
The birds fly in, the birds fly out,
And never touch a hair."

The second old whore from Baltimore said,
"Mine's as big as the moon.
The men jump in, the men jump out,
And never touch the womb."

The third old whore from Baltimore said,
"Mine's as big as the sea.
The ships sail in, the ships sail out,
And leave their rigging free."

The fourth old whore from Baltimore said,
"Mine's the biggest of all.
A man went in in the Springtime,
And didn't come out 'til Fall."

Five Nights Drunk I

Folklore usually has the cuckolded husband remain ignorant of his wife's gambols outside the marriage bed. This British ballad, reportedly one of the two or three most popular of the bawdy songs imported from the Old World, is the exception to the rule. Most of the printed versions suggest the little lady's dalliance delicately; this one is quite graphic and very straightforward.

When I came home last Saturday night,
As drunk as a skunk could be,
I saw a hat upon the rack
Where my hat ought to be.
I said, "Come here, honey.
Explain this thing to me.
How come this hat upon the rack
Where my hat ought to be?"

"Oh, you damn fool, you silly fool,
You're drunk as a skunk could be.
That's nothing but a chamber pot
My mother sent to me."
"Now in all my years of travel,
A million miles or more,
A John B. Stetson chamber pot
I never seen before."

6

When I came home last Saturday night,
As drunk as a skunk could be,
I saw some pants upon the chair
Where my pants ought to be.
I said, "Come here, honey.
Explain this thing to me.
How come these pants upon the chair
Where my pants ought to be?"
"Oh, you damn fool, you silly fool,
You're drunk as a skunk could be.
That's nothing but a bed quilt
My mother sent to me."
"Now in all my years of travel,
A million miles or more,
A fly hole on a bed quilt
I never seen before."

Now when I came home last Saturday
    night,
As drunk as a skunk could be,
I saw an ass upon the bed
Where my ass ought to be.
I said, "Come here, honey.
Explain this thing to me.
How come this ass upon the bed
Where my ass ought to be?"
"Oh, you damn fool, you silly fool,
You're drunk as a skunk could be.
That's nothing but a pumpkin
My mother sent to me."
"Now in all my years of travel,
A million miles or more,
An asshole on a pumpkin
I never seen before."

When I came home last Saturday night,
As drunk as a skunk could be,
I saw a head upon the bed
Where my head ought to be.
I said, "Come here, honey.
Explain this thing to me.
How come this head upon the bed
Where my head ought to be?"
"Oh, you damn fool, you silly fool,
You're drunk as a skunk could be.
That's nothing but a cabbage
My mother sent to me."
"Now in all my years of travel,
A million miles or more,
A mustache on a cabbage
I never seen before."

When I came home last Saturday night,
As drunk as a skunk could be,
I saw a cock in the hole
Where my cock ought to be.
I said, "Come here, honey.
Explain this thing to me.
How come this cock in the hole
Where my cock ought to be?"
"Oh, you damn fool, you silly fool,
You're drunk as a skunk could be.
That's nothing but a candle
My mother sent to me."
"Now in all my years of travel,
A million miles or more,
Bollocks on a candle
I never seen before."

7

Five Nights Drunk II

A second version of the classic ballad, one of the 305 anointed and duly certified by Francis James Child as an English or Scots popular ballad of traditional origin.

Well, it was Saturday night when I
    came home
    As drunk as I could be.
There on the hat-rack was a hat
    Where no hat ought to be.
So I turned to my wife
    And I said unto she,
"What's that hat a-doing there
    Where my hat ought to be?"
"Well, you blind fool, you stupid fool,
    You fool, why can't you see?
That ain't nothing but a chamber pot
    Your mother gave to me."
Now many miles have I traveled,
    A thousand miles or more,
But a chamber pot size six seven-eighths
    I never saw before.

Well, it was Saturday night when I
    came home
    A-buzzing like a bee.
There on the pillow was a head
    Where no head ought to be.
So I turned to my wife,
    And I said unto she,
"What's that head a-doing there
    Where my head ought to be?"
"Well, you blind fool, you stupid fool,
    You fool, why can't you see?
That ain't nothing but a cabbage
    Your mother sent to me."
Now many miles have I traveled,
    A thousand miles or more,
But a cabbage with a mustache
    I never saw before.

Well, it was Saturday night when I
    came home
    As drunk as I could be.
There in the stable I saw a horse
    Where no horse ought to be.
So I turned to my wife
    And I said unto she,
"What's that horse a-doing there
    Where my horse ought to be?"
"Well, you blind fool, you stupid fool,
    You fool, why can't you see?
That ain't nothing but a milk cow
    Your mother gave to me."
Now many miles have I traveled,
    A thousand miles or more,
But a milk cow with a saddle on
    I never saw before.

Well, it was Saturday night when I
    came home
    A-buzzing like a bee,
There in the parlor was a coat
    Where no coat ought to be.
So I turned to my wife
    And I said unto she,
"What's that coat a-doing there
    Where my coat ought to be?"
"Well, you blind fool, you stupid fool,
    You fool, why can't you see?
That ain't nothing but a blanket
    Your mother gave to me."
Now many miles have I traveled,
    A thousand miles or more,
But a blanket with buttons on it
    I never saw before.

The Tinker I

Popular belief in the British Isles once had it that gypsies—who are known as tinkers because of their traditional craft of metalworking—possessed, among other supernatural assets, the power of *glamour,* or an irresistible sex appeal. There is a venerable ballad, "The Gypsy Laddie," which recounts the story of one such tinker, the legendary Davey Faa, and his abduction-seduction of an impressionable young lady. Where "The Gypsy Laddie" is discreet and gentle, "The Tinker" is a cocksmith's delight. The tinker's attraction is explicitly based upon the size of his kidney-wiper, and not upon some supernatural charm, in the modern versions of the ballad.

There was a jolly tinker
And he came from Dungaree,
With a yard and a half of foreskin
Hanging down below his knee.

Chorus:

With his long dong-diddly-whacker,
Overgrown kidney-cracker,
Mother-fucking baby-fetcher
Hanging to his knees.

My lady she was dressing,
Dressing for the ball,
When she saw the jolly tinker
Lashing piss against the wall.

"Oh, tinker, oh, tinker,
I'm in love with you.
Oh, tinker, oh, tinker,
Will half a dollar do?"

Oh, he screwed her in the parlor;
He fucked her in the hall,
And the servant said, "By Jesus,
He'll be cramming on us all."

There were fifty naked women
Running up and down the hall,
Shouting, "Jesus Christ, Almighty,
Is he gonna fuck us all?"

"Oh, daughter, oh, daughter,
You were a silly fool,
To get busy with a man
With a tool like a mule."

"Oh, mother, oh, mother,
I thought I was able,
But he split me up the belly
From the cunt up to the navel."

Said the daughter to the mother,
"Why you God-damned whore!
If he gave you twenty inches,
You would ask for twenty more."

10

The Tinker II

The tinker's super-masculinity is expressed in another way in this version of the ballad. Having serviced everyone on the premises, he rides off unsatiated, "little drops of semen pitter-pattering at his feet."

The lady of the mansion
Was dressing for the ball
When she spied a tinker
Pissing up against the wall.

Chorus:
With his jolly great kidney-wiper,
And his balls the size of three,
And a yard of dirty foreskin
Hanging down below his knee.

The lady wrote a letter
And in it she did say,
"I'd rather be fucked by a tinker
Than my husband any day."

When the tinker got the letter
And in it he did read,
His balls began to fester
And his prick began to bleed.

So he mounted on his charger
And on it he did ride
With his balls slung o'er his shoulder
And his penis by his side.

Oh, he rode up to the mansion
And gave a loud call,
"Jesus!" yelled the lady,
"He has come to fuck us all!"

He fucked them in the kitchen.
He fucked them in the hall,
But when he fucked the butler,
'Twas the dirtiest trick of all.

He rode off from the mansion.
He rode into the street,
Little drops of semen
Pitter-pattering at his feet.

Oh, the tinker's dead and buried.
I'll bet he's gone to Hell.
He said he'd fuck the Devil,
And I'll bet he's done it well.

Samuel Hall

In 1701, an otherwise undistinguished chimney sweep by the name of Jack Hall was hanged at Tyburn Hill in London for the crime of burglary. As was the custom of the time, a hack writer dashed off some quick lines purporting to be the last sentiments of the dead man, and these were hawked in the streets even as Jack was being stretched.

This "last goodnight," as folklorists morbidly refer to the usually repentant ballads, passed into oral tradition. There, sometime after Jack had been elevated to his office (to borrow Francis Grose's phrase), a curious thing happened. Jack became Samuel—or more familiarly, Sam—and no longer remorseful. He was instead contemptuous, profane and disdainful of hangman, preacher, spectators and all.

Oh, my name is Samuel Hall, Samuel Hall.
My name is Samuel Hall, Samuel Hall.
My name is Samuel Hall
And I've only got one ball,
But it's better than none at all. Fuck 'em all.

Oh, I killed a man they said, so they said.
I killed a man they said, so they said.
I killed a man they said.
Christ, I bashed his bloody head
And I left him there for dead. Fuck 'em all.

Oh, they say that I must die, I must die.
They say that I must die, I must die.
They say that I must die,

12

And they'll hang me up so high.
Then I'll piss right in their eye. Fuck 'em all.

Oh, the parson, he will come, he will come.
The parson, he will come, he will come.
The parson, he will come
With his tales of Kingdom Come.
He can shove them up his bum. Fuck 'em all.

Oh, the sheriff will come too, will come too.
The sheriff will come too, will come too.
The sheriff will come too
With his motherfucking crew.
They've got fuck all else to do. Fuck 'em all.

I see Molly in the crowd, in the crowd.
I see Molly in the crowd, in the crowd.
I see Molly in the crowd,
And I feel so God damned proud
That I want to shout out loud, "Fuck 'em all."

In Kansas

Still another of the "Jack Hall" cycle or family, "In Kansas" is actually a mocking parody of a notably beautiful lament commemorating the Irish famines of the 1840's. The beauty of the song is only partly indicated by this stanza:

How I wish that we were geese, night and morn, night and morn.
How I wish that we were geese, night and morn.
How I wish that we were geese,
And could live and die in peace
'Til the hour of our release, eating corn, eating corn.

The stanza of the lament which probably inspired the American parody—often included although not in this version—is:

Oh, the praties, they grow small over here, over here.
Oh, the praties, they grow small over here.
Oh, the praties, they grow small,
And we eat them in the Fall.
Yes, we eat them skins and all over here, over here.

From that lament comes this screed.

Oh, the eagles, they fly high in Kansas.
Oh, the eagles, they fly high in Kansas.
Oh, the eagles, they fly high,
And they shit right in your eye.
Thank the Lord that cows don't fly in Kansas.

There's a shortage of good whores in Kansas.
There's a shortage of good whores in Kansas.
There's a shortage of good whores,
But there's keyholes in the doors,
And there's knotholes in the floors in Kansas.

Oh, they say to drink's a sin in Kansas.
Oh, they say to drink's a sin in Kansas.
Oh, they say to drink's a sin,
But they guzzle all they kin,
And the drys are voted in in Kansas.

They drink their whiskey neat in Kansas.
They drink their whiskey neat in Kansas.
They drink their whiskey neat
'Til it knocks them off their feet,
And it petrifies their meat in Kansas.

Oh, I chased a parson's daughter in Kansas.
Oh, I chased a parson's daughter in Kansas.
Oh, I chased a parson's daughter,
And I banged her when I caught her.
Now I cannot pass my water in Kansas.

14

There's no paper in the bogs in Kansas.
There's no paper in the bogs in Kansas.
There's no paper in the bogs.
They just sit there 'til it clogs,
Then they saw it off in logs in Kansas.

If you ever go to jail in Kansas,
If you ever go to jail in Kansas,
If you ever go to jail,
And you need a piece of tail,
The sheriff's wife is for sale in Kansas.

I Am Growing Old and Gray

This minor lament for a lost youth is another of the songs modeled upon the tune and stanzaic pattern of Jack Hall's last goodnight.

I am growing old and gray
Every year.
And I have less urge to play
Every year.
My head keeps getting thicker.
I can hold just that less liquor
And get drunk just that much quicker
Every year.

The women all are sweeter
Every year.
And they ask for much more peter
Every year.
But mine can get no bigger
And it's slower on the trigger
And cuts less and less a figure
Every year.

15

Sam MacColl's Song

Jack Hall's last goodnight is remarkable not only for its unrepentant nature, but also for its unparalleled progeny. Dozens of songs have either been modeled on the stanzaic pattern and rhyme scheme of Jack's ballad or have borrowed the melody which, in turn, led to a remolding of the host-text.

"Sam MacColl's Song" is one of those which deliberately followed the indelicate versification of "Jack Hall," using a tune which ultimately can also be traced to the gallows march of the chimney sweep.

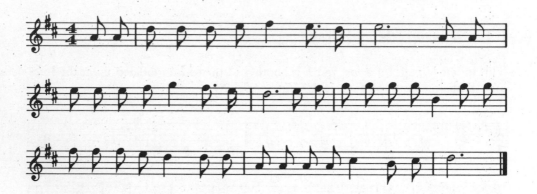

Oh, my name is Sam MacColl, Sam MacColl,
And I come from Donegal, Donegal.
Oh, my name is Sam MacColl,
And I come from Donegal,
And I have no balls at all, balls at all.

There can be no room for balls, room for balls,
When your pecker fills the halls, fills the halls,
So I kicked the walls all out,
And I chased the girls about,
And I skewered them with a shout, with a shout.

When it stands erect with pride, erect with pride,
All the girls want to hide, want to hide,
But they aren't so very meek;
At least once or twice a week,
They take a curious peek, curious peek.

Oh, the girls laugh and sing, laugh and sing,
At the length and breadth of my enormous thing, enormous thing,
For it fills them with delight
Through the day and through the night,
'Cause it fits secure and tight, secure and tight.

16

If the girls want no more, want no more,
Or they say they're very sore, very sore,
If the girls moan and weep,
Or they say they want to sleep,
I try horses, cows and sheep, cows and sheep.

The Darby Ram

Singers in Great Britain and the United States kept tacking on bawdy verses to the ritual song once sung by masked visitors who stopped at various homes in a village bringing luck upon the house during the year to come.

The lies and the bawdry grew more and more outrageous as time went on. When they finally slaughtered that fabulous beast, it took all the boys in Darby to carry away his bones and all the girls to roll away his stones.

In the United States, things were even worse. First, a military marching band during the Civil War used the tune on parade, and then Negro jazzmen refashioned the song into the New Orleans jazz standard, "Didn't He Ramble?" Following Gresham's law of folk balladry— bawdy verses drive out clean verses— "The Darby Ram" now salaciously celebrates the monster ram.

They brought a beast to Darbytown,
And drove him with a stock,
And all the girls in Darbytown
Paid a quarter to see his cock.

And when this beast got hungry,
They mostly fed him grass.
They didn't put it in his mouth;
They shoved it up his ass.

Chorus:

Maybe you don't believe me,
Maybe you think it's a lie,
But if you'd been down to Darbytown,
You'd see the same as I.

He did not care for grass so much;
He always wanted duck.
But every time he ate a bird,
He had to take a fuck.

The legs upon this monster,
They grew so far apart,
That all of the girls in Darbytown
Could hear him when he fart.

The garbage bill was awful,
And it cost us quite a bit,
But we had to keep a special truck
To haul away the shit.

The hair upon this monster,
It grew so very thick,
That none of the girls in Darbytown
Could see the head of his prick.

There's something else I'd like to say.
Now what do you think of this?
The folks would come from miles around
Just to watch him take a piss.

The horns upon this monster,
They grew up solid brass.
One grew out of his forehead
And the other grew out of his ass.

The girls that live in Darbytown
Will all sit in your lap.
One night a girlie sat on mine
And now I've got the clap.

17

A-Rovin'

Perhaps because of its fine tune, perhaps because of the sailor's intent which no amount of bowdlerizing can obscure, this is one of a handful of former sea songs with any currency ashore. It cannot be claimed "A-Rovin'" is now as popular or as frequently sung as it was in the days of sailing ships when it is said to have served as a chantey accompanying work aboard ship, but versions still turn up, far from the tradition which gave birth to the song, but close to the hearts of roisterers everywhere.

In Amsterdam there lived a maid.
Mark well what I do say.
In Amsterdam there lived a maid
And she was a mistress of her trade.
I'll go no more a-rovin' with you, fair maid.

Chorus:

A-rovin', a-rovin', since rovin's been my ruin.
I'll go no more a-rovin' with you fair maid.

I put my hand upon her knee.
Mark well what I do say.
I put my hand upon her knee.
She said, "Young man, you're rather free."
I'll go no more a-rovin' with you, fair maid.

18

I put my hand upon her thigh.
Mark well what I do say.
I put my hand upon her thigh.
She said, "Young man, you're rather high."
I'll go no more a-rovin' with you, fair maid.

I put my hand upon her snatch.
Mark well what I do say.
I put my hand upon her snatch.
She said, "Young man, that's my main hatch."
I'll go no more a-rovin' with you, fair maid.

She rolled me over on my back.
Mark well what I do say.
She rolled me over on my back
And fucked so hard my balls did crack.
I'll go no more a-rovin' with you, fair maid.

And then I slipped her on the blocks.
Mark well what I do say.
And then I slipped her on the blocks.
She said, "Young man, I've got the pox."
I'll go no more a-rovin' with you, fair maid.

And when she spent my whole year's pay,
Mark well what I do say.
And when she spent my whole year's pay,
She slipped her anchor and sailed away.
I'll go no more a-rovin' with you, fair maid.

The Gatesville Cannonball

Although "The Gatesville Cannonball" has little but the theme in common with "Bell Bottom Trousers," if the connecting link in the evolutionary scheme, "When I Was Young," is interposed, the relationship is clear enough.

As sung at Gatesville State School for Boys in Texas, "The Gatesville Cannonball" was apparently fashioned by someone who knew "When I Was Young" or another song quite like it.

Adapting the older song to a new environment—not uncommon in folk balladry —adding a few local touches, and borrowing a familiar tune from the jukeboxes, "The Wabash Cannonball," the unrepentant boys at Gatesville came up with a theme song.

Gather 'round me all you maidens,
And I will tell my tale,
Of how I got my ticket
On the Gatesville Cannonball.

From the honky tonks of Houston,
To the slums of San Antone,
To the great pool halls of Fort Worth,
Wherever I may roam,
You may have heard about me,
Of how I made my fall
And how I won my ticket
On the Gatesville Cannonball.

When I was young and handsome,
It was to my heart's delight
To go to balls and parties,
To stay out late at night.
It was at a ball I met her.
I asked her for a dance.
She could tell I was a Gatesville boy
By the way I wore my pants.

My stomps were neatly polished.
My ducks were neatly combed.
Before the dance was over,
I asked to walk her home.
Walking down the sidewalk,
You could hear the couples say,
"There goes the fair young maiden,
Just throwing her life away."

It was at her father's doorstep,
I asked if I may try.
It was at her mother's bedside,
I forced her down to lie.
I pulled her pants so gently.
I raised her dress so high.
I said, "I'll be a son of a bitch.
I'll go the rest or die."

It was the very next morning.
The sheets were spotted red.
Her mother said, "You son of a bitch,
You've got her maiden's head.
Gather 'round me all you fair maidens,
Listen to my plea.
Never trust a Gatesville boy
An inch above the knee."

20

When I Was Young

Change is the hallmark of oral tradition. In some cases, the changes are for the better; other times, the changes corrupt the song and lead eventually to its demise. In a relatively small number of instances, one song is so changed that it becomes a new effort, and both old and new songs continue side by side in oral currency. Such is the case with this American redaction of "Bell Bottom Trousers."

When I was young and foolish,
I used to take delight
Attending balls and dances
And staying out at night.

'Twas at a ball I met him.
He asked me for a dance.
I knew he was a sailor
By the buttons on his pants.

His shoes were neatly polished.
His hair was neatly combed.
And when the dance was over,
He asked to take me home.

As we walked home together,
I heard the people say,
"There goes another girlie
That's being led astray."

'Twas on my father's doorstep
That I was led astray.
'Twas in my mother's bedroom
That I was forced to lay.

He laid me down so gently.
He raised my dresses high.
He said, "Now, Maggie, darling,
Take it now or die."

"Here is half a dollar
For the damage I have done,
For soon you will have children,
A daughter or a son.

"If it is a daughter,
Take her on your knee.
But if it is a son, then
Send him out to sea.

"I hope next time I see you
That you'll remember me,
And thank God for the blessing
That I have brought to thee."

The Fire Ship

In a sanitary version, this sailor's ballad was recently revived as a popular song. Needless to say, the popular recording lacked the realism of seventeenth-century versions which contained verses such as:

> She gave to me a syrup sweet
> [That] was in her placket box,
> But e'er three minutes went about
> It proved the French-pox.
>
> The fire ship she did blow me up
> As my effigy shows,
> And all may read upon my face
> The loss of teeth and nose.

Modern-day bawdy texts also avoid this graphic detail, the singers apparently preferring to treat venereal disease humorously.

As I stepped out one evening upon a night's career,
I spied a lofty clipper ship and after her I steered.
I hoisted up my sig-in-als which she so quickly knew,
And when she seen my sig-in-als fly, she immediately hove to.

Chorus:

She had a dark and a rovin' eye,
And her hair hung down in ring-a-lets.
She was a nice girl, a proper girl,
But one of the rakish kind.

Oh, sailor, please excuse me for being out so late,
But if my parents knew of it, oh, sad would be my fate.
My father is a minister, a good and honest man.
My mother is a Methodist; I do the best I can.

I eyed that girl both up and down for I'd heard such talk before,
And when she moored herself to me, I knew she was a whore.
But still she was a pretty girl; she shyly hung her head.
"I'll go along with you, my lad," this to me she said.

I took her to a nice hotel; I knew she wouldn't mind.
But little did I ever think she was one of the rakish kind.
I played with her for quite some time, and learned to my surprise,
She was nothing but a fire ship rigged up in a disguise.

So up the stairs and into bed I took that maiden fair.
I fired off my cannon into her thatch of hair.
I fired off a broadside until my shot was spent,
Then rammed that fire ship's waterline until my ram was bent.

Then in the morning she was gone; my money was gone too.
My clothes she'd hocked; my watch she stole; my sea bag was gone too.
But she'd left behind a souvenir, I'd have you all to know,
And in nine days, to my surprise, there was fire down below.

Now all you jolly sailormen who sail upon the sea
From England to Amerikay take warning now from me.
Beware of lofty fire ships, they'll be the ruin of you.
They'll empty out your shot locker and pick your pocket too.

My God, How the Money Rolls In

One of a handful of the most popular bawdy songs, this urban ditty can ultimately be traced to an Irish and Scots tinkers' song, the first stanza of which is:

My father was hung for sheep-stealing.
My mother was burnt for a witch.
My sister's a bawdy-house keeper,
And I am a son-of-a-bitch.

The bawdy parent text seems to have reached American shores in its unexpurgated form, but has not flourished. "My God" meanwhile pops up everywhere, carolled to the innocent melody of "My Bonnie Lies Over the Ocean."

My father makes illegal whiskey.
My mother makes illegal gin.
My sister sells sin in the corner.
My God, how the money rolls in!

Chorus:

Rolls in. Rolls in.
My God, how the money rolls in, rolls in.
Rolls in. Rolls in.
My God, how the money rolls in.

We've started an old-fashioned gin shop,
A regular palace of sin.
The principal girl is my grandmother.
My God, how the money rolls in!

My brother's a curate in Sydney.
He's saving poor girlies from sin.
He'll save you a blonde for a dollar.
My God, how the money rolls in!

Grandmother makes cheap prophylactics;
She punctures the end with a pin.
Grandfather performs the abortions.
My God, how the money rolls in!

My bonnie has tuberculosis;
My bonnie has only one lung.
My bonnie spits blood in her pocket
And uses it for chewing gum.

My uncle whittles out candles
With wax especially soft.
He says it will come in handy,
If ever his business drops off.

My sister was once a virgin;
She didn't know how to begin.
I showed her the tricks of the trade.
My God, how the money rolls in!

24

The Monk of Great Renown I

Priestly celibacy has not always been as strictly observed as canonical law would have it. Medieval and Renaissance folklore is full of stories of men of the cloth who momentarily disrobed, though the tales were probably no more numerous than the clerical indiscretions. The situation has changed a good deal since then, and clerical incontinence is much less frequent than it once was.

Still, various anti-Catholic tracts occasionally turn up—scurrilous end-pieces from a roll of whole cloth—chronicling monotonous orgies of priests and nuns, the local bishop presiding. "The Monk of Great Renown" is not of that stripe. Unlike the hypocritical *agit-prop,* "The Monk" is good humored, even approving of "the dirty old man."

There was a monk of great renown.
There was a monk of great renown.
There was a monk of great renown.
He fucked the girls around the town.

Spoken:

The dirty old man. The dirty old man.
The bastard deserves to die. Fuck him.

Chorus:

Brothers, let us pray.
Glory, glory, hallelujah.

He met a girl with lily-white thighs,
He met a girl with lily-white thighs,
He met a girl with lily-white thighs,
And teats that grew to enormous size.

He laid her on a downy bed,
He laid her on a downy bed,
He laid her on a downy bed,
And busted in her maidenhead.

He shoved it in until she died,
He shoved it in until she died,
He shoved it in until she died,
And then he tried the other side.

He carried her to the burial ground.
He carried her to the burial ground.
He carried her to the burial ground.
He thought he'd go another round.

The monk lamented his grief and shame,
The monk lamented his grief and shame,
The monk lamented his grief and shame,
So he fucked her back to life again.

25

The Monk of Great Renown II

Another version, this with a vastly different ending in which the punishment fits the crime:

There was an old monk of London town. (3x)
He fucked all the women of great renown.

Chanted: *Chorus:*

The old sod. The old sod.   Let us pray.
The bastard deserves to die. Fuck him.   Glory, glory hallelujah.

His brother monks cried out in shame. (3x)
So he rolled the women over and did it again.

His brother monks said, "We'll stop his frolics." (3x)
So they rolled him over and cut off his bollocks.

The Foggy Dew

This is one of the most beautiful of British love songs, delicately suggestive of the sexual, perhaps the most non-bawdy of the bawdy songs in this collection. In spite of this, the most frank of its verses, the third, has been censored on numerous occasions. While this censorship does not harm the beauty of the song, it does destroy its direct honesty.

Now, I am a bachelor; I live by myself
And I work at the weaver's trade.
The only thing I ever did wrong
Was to woo a fair, young maid.
    I wooed her in the summer time,
    And part of the winter time too;
    But the only thing that I ever did wrong
    Was to keep her from the foggy, foggy dew.

One night this maid came to my bed
Where I lay fast asleep.
She laid her head upon my chest
And then she began to weep.
    She sighed, she cried, she damn near died.
    She said, "What shall I do?"
    So I took her into bed and I covered up her head
    Just to keep her from the foggy, foggy dew.

All through the first part of the night,
We did laugh and play.
And through the latter part of the night,
She slept in my arms 'til day.
    Then when the sun shone down on our bed,
    She cried, "I am undone."
    "Hold your tongue, you silly girl.
    The foggy dew is gone."

Now I am a bachelor; I live with my son.
I work at the weaver's trade,
And every time I look into his face
He reminds me of the fair young maid.
    He reminds me of the summer time
    And part of the winter time too,
    And the many, many times I took her in my arms
    Just to keep her from the foggy, foggy dew.

O'Reilly's Daughter

Beyond a doubt, this is one of the most popular of bawdy songs, especially amongst college students. A British import, "O'Reilly's Daughter" or "One-Eyed Riley" has survived in oral tradition relatively unchanged for at least a hundred years. One reason perhaps for this lack of change is the fact that the story is told in traditional ballad style, economically, with only the sparest of details. There simply is not much meat to cut from the bare bones and adding stanzas would only encumber the narrative.

As I was sitting in O'Reilly's bar,
Listening to tales of blood and slaughter,
Suddenly a thought came to my mind:
Thought I'd shag O'Reilly's daughter.

Chorus:

Rubba-dub-dub. Rubba-dub-dub.
Let's give a cheer for the one-balled Reilly.
Rubba-dub-dub. Balls. Balls.
Rubba-dub-dub. Shag on.

Grabbed that bitch by the teats,
Then I threw my left leg over.
Shag, shag, shag some more,
Shagged all night 'til the fun was over.

Came a knock at the door.
Who could it be but her God-damned father?
Two horse pistols in his hands,
Coming to see who was shagging his daughter.

28

I grabbed that bastard by the neck,
Stuck his head in a pail of water,
Shoved those pistols up his butt
A damn sight further than I shagged his daughter.

As I go walking down the street,
People shout from every corner,
"There goes that God-damned son-of-a-bitch
Who did shag O'Reilly's daughter."

Horse Shit

In spite of the dramatic title, this is still another version of "The Monk of Great Renown." The monk has become a pilot and the story, however elemental, has disappeared, but the derivation of "Horse Shit" is plain enough.

There was a pilot of great renown.
There was a pilot of great renown.
There was a pilot of great renown,
Until he fucked a girl from our town,
    Fucked a girl from our town.
    Ha, ha, ha. Ho, ho, ho.
    Horse shit.

He laid her down beside a stump.
He laid her down beside a stump.
He laid her down beside a stump,
And then he missed her cunt and split the stump,
    Missed her cunt and split the stump.
    Ha, ha, ha. Ho, ho, ho.
    Horse shit.

Successive verses follow the same pattern, substituting:

He laid her in a feather bed,
And then he twisted in her maidenhead.

He laid her on a winding stair,
And then she shoved it in clear up to there.

He laid her down beside a pond,
And then he fucked her with his magic wand.

Bollochy Bill the Sailor

This song, unlike so many folk songs, has little to recommend it. Its melody is monotonous; its lyrics are repetitious to the point of idiocy. But, weak tune and foolish lyrics notwithstanding, the song has an appeal all its own. Singers can add new lyrics as they go, unburdened by the necessity of observing rhyme schemes; the repetitive tune is easily learned and seems to gather momentum as the song goes on. So for a hundred or more years, Bollochy Bill has been paying his visit to the fair young maiden.

"Who's that knocking at my door?
Who that knocking at my door?
Who's that knocking at my door?"
Cried the fair young maiden.

"It's only me from over the sea,"   "Just open the door and lay on the floor,"
Said Bollochy Bill the sailor.   Said Bollochy Bill the sailor.
"It's only me from over the sea,"
Said Bollochy Bill the sailor.

"I'll come down and let you in,"   "What if Ma and Pa should see?"
Cried the fair young maiden.   Cried the fair young maiden.
"I'll come down and let you in,"
Cried the fair young maiden.

30

"We'll fuck your ma and shoot your pa,"
Said Bollochy Bill the sailor.

"What if we should have a child?"
Cried the fair young maiden.

"We'll dig a ditch and bury the bitch,"
Said Bollochy Bill the sailor.

"Stop shouting at the door,"
Cried the fair young maiden.

"I just got paid and want to get laid,"
Said Bollochy Bill the sailor.

"What's that thing between your legs?"
Cried the fair young maiden.

"It's only a pole to shove up your hole,"
Said Bollochy Bill the sailor.

"What's that fur around the pole?"
Cried the fair young maiden.

"It's only some grass to tickle your ass,"
Said Bollochy Bill the sailor.

Ball of Yarn

There are any number of disingenuous, if not downright obscure euphemisms
for sexual intercourse in folk balladry. In some songs, a soldier plays his fiddle;
in others, the girl's thyme is stolen away. Rest assured whatever the device chosen,
it will sound wondrously innocent to the uninitiated. Were it not for the rather
frank story of this song, the true meaning of "winding up that little ball of yarn"
might be similarly vague.

31

In the merry month of May when the lambs did sport and play,
I went to take a walk around the town.
I met a pretty miss and politely asked her this:
"Will you let me wind your little ball of yarn?"

Chorus:

Ball of yarn, ball of yarn,
It was then I wound her little ball of yarn.
Ball of yarn, ball of yarn,
It was then I wound her little ball of yarn.

With my arm about her waist, we went to a quiet place,
And I gently laid her down upon the grass.
While the birdies and the bees did the same among the trees,
She let me wind her little ball of yarn.

It was shortly after this I went out to take a piss
And to see if she had done me any harm.
With her crack beneath her lap, she had given me the clap
When she let me wind her little ball of yarn.

It was nine months after that in a bar room where I sat,
A policeman put his hand upon my arm.
Said the officer in blue, "Now, young man, we're after you
Just for winding up that little ball of yarn."

To the judge straightway we went, and I offered to repent,
But the judge said, "I do not give a darn.
Guilty in the first degree! To the penitentiary
Just for winding up that little ball of yarn."

In the jailhouse I sit with my fingers dipped in shit,
And the bedbugs play billiards with my balls.
And the women as they pass stick their hatpins up my ass
Just for winding up that little ball of yarn.

Bell Bottom Trousers

Sailors, tinkers, lawyers, millers and tailors have fearful reputations in British folklore. Tailors are inevitably cowards; millers and lawyers are just as inevitably dishonest. Tinkers are oversexed, and sailors are seducers of innocent maidens. The once numerous songs about lawyers, millers and tailors have not survived the wear and tear of oral transmission, but those about tinkers and sailors thrive. None is more popular than "Bell Bottom Trousers."

When I was just a serving maid who lived in Drury Lane,
My master he was kind to me; my mistress was the same.
When along came a sailor boy with laugh so bright and gay,
And he was the source of all my misery.

Chorus:

With his bell bottom trousers, coat of navy blue,
He would climb the riggin' like his daddy used to do.

He asked me for a candle to light him to his bed.
He asked me for a nightcap to put upon his head.
Now I was just a simple lass and didn't mean no harm,
So I hopped into the sailor's bed to keep the sailor warm.

In the morning he was gone and he left a five pound note,
With a bit of writin', and this is what he wrote:
"Now you may have a daughter, lass. You may have a son,
And this should help to pay for the trouble I have done.
Now if you have a daughter, you can bounce her on your knee,
But if you have a son, you can send him off to sea."

The Ball of Kirriemuir

Reportedly, "The Ball of Kirriemuir" was written in the 1880's to celebrate the comings, goings and doings at an actual social event in the Kirriemuir district of Scotland.

According to James Barke, young men of lusty tempers took advantage of the fact that few women of the day wore what are now known as "panties," and the few styles on the market sported open crotches. The men sprinkled the earthen floor with the burred seeds of ripened roses. Once the music started, the seeds and dust swirled. The seeds lodged in the nether brush of the ladies present, setting up a fierce itch.

Not content with this external irritation, the men topped off the punch with a soupçon of Spanish fly. Finally, they rigged the hanging paraffin lamp to burn out at about the same time that rose seeds and cantharides took effect.

The result was the most sung-about orgy in the history of the Western world.

"The Ball" became one of the most popular of soldiers' songs, Barke says, first during World War I and again with World War II. When the Highland Division entered Tripoli at the end of the North African campaign, the troops marched past the reviewing stand—with Winston Churchill the reviewing officer, no less —singing "The Ball of Kirriemuir." At first puzzled, Churchill grinned broadly. The BBC's disc recording of the historic event was scrapped.

Just how much of the original ballad remains in this version is impossible to tell. A good version now will contain fifteen to twenty stanzas, but the actual number of stanzas in oral tradition may run as high as fifty.

34

'Twas the gathering o' the clans,
And all the Scots were there,
A-skirlin' on their bagpipes,
And strokin' pussy hair.

Chorus:
Singing, "Who hae ye, lassie,
Who hae ye noo?
The ane that hae ye last time
He canna hae ye noo."

Maggie McGuire, she was there
A-showin' the boys some tricks,
And ye canna hear the bagpipes
For the swishin' o' the pricks.

Sandy MacPherson, he was there
And on the floor he sat,
Amusin' himself by abusin' himself
And catchin' it in his hat.

The factor's wife, she was there,
Ass against the wall,
Shoutin' to the laddie boys,
"Come ye one an' all."

The factor's daughter, she was there,
Sittin' down in front,
A wreath of roses in her hair,
A carrot up her cunt.

The mayor's daughter, she was there
And kept the crowd in fits
By jumpin' off the mantle piece
And landin' on her tits.

The village idiot, he was there;
He was a perfect fool.
He sat beneath the oak tree
And whittled off his tool.

The chimney sweep, he was there,
But soon he got the boot,
For every time he farted,
He filled the room with sóot.

Johnny McGregor, he was there,
A lad so brave and bold.
He pulled the foreskin over the end
And whistled through the hole.

Down in the square,
The village dunce he stands,
Amusin' himself by abusin' himself
And usin' both his hands.

There was fuckin' in the parlor.
There was fuckin' in the ricks.
Ye canna hear the music
For the swishin' o' the pricks.

There was fuckin' in the bedroom,
Fuckin' on the stair.
Ye canna see the carpet
For the come and curly hair.

The elders of the church,
They were too old to firk,
So they sat around the table
And had a circle jerk.

The bride was in the corner
Explainin' to the groom
The vagina, not the rectum,
Is the entrance to the womb.

The groom was excited
An' racin' 'round the hall
A-pullin' on his pecker
An' showin' off his balls.

The king was in the countin' house
A-countin' out his wealth.
The queen was in the parlor,
A-playin' wi' herself.

The queen was in the kitchen,
Eatin' bread and honey.
The king was in the kitchen maid
And she was in the money.

John Brown, the parson
Was quite annoyed to see
Four and twenty maidenheads
A-hangin' from a tree.

And when the ball was over,
The opinion was expressed:
Although they liked the music,
The fuckin' was the best.

35

The Wayward Boy

This ballad is widely known, and probably owes some of its popularity to the catchy melody, the familiar "The Girl I Left Behind Me," and some to the sprightly internal rhymes. Whatever the reason, the song itself is interesting; the wayward boy seemingly dismisses his painful injury at the hands of the girl's father, then applauds or tacitly approves of the girl's promiscuity. No double standard in bawdry.

I walked the street with my prick to my feet.
I heard a voice come to me.
A lovely maid looked out and said,
"I need someone to screw me."
Said I, "My dear, you needn't fear,
For I have heard your pleading.
It's very plain I can ease your pain.
I've got just what you're needing."

"I've heard of you, my wayward boy.
Your name is known quite widely,
But I can't come down, I'm sad to say.
My door is bolted tightly.
My father is a minister,
My maidenhead does cherish,
So every night he locks me tight,
So horny I do perish."

36

She stood out there in the midnight air
With the wind blowing up her hinder,
And her ass all bare and her cunt all hair,
So I climbed right up behind her.
Said I, "Young maid, don't be afraid.
The pleasures can be thrilling.
If you're someone who wants some fun,
The wayward boy is willing."

She jumped into bed and she covered up her head
And she swore I couldn't find her,
But I knew damn well she lied like hell,
So I jumped right in behind her.
I shoved old Pete right through the sheet
And up her organ grinder.
The white of an egg ran down her leg,
But the rest remained inside her.

On the very next stroke, the damn bed broke.
Her father came a-gunning.
I hit the floor with my prick all sore.
I got to my feet a-running.
I left that lass in my bare ass
As a shotgun blast did find me.
For weeks in bed, I was picking out lead
With a mirror held behind me.

As years went by, I thought with a sigh,
When fancy did remind me.
So one fine day I made my way
To the girl I left behind me.
She was still locked in to keep off men.
She didn't look much older,
But she'd had her joys: three girls, four boys
And a baby on her shoulder.

The Bastard King of England

It's really a very good story; backstairs gossip about palace intrigue is always interesting. The way the story goes, Rudyard Kipling wrote "The Bastard King of England" (pronounced "En-ga-land") and that authorship cost him the poet laureate's knighthood. It is too bad that the attribution is apparently spurious; "The Bastard King" would undoubtedly be Kipling's most popular work.

Oh, the minstrels sing of an English king
Who lived long years ago,
And he ruled his land with an iron hand,
But his mind was weak and low.
He used to hunt the royal stag
Within the royal wood,
But better than this he loved the bliss
Of pulling his royal pud.

Chorus:

He was dirty and lousy and full of fleas.
His terrible tool hung to his knees.
God save the bastard king of England.

Now the Queen of Spain was an
  amorous dame,
A sprightly dame was she,
And she longed to fool with his
  majesty's tool
So far across the sea.
So she sent a royal message
With a royal messenger
Inviting the king to bring his ding
And spend the week with her.

When news of this reached Philip of
  France,
He swore before his court,
"The queen prefers my rival
Just because my dork is short."
So he sent the Duke of Zippity-Zap
To slip the queen a dose of clap
To pass it on to the bastard
King of England.

When news of this foul, dastardly deed
Reached fair Windsor Hall,
The king swore by the royal whore
He'd have the Frenchman's balls.
So he offered half his kingdom
And the hole of Queen Hortense
To any loyal Briton
Who would nut the King of France.

So the loyal Duke of Essexshire
Betook himself to France.
When he swore he was a fruitier,
The king took down his royal pants.
Then around his prong he tied a thong,
Leaped on his horse and galloped along,
Dragging the Frenchman
Back to England.

Now the king threw up his breakfast
And he shit all over the floor,
For during the ride, the Frenchman's
    pride
Had stretched a yard or more.
And all the maids of England
Came down to London town,
And shouted round the battlements,
"To hell with the British crown."

Last chorus:

So the King of France usurped the
    throne.
His sceptre was his royal bone.
Hail to the bastard King of England.

She Was Poor But She Was Honest

Originally, this was a bathetic lament, sung with tongue in cheek by English music hall singers. The mock lament of "It's the Same the Whole World Over," popularized the world over by British troops, was quickly cut down. This parody captures the sentiment of the original, but it makes its point in more forthright fashion.

She was poor but she was honest,
Victim of a rich man's whim.
He was rich and he seduced her,
And she had a child by him.

See him riding in his carriage,
See him going to the hunt,
Thinking nothing of a marriage,
Only of a piece of cunt.

Now she stands in Picadilly,
Selling matches by the box.
Anyone who buys those matches
Gets a hellfire dose of pox.

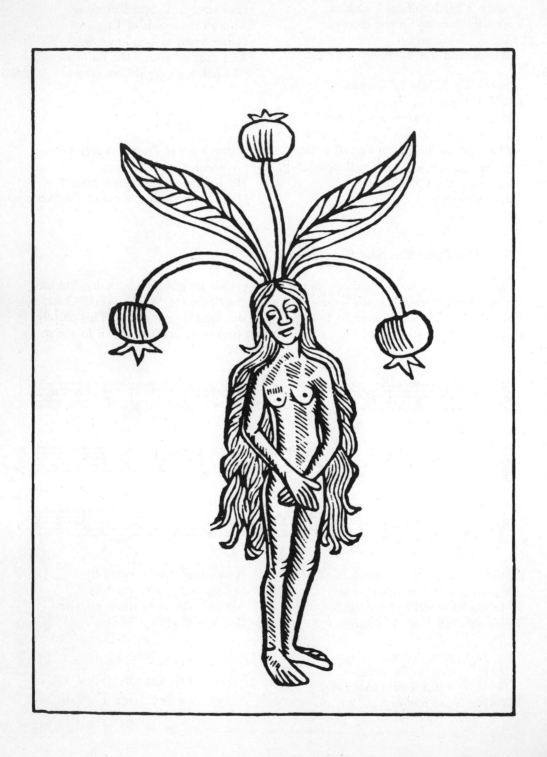

AS AMERICAN AS MOM'S APPLE PIE

Here's to America, land of the push,
Where a bird in the hand is worth two in the bush,
But if in that bush a fair maiden should stand,
Then a push in the bush is worth two in the hand.

Not to be outdone, the colonists have produced more than their fair share of bawdy songs. Few have anything like the sturdy lineage of the ballads from the British Isles, but many have gained the same world-wide popularity the older songs enjoy. Blame the American GI, who has proved himself capable of some truly inspired debauchery.

On the whole, American tradition, bawdy or otherwise, has produced far fewer ballads narrating a single event than has the British, but it has fashioned far more parodies, loosely grouped jokes in rhymed form, and items of social commentary and description. The reason for this is at least partly a result of the speed-up in the tempo of contemporary life. People are less inclined, and perhaps even have less time, to patiently listen to a song which may take five or ten minutes to sing. The pattern of entertainment, especially of the all-pervasive popular music, is for short songs, following one upon the other. At the end of each, the audience applauds the fact that its patience and intelligence have not been unduly taxed.

The cultural imperatives create a model which even the underground of bawdry follows. The older, longer ballads are truncated. Songs of more recent vintage "get on and get off" quickly.

Frankie and Johnny

"Frankie and Johnny" must certainly be one of the most popular of American folk songs. Only "John Henry" has as many devoted disciples to sing its praises, so many tireless scholars anxious to root out every last version of this American tragedy.

Apparently, there was a Frankie—general consensus would have her a hustler in St. Louis—and apparently she supported a natural-born easeman named Albert or Johnny. (The various versions have him by both names.) But Albert or Johnny ran out of luck and he died, as they said along the river before the turn of the century, from a sudden attack of lead poisoning.

Sometime after the fact, prostitutes in St. Louis were singing this song, accompanied by the barrelhouse pianos of a hundred cribs and bars. Eventually, an expurgated version made the hit parade and the tragedy of Frankie became a national treasure. That isn't half bad for a fifty-cent whore.

Frankie and Johnny were lovers;
Oh Lordy, how they made love.
Swore to be true to each other,
True as the stars above,
    For he was her man,
    But he done her wrong.

Frankie was a good girl,
Most everybody knows.
She gave a hundred dollars
To Johnny for a suit of clothes,
    'Cause he was her man,
    But he done her wrong.

Frankie worked in a crib-joint
Behind a grocery store.
She gave all her money to Johnny;
He spent it on high-tone whores.
    God damn his soul.
    He done her wrong.

Frankie was a fucky hussy,
That's what all the pimps said,
And they kept her so damn busy,
She never got out of bed.
    But he done her wrong.
    God damn his soul.

Frankie she knowed her business,
She hung out a sign on the door:
"Fresh fish cost you a dollar here,
Fancy fuck'ing cost ten cents more."
    He was her man.
    He done her wrong.

Frankie went looking for Johnny.
She hung out a sign on the door:
"No more fish for sale now,
Go find you another whore."
    He was her man.
    But he done her wrong.

Frankie went down Fourth Street.
She ordered a glass of beer,
Said to the big bartender man,
"Has my ever-lovin' man been here?"
    God damn his soul.
    He done her wrong.

"I couldn't tell you no story.
I couldn't tell you no lie.
I saw your Johnny an hour ago
With a whore called Alice Bly.
    God damn his soul,
    He was doin' you wrong."

Frankie ran back to her crib-joint,
Fixin' to do him some harm.
She took out a bindle of horse
And shot it right up her arm.
    God damn his soul.
    He was doing her wrong.

Frankie put on her kimono;
This time it wasn't for fun
'Cause right underneath it
Was a great big forty-four gun.
    God damn his soul.
    He done her wrong.

She ran along Fish Alley,
Looked in a window so high,
Saw her lovin' Johnny
Finger-fucking Alice Bly.
    He was doing her wrong.
    God damn his soul.

Frankie went to the front door.
She rang the whorehouse bell.
"Stand back you pimps and whores
Or I'll blow you straight to hell.
    I'm hunting my man.
    Who's doin' me wrong."

Frankie drew back her kimono,
Pulled out her big forty-four.
Rooty-toot-toot, three times she shoot,
Left him lyin' on that whorehouse floor.
    She shot her man
    'Cause he done her wrong.

"Roll me over, Frankie,
Roll me over slow.
A bullet got me in my right side,
Oh God, it hurts me so.
    You killed your man
    'Cause I done you wrong."

Frankie ran back to her crib-joint.
She fell across the bed,
Saying, "Lord, oh Lord, I've shot my man.
I've shot my Johnny dead.
    He was my man.
    God damn his soul."

Three little pieces of crêpe
Hanging on the crib-joint door
Signifies that Johnny
Will never be a pimp no more.
    God damn his soul.
    He done her wrong.

"Bring out your rubber-tired buggy.
Bring out your rubber-tired hack.
I'm taking my man to the graveyard;
I ain't gonna bring him back.
    He was my man
    But he done me wrong."

They brought a rubber-tired buggy,
And brought out a rubber-tired hack.
Thirteen pimps went to the cemetery
But only twelve of them came back.
    He's dead and gone,
    He was doing her wrong.

Frankie went out to the graveyard,
Sorry as she could be,
Ridin' behind a whorehouse band
Playin' "Nearer My God to Thee."
    He was her man.
    He was doing her wrong.

Frankie stood up in the courtroom.
"I'm not tellin' no sass.
I didn't shoot Johnny in the first degree.
I shot him in his big black ass.
    He was my man.
    He was doin' me wrong."

The judge said, "Stand up, Frankie.
Stand up and dry your tears.
You know murder's a hangin' crime
But I'll give you ninety-nine years.
    He was your man.
    He was doin' you wrong."

The last time I seen Frankie
She was ridin' on that train
Takin' her to the jail house,
Never bring her back again.
    He was her man.
    God damn his soul.

Stackolee

Stackolee, or Stagolee, or Stackerlee, or Stagger Lee, or Stack-o'-Dollars—he's known by all five names—is one of the legendary giants of Negro folklore. Not only is he celebrated in this ballad, but Stack' can boast of dozens of tales and legends which circulate about him. His prodigious feats far surpass those of his Bunyanesque rivals, for who among them can claim to have caused the San Francisco earthquake merely by pulling out the water pipes in a local saloon?

Stackolee's strength was that of ten, not because his heart was pure, but because the Devil made a bargain with him. In exchange for Stack's soul, Old Scratch gave the badman a magic John B. Stetson hat. When a rival tough stole or won the hat in a card game, Stack' killed him.

Like John Hardy, another of his ilk, Stackolee can count on his friends when he is clapped in the local hard-rock hotel. His cronies come down to say goodbye; his girl friend hustles to make his bail. This is loyalty.

Stackolee was a bad man;
Everybody knows
Spent one hundred dollars
On them high-tone, fancy whores.
    They all loved Stackolee.

Billy Lyons said, "Stackolee,
Please don't take my life.
You make an orphan of my son,
And a widow of my wife."
    Mean old bad man, Stackolee.

"I don't give a damn for your son.
I don't give a damn for your wife.
You done stole my Stetson hat.
I'm going to take your life."
    Mean old bad man, Stackolee.

What do you know about this?
What the hell you know about that?
Stackolee killed Billy Lyons
Over a damned old Stetson hat.
    Poor old Stackolee.

They took him to the jailhouse
And they threw his ass in a cell.
All the pimps and whores went on down
To bid poor Stack farewell.
    Poor old Stackolee.

Policeman said to Stackolee—
His eyes all filled with tears—
"The judge sure won't be hard on you;
He'll just give you ninety-nine years."
    Poor old Stackolee.

Stack's girl was a good girl,
None of that low-down trash.
"I'll make the bail for Stackolee,
Give that sheriff a piece of ass."
    Poor old Stackolee.

She hustled in the morning.
She hustled in the night.
She got so thin from hustling
She was an awful sight.
    She'd get the dough for Stackolee.

One night it rained like hell
And she had an awful time.
She said, "I won't break Stackolee's luck."
She shook her fanny for a dime,
    Making bail for Stackolee.

Then she got a dirty old crib
Right behind the jail.
She hung a sign on the front door:
"Fresh fish here for sale."
    She'd get the bail for Stackolee.

One night she had more bad luck.
An old nigger give her a buck.
She said, "You know I got no change,
So give yourself another fuck
    For poor old Stackolee."

The judge then said to Stackolee,
"I know why you're standing there.
You done shot Billy Lyons.
You going to the electric chair,
    Poor old Stackolee."

One night there came a telephone call
And everybody cried.
It said that at nine o'clock
Poor old Stack had fried.
    Means a funeral for Stackolee.

When Stackolee's girl friend
Heard this awful news,
She was lyin' on the torn bedspread
Havin' the electric chair blues,
    Havin' the blues for Stackolee.

When they got to the graveyard
And saw that awful hole,
Those pimps and whores fell on their knees
And asked the Lord to save their souls.
    Poor old Stackolee.

A high yeller pimp stepped out,
Said, "I ain't got much to say,"
Pulled a bindle and took a shot,
Said, "Like Stack, I'm on my way."
    Poor old Stackolee.

They laid out poor old Stackolee
And laid him in his last hole.
All the whores and pimps gathered 'round and said
"Lord have mercy on his soul.
    Poor old Stackolee."

Blinded by Turds

Sexual subjects dominate in bawdy songlore true, but there are some ballads concerning that equally natural and equally tabooed function, excretion. The melody for this sally into the outhouse is "Sweet Betsy from Pike."

There was an old lady who lived in our town
Whose asshole was stuffed with the great smelly brown.
She took a large dose without reading the box.
Before she could strip, turds were flying like rocks.

Chorus:

Singing tur-ra-la, tur-ra-la, tur-ra-la-lay.

She ran to the window and stuck out her ass,
When just at that moment a stranger did pass.
He smelled a strong fart settle down on that place
When a fucking big turd hit him right in the face.

He ran to the east and he ran to the west
When a fast flying turd landed right on his chest.
He ran to the north and he ran to the south
When another big turd hit him right in the mouth.

So the next time you walk out be careful of shit.
Look out where you walk and don't step in it,
And pity the beggar whose sign bears these words:
"I am an old man who was blinded by turds."
    And as you pass by, please contribute a bit
    To the sorrowful fellow who's blinded by shit.

The Big Black Bull

Considering the fact that, until recent times, the United States was predominantly rural, it is surprising that there are not more barnyard epics such as this. "The Big Black Bull," however, is apparently the only such pastorale still in oral circulation, and its popularity depends not upon the poetry as such, but upon the linking of the words with a somewhat solemn, easily-sung tune.

The big, black bull came down from the mountain,
Houston, Sam Houston.
The big, black bull came down from the mountain
Long time ago.

Chorus:

Long time ago.
Long time ago.
The big, black bull came down from the mountain
Long time ago.

He spied a heifer in the pasture,
Houston, Sam Houston.
He spied a heifer in the pasture
Long time ago.

Chorus:

Long time ago.
Long time ago.
He spied a heifer in the pasture
Long time ago.

He jumped the fence and he jumped that heifer,
Houston, etc.

He missed his mark and *ffftt* in the pasture,
Houston, etc.

His tool ran dry and his balls grew hollow,
Houston, etc.

Wiped his cock on a hickory sapling,
Houston, etc.

The big black bull went back to the mountain,
Houston, etc.

One hung low and the other hung lower,
Houston, etc.

The Sexual Life of the Camel

The Sphinx is one of the seven wonders of the world. This commonly-found American ditty does not rank quite so high.

Oh, the sexual life of the camel
Is stranger than anyone thinks.
In moments of amorous passion,
He frequently buggers the Sphinx.

But the Sphinx's posterior passage
Is clogged with the sands of the Nile,
Which accounts for the hump on the camel,
And the Sphinx's inscrutable smile.

Casey Jones

This native American ballad exists in two very distinct versions. One is the story of the fatal train wreck; the other is a mélange of verses concerning Casey's sexual adventures. It would be a toss-up as to which is the more popular, though the ballad of the train wreck wins hands down when it comes to public performances.

Casey Jones was a son-of-a-bitch,
Drove a hot steam engine through a forty foot ditch,
Pissed on the whistle and he shit on the bell
And he went through Chicago like a bat out of hell.

Chorus:

Casey Jones mounted to his cabin.
Casey Jones had his pecker in his hand.
Casey Jones mounted to his cabin,
Said, "Look out, ladies, I'm a railroad man."

It happened one morning about a quarter to four,
Pulled up in front of a whorehouse door,
Climbed through the window with his cock in his hand
And said, "I'll prove I'm a railroad man."

50

He lined a hundred whores up against the wall,
And he bet ten dollars he could fuck them all.
He fucked ninety-eight and his balls turned blue.
He took a shot of whiskey and he fucked the other two.

Casey Jones was a son-of-a-bitch.
His balls were covered with the whorehouse itch.
He went to the door with his pecker in his hand,
Says to the lady, "I'm a railroad man."

Casey Jones said before he died
There were five more things he'd like to ride:
Bicycle, tricycle, automobile,
Bow-legged woman and a ferris wheel.

Casey Jones said before he died
There were two more drinks he'd like to try.
"Well, tell me, Casey, what can they be?"
"A cup of coffee and a cup of tea."

They were rolling down the line 'bout half past two.
Casey pissed in the fire and the boiler blew.
The fireman drowned in a yellow stream
And for miles around you could see yellow steam.

The Old Gray Bustle

Another of America's sentimental favorites redone to a fare-thee-well
sung to the tune of *Put on Your Old Gray Bonnet*.

Put on your old gray bustle and get out and hustle
For tomorrow there's a mortgage coming due.
Just put your ass in clover, let the boys look it over,
If you can't get five, take two.

Put on that old blue ointment, the crabs' disappointment,
And we'll kill the bastards where they lay.
Though it scratches and itches, it will kill the sons-of-bitches
In the good old-fashioned way.

Put on those old red panties that once were your auntie's,
And let's go play in the hay,
And while they're out there hayin', we'll be in here layin'
In the good old-fashioned way.

No Balls at All

The theme of the young girl forced to marry the much older man—often for financial reasons—is not infrequent in folklore and song. The girl usually manages to find solace for her empty marriage bed in the arms of a more virile companion, folk singers being a rather sympathetic lot. "No Balls at All" is unusual only in that the cuckoldry extends to the second generation.

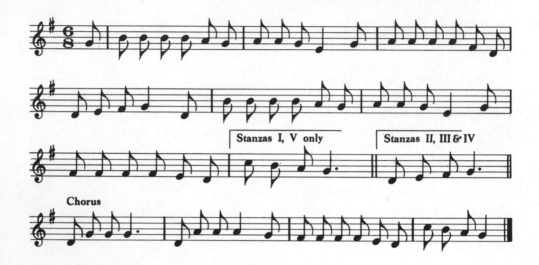

Oh, listen, my children, a story you'll hear.
A song I will sing you; 'twill fill you with cheer.
A charming young maiden was wed in the Fall.
She married a man who had no balls at all.

Chorus:

No balls at all. No balls at all.
She married a man who had no balls at all.

The night of the wedding she leaped into bed.
Her breasts were a-heaving; her legs were well spread.
She reached for his penis; his penis was small.
She reached for his balls; he had no balls at all.

"Oh mother, oh mother, oh, what shall I do?
I've married a man who's unable to screw.
For many long years, I've avoided the call,
Now I've married a man who has no balls at all."

"Oh daughter, oh daughter, now don't feel so sad;
I had the same trouble with your dear old dad.
There are lots of young men who will answer the call
Of the wife of a man who has no balls at all!"

Now the daughter she followed her mother's advice,
And she found the proceedings exceedingly nice,
And a bouncing young baby was born in the Fall
To the wife of the man who had no balls at all.

Spoken: No testicles whatsoever!

In the Shade of the Old Apple Tree

There is a certain perversity in the traditional muse that makes folk singers
inevitably parody all the sentimental favorites of the Gay Nineties and the early
1900's. The originals are still sung in alcoholic comraderie, but more than one
person has a knowing grin when they get around to "Sweet Adeline," "In the
Shade of the Old Apple Tree" or "The Band Played On." He remembers another set of lyrics, one perhaps not so suited for mixed company, certainly not
in public. And he doesn't have to refer to song sheets either; he might have
forgotten the original words, but he isn't likely to forget the bawdy version.

In the shade of an old apple tree,
A pair of fine legs I can see,
A little red dot,
With a hole on top,
It looked like a tarbrush to me.

In the shade of the old apple tree,
That's where Zelda first showed it to me.
It was hairy and black,
And she called it her crack,
But it looked like a subway to me.

So I pulled out my pride of New York.
It fitted in just like a cork.
And I said, "Oh, lady, don't scream,
While I dish out the cream,
In the shade of an old apple tree."

53

Bang Away, Lulu I

Lulu is one of the legendary girls in American folk song, rivaled in her sexual capacities only by the equally well-known Cindy. There is no standard version of "Lulu"; like so many other songs from the Southern Appalachians, "Lulu" has hundreds of verses. Each singer knows only a handful, to which he will add new stanzas as he thinks of them or as his neighbors sing them.

I wish I was a diamond upon my Lulu's hand,
And every time she wiped her ass, I'd see the promised land,
Oh, Lordy.

Chorus:
Bang away, my Lulu; bang away good and strong.
Oh, what'll we do for a damn good screw when our Lulu's dead and gone?

I wish I was the pee-pot, beneath my Lulu's bed,
For every time she took a piss, I'd see her maidenhead,
Oh Lordy.

My Lulu had a baby. She named it Sunny Jim.
She dropped it in the pee-pot to see if he could swim,
Oh, Lordy.

First it went to the bottom, and then it came to the top,
Then my Lulu got excited and grabbed it by the cock,
Oh, Lordy.

I wish I was a candle, within my Lulu's room,
And every night at nine o'clock, I'd penetrate her womb,
Oh, Lordy.

54

My Lulu's tall and sprightly. My Lulu's tall and thin.
I caught her by the railroad track jacking off with a coupling-pin,
Oh, Lordy.

I took her to the Poodle Dog, upon the seventh floor.
And there I gave her seventeen raps and still she called for more,
Oh, Lordy.

My Lulu was arrested; ten dollars was the fine.
She said to the judge, "Take it out of this ass of mine,
Oh, Lordy."

Sometimes I got a nickel and sometimes I got a dime,
But when I got a quarter, Lulu lays it on the line,
Oh, Lordy.

Pappy loved my mammy; mammy loved the men.
Now mammy's full of buckshot and pappy's in the pen,
Oh, Lordy.

Lulu got religion; she had it once before.
She prayed to Christ with the minister while they did it on the floor,
Oh, Lordy.

My Lulu went to Boston, and there she met a trucker,
She high-balled to the bedroom cryin', "Double-clutch me,
Mother-fucker."

My Lulu had a sister who lived up on a hill.
If she hadn't died of syphilis, we'd be banging still,
Oh, Lordy.

Some girls work in offices; some girls work in stores,
But Lulu works in a hotel with forty other whores.
Oh, Lordy.

Bang Away, Lulu II

A slightly different version, this one depends upon the deliberately unfinished
last line of each verse for its humor.

Lulu's got a rooster.
Lulu's got a duck.
She put them in the bathtub
To see if they would.

Chorus:

Bang, bang Lulu.
Lulu's gone away.
Who we gonna bang, bang
Since Lulu's gone away?

Lulu's got two boy friends.
They are very rich.
One's the son of a banker,
The other's a son-of-a

Cows wear bridles.
Horses wear bits.
Lulu wears a sweater
To cover up her.

Lydia Pinkham

Until the passage of the Pure Food and Drug Act of 1906, manufacturers of patent medicines could make the most extravagant claims for their products. "It's good for what ails you and if nothing ails you, it's good for that, too," howled the pitchmen. The Original Dr. Jones' Genuine Stump Water Indian Tonic Certified Double Strength was guaranteed to cure everything from arthritis to scarlet fever; two bottles would put tuberculars back on their feet.

Lydia Pinkham's potion was not the most blatant in its claims, but it was one of the better sellers—along with Carter's Little Liver Pills—and the tonic was said to relieve what are euphemistically known as "feminine ills." So it is natural that the claims of the makers should come in for some satirizing, first as a popular song, then as a bawdy parody even funnier than the original.

Mrs. Jones had rotten kidneys;
Poor old lady couldn't pee,
So she took, she swallowed, she gargled
Some vegetable compound,
And now they pipe her out to sea.

Chorus:

Then we'll sing, we'll sing,
We'll sing of Lydia Pinkham,
Savior of the human race.
How she makes, she bottles,
She sells her vegetable compound,
And the papers publish her face.

Geraldine, she had no breastworks,
And she couldn't fill her blouse,
So she took, she swallowed, she gargled,
Some vegetable compound,
And now they milk her with the cows.

Widow Brown, she had no children,
Though she loved them very dear,
So she took, she swallowed, she gargled
Some vegetable compound,
And now she has them twice a year.

Arthur White had been castrated
And had not a single nut,
So he took, he swallowed, he gargled
Some vegetable compound,
And now they hang all 'round his butt.

Willie Smith had peritonitis,
And he couldn't piss at all,
So he took, he swallowed, he gargled
Some vegetable compound,
And now he's a human waterfall.

Billy Black lacked hair on his balls,
And his pecker wouldn't peck,
So he took, he swallowed, he gargled
Some vegetable compound,
Now it's as long as a gy-raffe's neck.

57

Thais

Scholars might argue as to whether or not this is a true folk song. The words were written by the very contemporary New York attorney and opera lover, Newman Levy, as a satire on Massenet's opera of the same name. The tune, a version of "The Son of a Gambolier," or, as it is more commonly known, "The Rambling Wreck from Georgia Tech," was later attached by someone who felt Levy's poem too good to be confined to the printed page. Now, as the song has circulated, the words of Levy's poem have undergone some change—not greatly, true—but certainly in the tradition of all songs the folk consider to be their own.

One time in Alexandria, wicked Alexandria,
The night life was exciting in that city by the Nile,
There lived, historians report, the pride of Nile's famed resort,
The pride of Pharoah's noble court, and Thais was her name.

Nearby, in peace and piety, avoiding all society,
There dwelt a band of holy men who'd built a refuge there,
And in the desert's solitude, they spurned all earthly folly to
Devote their days to holy works, to fasting, and to prayer.

Now, one monk whom I solely mention of this group of holy men
Was known as Athaneal; he was famous near and far.
At fasting bouts or prayer with him, no other could compare with him.
At grand and lofting praying he could do the course in par.

One night while sleeping heavily (from fighting with the Devil, he
Had gone to bed exhausted while the sun was shining still),
He had a vision Freudian and though he was annoyed he an-
Alyzed it in the well-known style of Doctors Jung and Brill.

58

He dreamed of Alexandria, of wicked Alexandria.
A crowd of men were cheering in a manner somewhat rude
At Thais, who was dancing there, and Athaneal, glancing there,
Observed her do the shimmy in what artists call the nude.

Said he, "This dream fantastical disturbs my thoughts monastical.
Some unsuppressed desire, I fear, has found my monkish cell.
I blushed up to the hat o' me to view this girl's anatomy.
I'll go to Alexandria and save her soul from hell."

So pausing not to wonder where he'd put his summer underwear,
He quickly packed his evening clothes, his toothbrush and a vest,
And to guard against exposure, he threw in some woolen hosiery,
And bidding all the boys goodbye, he started on his quest.

This monk, though warned and fortified, was deeply shocked and mortified
To find on his arrival wild debauchery in sway.
While some lay in a stupor sent by booze of more than two percent,
The others were behaving in a most immoral way.

Said he to Thais, "Pardon me, although this job is hard on me,
I gotta put you wise to what I come down here to tell.
What's all this sousin' gettin' you? Cut out this pie-eyed retinue.
Let's hit the trail together, kid, and save your soul from hell."

Although this bold admonishment caused Thais some astonishment,
She coyly answered, "Say, you said a heaping mouthful, Bo.
This burg's a frost, I'm telling you. The brand of hooch they're selling you
Ain't like the stuff we used to get, so let's pack up and go."

So forth from Alexandria, from wicked Alexandria,
Across the desert sands they go beneath the blazing sun,
Till Thais, parched and sweltering, finds refuge in the sheltering
Seclusion of a convent and the habit of a nun.

But now the monk is terrified to find his fears are verified.
His holy vows of chastity have cracked beneath the strain.
Like one who has a jag on, he cries out in grief and agony,
"I'd sell my soul to see her do the shimmy once again."

Alas! his pleadings clamorous, though passionate and amorous,
Have come too late; the courtesan has danced her final dance.
The monk says, "That's a joke on me, for that there dame to croak on me.
I hadn't oughter passed her up the time I had the chance."

Acknowledgment: From OPERA GUYED, by Newman Levy. Copyright 1923 and renewed 1951 by Newman Levy. Reprinted by permission of Alfred A. Knopf, Inc.

The Ring-Dang-Doo

Sometime around the age of twelve or thirteen, boys seem to learn this song, just as their fathers did before them, and their fathers before them. From generation to generation, the song has changed, but the various versions will almost invariably contain the description of the ring-dang-doo (here called the "ring-a-rang-roo") as being "soft and round like a pussy cat." No one has yet suggested that the euphemism for the vagina, "pussy," comes from this song, but it's an interesting theory.

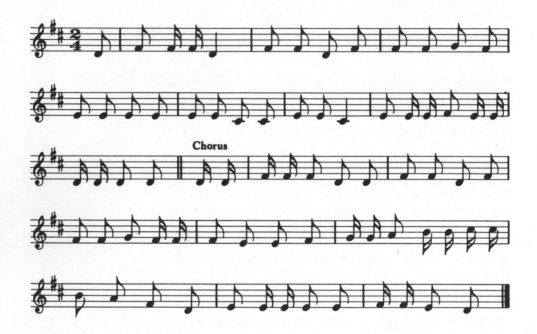

When I was a lad in my teens,
I met a gal from New Orleans.
She had blond hair and blue eyes too.
She let me ride on the ring-a-rang-roo.

Chorus:

Oh, the ring-a-rang-roo, now what is that?
It's soft and round like a pussy cat.
It's got a hole in the middle and split in two,
And that's what they call the ring-a-rang-roo.

She took me down into her cellar,
And said that I was a mighty fine feller.
She fed me wine and whiskey too.
She let me ride the ring-a-rang-roo.

60

Her father came and angrily said,
"You have lost your maidenhead.
Well, pack your bags and your Kotex too,
And make your living off your ring-a-rang-roo."

So she went off to be a whore,
And hung this sign above her door:
"One dollar each and three for two
To take a crack at my ring-a-rang-roo."

They came by twos, they came by fours,
Until at last they came in scores,
But she was glad when they were through
For they had ruined her ring-a-rang-roo.

Now along came Pete, the son-of-a-bitch.
He had blue balls and the seven-year itch.
He had the clap and the syphilis too,
And he put them all in the ring-a-rang-roo.

And now she lies beneath the sod;
Her soul, they say, is gone to God,
But down in Hell, when Satan's blue,
He takes a whirl at her ring-a-rang-roo.

Minnie the Mermaid

Another of the parodies of popular songs of another day, "Minnie" wasn't much
of a song to begin with, and the bawdy parody has happily outlasted the original.

Oh, what a time I had with Minnie the Mermaid
Down at the bottom of the sea.
Down amongst the corals where she lost her morals,
My, but she was good to me.
Oh, what a time I had with Minnie the Mermaid
Down in her seaweed bungalow.
Ashes to ashes, dust to dust;
Two twin beds and only one of them mussed.
Oh, what a gal was my Minnie the Mermaid,
Down at the bottom of the sea.

61

The Chisholm Trail

John A. Lomax, certainly one of the most active collectors of folk songs in the United States, thought that this song was close to being *the* cowboy epic. Stretched end to end, the verses reached from the Panhandle to the rail heads of Kansas, chronicling the hero's misfortunes as he drives the 2-U (or "goddam") herd up the trail.

Now gather 'round, boys, and listen to my tale,
And I'll tell you my troubles on the old Chisholm Trail.

Chorus:

Singing, ki-yi-yippy, yippy-yay, yippy-yay,
Singing, ki-yi-yippy, yippy-yay.

Alternate Chorus:

Gonna tie my pecker to my leg, to my leg,
Gonna tie my pecker to my leg.

My name's Bill Taylor and my love's a squaw,
Livin' on the banks of the muddy Washita.

I come from Texas with the longhorn cattle
On a ten-dollar horse, and a forty-dollar saddle.

Sittin' in the saddle with my hand on my dong,
Shootin' jism on the cows as we go along.

We left Texas on October twenty-third,
And traveled up the trail with the 2-U herd.

We didn't reach town 'til Winter, Eighty-two.
My ass was draggin' and my pecker was too.

I went huntin' tail from a parlor house whore,
But I didn't have enough, so they kicked me out the door.

With my ass in the saddle and my pecker all sore,
I spied a little lady in the whorehouse door.

I asked for tail and I gave her a quarter,
And she says, "Young man, I'm a minister's daughter."

I took out a dollar and I put it in her hand,
And she says, "Young man, will your long pecker stand?"

I grabbed right hold and I throwed her on the grass.
My toe-hold slipped and I rammed it in her ass.

I fucked her standin' and I fucked her lyin';
If she'd a-had wings, I'd a-fucked her flyin'.

Five days later, my prick turned blue.
I ran to the doctor and he didn't know what to do.

So I went to another and he said, "Cough."
I coughed so hard my balls dropped off.

I went to another 'cause my pecker was sore;
"By God," said the doctor, "It's that same damn whore."

So I sold my horse and I sold my saddle,
And I bid goodby to the longhorn cattle.

The last time I seen her and I ain't seen her since,
She was scratchin' her cunt on a barbed wire fence.

The Band Played On

Certainly among the most popular of the old favorites, "The Band Played On"
could not go long without a parody.

Casey got hit with a bucket of shit
And the band played on.
He waltzed 'round the floor and got hit with some more
And the band played on.
His balls were so loaded, he nearly exploded.
The poor girl shook with alarm.
He married the bitch with the seven-year itch
And the band played on.

The Lehigh Valley I

How Victorian hearts fluttered when popular singers of the day sang of innocent maidens seduced from their proper parlors by dastardly villains. The immorality plays of the period presented their own prim estimate of crime and punishment. If the girl fell into sinful ways, she inevitably had to die repentant at the end of the piece. If she remained pure and simple in spite of the temptations thrust upon her, the hero would just as inevitably arrive on the scene to save both the day and her virtue.

In the harsh light of reality, this sort of melodrama is not going to last very long. Once "The Tramp's Lament" left the overstuffed drawing rooms, the bathetic agonies were quickly trimmed away. In the original "Tramp's Lament," the narrator informs the listener that he was once a blacksmith, and having put aside his anvil, he is hammer and tongs after the city slicker who stole his innocent daughter Nellie from hearth and fireside.

> Well, it's the same old story,
> Common enough, you'll say,
> But he was a soft-tongued devil
> And got her to run away.
>
> More than a month, or later,
> We heard from the poor young thing.
> He had run away and left her
> Without any wedding ring.

Nellie returns home to die of a raging fever—naturally—and dad is off to hunt the scoundrel who ruined his daughter.

This is all very well and good, but no self-respecting hobo could leave such an easy target alone. The result is one of the classics of hobo balladry.

Don't look at me that way, stranger,
I didn't shit in your seat.
I just come down from the mountains
With my balls all covered with sleet.

I've been up in the Lehigh Valley,
Me and my old pal, Lou,
A-pimpin' for a whorehouse
And a God damned good one too.

It was there that I first fucked Nellie;
She was the village belle.
I was only a lowdown pander
But I loved that girl like hell.

But along came a city slicker,
All handsome, gay and rich,
And he stole away my Nellie,
That stinkin' son-of-a-bitch.

I'm just restin' my ass a moment,
And then I'm on my way.
I'll hunt the runt that swiped my cunt
If it takes 'til Judgment Day.

The Lehigh Valley II

Another tear-jerker with the same roots, sung to the same tune.

It was down in the Lehigh Valley,
In early sixty-three,
We were panning sand in the Rio Grande,
Cross-eyed Bill and me.

When Bill got stuck on a gal named Nell,
Well, she warn't so goldurned bad,
But he brought her up to the house to live,
And I was a rooty lad.

While cross-eyed Bill was panning in the creek
As it trickled through the trees near by,
Nell and I'd be at it,
A-tearing off a tick on the sly.

Well, Spring rolled by in the old Lehigh
And Nell dropped twins, you see,
One was a cross-eyed son-of-a-bitch
And the other looked just like me.

Aimee McPherson

Combining the showmanship of a Ziegfeld with the fervid preaching of a hard-shell fundamentalist, Sister Aimee McPherson had built a $1.5 million temple, acquired a personal fortune worth an estimated $1.25 million and shaken Los Angeles' more orthodox clergy to the very bottom of their collection boxes.

And then, on May 18, 1926, the flamboyant evangelist disappeared.

For 36 days her flock of 40,000 fretted anxiously, torn by rumors of foul play, gladdened by whispers of her reincarnation. She reappeared in Agua Prieta, Mexico, not far from Douglas, Arizona, with a thin tale of being kidnapped and making a daring escape across the desert.

To the fanfare of newspaper headlines, Sister Aimee returned to her overjoyed congregation. More skeptical and less devoted, newspaper reporters and investigators for the district attorney began looking into her penny-dreadful tale.

No one ever proved anything—in spite of a long trial on charges of obstructing justice which sputtered to an indecisive end—but some believe Sister Aimee had spent ten days in the fashionable resort of Carmel, California, with a man believed to be the Four Square Gospel's former radio engineer, Kenneth G. Ormiston. (His name is wrong in the song.)

Sister Aimee's Carmel capers marked the beginning of the end of the Four Square Gospel Church. Her temple still offers its pulpit to traveling evangelists, but the pews are no longer crowded with devoted parishioners. The brass band, the huge women's choir, the gaudy wardrobe have disappeared. A handful of her former parishioners with warm memories, the now-silent temple, and this song are about all that remain of America's most famous female evangelist.

Did you ever hear the story 'bout Aimee McPherson,
Aimee McPherson, that wonderful person?
She weighed a hundred-eighty and her hair was red,
And she preached a wicked sermon so the papers all said.

Chorus:
Heigh-dee, heigh-dee, heigh-dee, heigh,
Ho-dee, ho-dee, ho-dee, ho.

Aimee built herself a radio station
To broadcast her preachin' to the nation.
She found a man named Armistead who knew enough
To run the radio while Aimee did her stuff.

She held a camp meetin' out at Ocean Park,
Preached from early mornin' 'til after dark,
Said the benediction, folded up the tent,
An' nobody knew where Aimee went.

When Aimee McPherson got back from her journey,
She told her story to the district attorney.
Said she'd been kidnapped on a lonely trail;
In spite of a lot of questions, she stuck to her tale.

Well, the Grand Jury started an investigation,
Uncovered a lot of spicy information,
Found out about a love nest down at Carmel-by-the-Sea,
Where the liquor was expensive and the lovin' was free.

They found a cottage with a breakfast nook,
A foldin' bed with a worn-out look.
The slats were busted and the springs were loose,
And the dents in the mattress fitted Aimee's caboose.

Well, they took poor Aimee and they threw her in jail.
Last I heard, she was out on bail.
They'll send her up for a stretch, I guess.
She worked herself up into an awful mess.

Now Radio Ray is a goin' hound;
He's goin' yet and he ain't been found.
They got his description, but they got it too late;
Since they got it, he's lost a lot of weight.

Now, I'll end my story in the usual way,
About this lady preacher's holiday.
If you don't get the moral then you're the gal for me
'Cause they got a lot of cottages down at Carmel-by-the-Sea.

Hallelujah, I'm a Bum

Rightfully considered an American classic, this hobo-bum-tramp's song could not fairly be called a "bawdy song," but only one with some off-color verses.

The fourth stanza of this version has a neat play-upon-words dependent upon the music and all but lost on the printed page. The sixth stanza, with its mention of the bedroom appliance, may give some indication of the age of the text.

Oh, why don't you work like other men do?
How the hell can I work when there's no work to do?

Chorus:

Hallelujah, I'm a bum,
Hallelujah, bum again.
Hallelujah, give us a handout
To revive us again.

Springtime is here and I'm just out of jail,
The whole winter in without any tail.

I went to a house and I knocked on the door,
My cock sticking straight out, my balls on the floor.

I asked for a piece of bread and some food.
The lady said, "Bum, you will eat when I'm screwed."

When I left that lady, my cock it was sore,
My belly was full, her ass it was tore.

68

I went to another and I asked her for bread.
She emptied the peepot all over my head.

Be happy and glad for the Springtime has come.
We'll throw down our shovels and go on the bum.

Why don't you fuck like other men do?
How the hell can I fuck when there's no broads to screw?

Red Wing

As long as we are on the subject of women, some kind words should be added about "Red Wing." At one time, the song of the Indian maid was a sentimental tearjerker, but no more. That hearthside ballad was parodied and re-parodied. The longest of these bawdy parodies are hard to come by now; this one stanza seems to be all most singers of this generation know. It's enough.

There once was an Indian maid
Who was a whore by trade.
For a dime at a whack,
She'd lie on her back
And let the cowboys shove it up her crack.
    One day, to her surprise,
    Her belly began to rise.
    Her cunt gave a grunt
    And out jumped a runt
    With his balls between his eyes.

69

Abdul the Bulbul Emir

The Crimean War stimulated a good deal of interest in things oriental and pseudo-oriental during the middle of the nineteenth century. The influence of the *ersatz* was felt throughout the popular arts, was absorbed in the styles and designs of the period, and, in no little way, was reflected in what are now objets d'art but were once common household goods—the overstuffed furniture, the tasseled antimacassars, the Tiffany glasses, the colored glass lampshades.

The original "Abdul" concerned the fateful duel between Ivan and the Emir, the pair doing each other in, snick and snee. However, that light-hearted lampoon of Russo-Turkish relations was turned to a contest of a different sort.

In the harems of Egypt no infidels see
The women more fairer than fair;
But the fairest, a Greek, was owned by a sheik
Called Abdul the Bulbul Emir.

A traveling brothel came into the town,
Run by a pimp from afar
Whose great reputation had traveled the nation,
'Twas Ivan Skavinsky Skavar.

Abdul the Bulbul arrived with his bride,
A prize whose eyes shone like a star.
He claimed he could prong more cunts with his dong
Than Ivan Skavinsky Skavar.

A great fucking contest was set for the day
A visit was planned by the czar,
And the curbs were all lined with harlots reclined
In honor of Ivan Skavar.

They met on the track with their tools hanging slack,
Dressed only in shoes and a leer.
Both were fast on the rise, but they gasped at the size
Of Abdul the Bulbul Emir.

The cunts were all shorn and no rubbers adorned
The prongs of the pimp and the peer,
But the pimp's steady stroke soon left without hope
The chance of the Bulbul Emir.

They worked through the night till the dawn's early light.
The clamor was heard from afar.
The multitudes came to applaud the ball game
Of Abdul and Ivan Skavar.

When Ivan had finished he turned to the Greek
And laughed when she shook with great fear.
She swallowed his pride; he buggered the bride
Of Abdul the Bulbul Emir.

When Ivan was done and was wiping his gun,
He bent down to polish his gear.
He felt up his ass a hard pecker pass;
'Twas Abdul the Bulbul Emir.

Now the crowds looking on proclaimed who had won.
They were ordered to part by the czar.
But fast were they jammed. The pecker was crammed
In Ivan Skavinsky Skavar.

Now the cream of the joke when apart they were broke
Was laughed at for years by the czar,
For Abdul the Bulbul left most of his tool
In Ivan Skavinsky Skavar.

The fair Grecian maiden a sad vigil keeps
With a husband whose tastes have turned queer.
She longs for the dong that once did belong
To Abdul the Bulbul Emir.

Bye Bye Blackbird

The original was a favorite of flappers during the halcyon decade of the Twenties. The parody circulated some ten years later.

Back your ass against the wall.
Here I come, balls and all.
    Bye, bye, cherry.
I may not have a helluva lot,
But what I got will fill your twat.
    Bye, bye, cherry.
First you took me out into the wildwood,
Then you took advantage of my childhood.
Hoist your ass and shake a teat.
Guide my prick into your slit.
    Cherry, bye, bye.

Kathusalem

In the original song, published in 1866, the heroine falls in love with an infidel, much to the displeasure of her father, the Baba of Jerusalem. One night, when the lovers are together, papa Baba greases a cord with goozalem and garrotes the two. And now the ghosts of the pair float over Jerusalem's wailing wall.

Like "Abdul the Bulbul Emir," "Kathusalem" was a beer parlor favorite. In such company, it is no wonder that by 1918—perhaps earlier—the original story had fallen upon such evil ways as these.

In days of old there was a dame
Who plied a trade of ancient fame.
It was a trade of ill repute;
In fact, she was a prostitute.

When the Jewish army came to town,
The price went up and she went down,
And took them on, white, black or brown,
This harlot of Jerusalem.

Chorus:

Hi, ho, Kathusalem,
The harlot of Jerusalem,
Prostitute of ill repute,
The daughter of the rabbi.

And now within this city's wall
There dwelt a priest both lean and tall,
And he could fornicate them all,
The maidens of Jerusalem.

Kathusalem was a sly old witch,
A dirty whore, a fucking bitch,
Who maketh all the pricks to twitch,
This harlot of Jerusalem.

One night, returning from a spree,
His customary hard had he,
And on the street he chanced to meet
This harlot of Jerusalem.

It was a fact: she had a crack
With hair so black; it could contract
To fit the tool of any fool
Who fucked in all Jerusalem.

She took him to a shady nook,
And from its hiding place she took
His penis curved into a hook,
The pride of all Jerusalem.

72

He laid her down upon the grass,
Lifted her dress above her ass;
He grabbed his prick and made a pass
At the fuck-hole of Kathusalem.

But she was low and underslung;
He missed her twat and hit her bung,
Planting the seeds of many a son
In the ass-hole of Kathusalem.

Kathusalem, she knew her part;
She spread her legs; she blew a fart,
And blew the bastard all apart,
All o'er the walls of Jerusalem.

Now the bastard's down in hell,
They say he's doing rather well,
And you can tell him by the smell
Of the asshole of Kathusalem.

In days to come she bore a brat,
A son-of-a-bitch, a dirty rat,
Who masturbated with a cat,
The bastard of Kathusalem.

The Winnipeg Whore

Lurking somewhere between the lines of this song, there is a grain of fact. The Winnipeg whore was probably a real woman, raised to mythic heights by lumberjacks. They borrowed a dance tune now known to school children as "Reuben, Reuben, I've Been Thinking" and to infants as "Ten Little Indians," hanging upon it an elegy in honor of the lady. The Winnipeg whore may be Canadian by birth, but she has become a naturalized citizen of the English-speaking world.

My first trip to Canadian borders,
My first trip to Canadian shores,
Met a gal named Rosie O'Grady,
Better known as the Winnipeg whore.

Said, "My faith! you look familiar,"
Flopped her ass on my knee,
Said she'd meet me in the northeast
    corner,
Dollar and a half would be her fee.

Some were fiddling, some were fie-deling,
Some were fucking on the bar room floor,
But I was up in the northeast corner
Putting it to the Winnipeg whore.

Fucked her once, fucked her twice,
Then I fucked her one time more.
She gave a shout, and then she fainted.
That was the end of the Winnipeg whore.

73

I-Yi-Yi-Yi

For sheer length, this is the champion bawdy song of all time. At any bawdy song swap, this is likely enough to run on for 25 or 30 verses, and that barely scratches the surface. The standard collection of limericks—only recently offered for public sale in the United States—has 1739 different limericks, any one of which might turn up as a verse in "I-Yi-Yi-Yi."

The song also has a number of different choruses, each popular in its own locale; two of the best-known are included here, with their variations. The first is set to a part of the chorus of "Cielito Lindo," a handsome complement to the music for the verses—also used by "The Gay Caballero." The alternate chorus is borrowed from a stage song of the last century.

Chorus:
I-yi-yi-yi,
In China, they never eat chili.
So here comes another verse worse than the other verse,
So waltz me around again, Willie.

74

Alternate chorus:
Sweet violets, sweeter than all the roses,
Covered all over from head to toe,
Covered all over with (shit)*

There was a young man from Racine,
Who invented a fucking machine.
Concave or convex,
It would fit either sex,
And jack itself off in between.

There once was a whore from the Azores,
Whose cunt was all full of big sores.
The dogs in the street
Lapped up the green meat
That hung in festoons from her drawers.

A scholarly fellow from Duckingham
Wrote a treatise on women and fucking 'em.
But he was a beat by a Turk
With a twelve-volume work
On cunts and the fine art of sucking 'em.

There was a young lady from Munich
Who was ravished one night by a eunuch.
At the height of her passion,
He slipped her a ration
From a squirt gun concealed in his tunic.

When she wanted a new way to futter,
He greased her behind with butter.
Then with a sock,
In went his jock,
And they carried her home on a shutter.

A mathematician named Fine
Always showed her classes a good time.
Instead of multiplication,
She taught fornication,
And never got past sixty-nine.

There was a man from De Grasse
Whose balls were made of brass.
In inclement weather,
He'd knock them together,
And sparks would fly out of his ass.

---

* The parenthetical word can be omitted.

There once was a man from Blatz
Whose balls were constructed of glass.
When they clanked together,
They played "Stormy Weather,"
And lightning shot out of his ass.

There once was a man from Boston
Who drove around in an Austin.
There was room for his ass
And a gallon of gas,
So his balls hung out and he lost them.

There was a young girl named Myrtle
Who had an affair with a turtle.
Her swelling abdominal
Was considered phenomenal
'Til they discovered the turtle was fertile.

An unfortunate fellow named Chase
Had an ass that was badly misplaced.
He showed indignation
When an investigation
Proved that few persons shit through their faces.

There was a young man named Hentzel
Who had a terrific long pencil.
He went through an actress,
Two sheets and a mattress,
And shattered the family utensil.

There once was a man from Nantuckett
With a cock so long he could suck it.
Said he, with a grin,
As he wiped off his chin,
"If my beard was a cunt, I would fuck it."

There once was a hermit named Dave
Who kept a dead whore in his cave.
He said, "I admit
I'm a bit of a shit,
But think of the money I save."

There was a young fellow from Kent
Whose dong was so long that it bent.
To save himself trouble,
He put it in double,
And instead of coming, he went.

There once was a maid from Cape Cod
Who thought babies came from God,
But it wasn't the Almighty
Who lifted her nighty,
But Roger the lodger, by God.

There once was a rabbi from Keith
Who circumcised men with his teeth.
It was not for the treasure,
Nor sexual pleasure,
But to get at the cheese underneath.

There once was a man from Iraq
Who had holes down the length of his cock.
When he got an erection,
He would play a selection
From Johann Sebastian Bach.

There was a young lady from Dee
Whose hymen was split into three,
And when she was diddled,
The middle string fiddled
"Nearer My God to Thee."

There was a young man from Leeds
Who swallowed a package of seeds.
Great tufts of grass
Grew out of his ass,
And he couldn't sit down for the weeds.

While Titian was mixing rose madder,
He espied a nude girl on a ladder.
Her position to Titian
Suggested coition
So he climbed up the ladder and had 'er.

There was a lady named Wild
Who kept herself quite undefiled.
By thinking of Jesus,
Contagious diseases,
And the bother of having a child.

There was a couple named Kelly
Who were stuck belly to belly
Because, in their haste,
They used library paste
Instead of petroleum jelly.

There once was a novice at Chichester
Whose form made the saints in their niches stir.
One morning at matins,
Her bosom 'neath satins
Made the Bishop of Chichester's britches stir.

There once was a lady named Alice
Who used a dynamite stick for a phallis.
They found her vagina
In North Carolina,
And the rest of her body near Dallas.

A Roman who hailed from Gazondom
Used a dried hedgehog's hide for a condom.
His mistress did shout
As he pulled the thing out,
"De gustibus non disputandum!"

There was a young lawyer named Rex
With diminutive organs of sex.
When hauled in for exposure,
He replied with composure,
"De minimis non curat lex."

There was a biologist named Reba
Who loved a sexy amoeba.
This primordial jelly
Would crawl on her belly
And murmur, *"Ich liebe. Ich liebe."*

On the breast of a lady named Gail
Was tatooed the price of her tail.
And on her behind,
For the sake of the blind,
Was the same information in Braille.

There was a young man named Adair
Who was fucking a girl on the stair.
The bannister broke
And by doubling his stroke,
He finished her off in mid-air.

An Argentine gaucho named Bruno
Said, "Fucking is one thing I do know.
All women are fine,
And sheep are divine,
But llamas are *numero uno.*"

A wealthy old maid from Twickenham
Had a butler without any prick on him.
On her knees every day
To God she would pray
To lengthen and strengthen and thicken him.

There was a young lady named Ransom
Who was loved three times in a hansom.
When she asked for more,
Came a voice from the floor,
"My name is Simpson, not Sampson."

There once was a queer from Khartoum
Who invited a whore [dyke] to his room.
They argued all night
As to who had the right
To do what, and with which and to whom.

She wasn't what one would call pretty,
And other girls offered her pity.
So nobody guessed
That her Wasserman test
Involved half of Oklahoma City.

A lady astrologist in Vancouver
Once captured a man by maneuver.
Influenced by Venus,
She jumped on his penis,
And nothing on earth could remove her.

There was a young lady from France
Who decided to take just once chance.
For an hour or so,
She just let herself go,
And now all her sisters are aunts.

There was a young lady from Maine
Who enjoyed copulating on a train.
Not once, I maintain,
But again and again
And again and again and again.

An Eskimo on his vacation
Took a night off to succumb to temptation.
'Ere the night was half through,
The Eskimo was, too,
For their nights are of six months duration.

The Hermit

Properly speaking, "The Hermit" is not a bawdy song at all. One might call it "improper" or "saucy," but not "dirty."

A hermit once lived in a beautiful dell,
And it is no legend, this story I tell,
So my father declared, who knew him quite well,
    The hermit.

He lived in a cave by the side of the lake,
Decoctions of herbs for his health he would take,
And only of fish could this good man partake
    On Friday.

And most of his time he spent in repose.
Once a year he would bathe both his body and clothes.
How the lake ever stood it, the Lord only knows,
    And He won't tell.

One day as he rose, dripping and wet,
His horrified vision three pretty girls met;
In matters of gallantry, he wasn't a vet,
    So he blushed.

He grabbed up his hat that lay on the beach,
And covered up all that its wide brim would reach,
Then he cried to the girls in a horrified screech,
    "Go away."

But the girls only laughed at his pitiful plight,
And begged him to show them the wonderful sight,
But he clung to his hat with all of his might
    To hide it.

80

But just at this moment a villainous gnat
Made the hermit forget just where he was at.
He struck at the insect, and let go of the hat—
 "Oh, horrors!"

And now I have come to the crux of my tale.
At first he turned red, then he turned pale,
Then he offered a prayer, for prayers never fail,
 So 'tis said.

Of the truth of this tale, there is no doubt at all.
The Lord heard his prayer and He answered his call:
Though he let go the hat, the hat didn't fall.
 A miracle!

Doodle-De-Doo

Much of American popular music simply begs for parody (much of it, too, is already a parody of itself). There is usually someone willing to oblige; witness this take-off on the nonsensical song which pleased an earlier generation.

Do it to me, like you did to Marie,
Last Saturday night on the davenport couch.
First you caressed her, and then you undressed her,
Last Saturday night on the davenport couch.
 Roses are red and ready for pluckin',
 I am sixteen and ready for high school.
 Doodle-de-doo, doodle-de-doo,
 Doodle-de-doodle-de-doo.

Showed it to me, her lily-white knee
And her doodle-de-doo, her doodle-de-doo.
She showed me her chest but the part I liked best
Was her doodle-de-doo, her doodle-de-doo.
 Under the cover, she'll shake it and shake it,
 With all of her shaking it's a wonder she don't break it.
 Doodle-de-doo, doodle-de-doo,
 Doodle-de-doodle-de-doo.

The Sterilized Heiress

Purportedly the recounting of a true occurrence, this has survived all but the faintest memory of the incident it laments.

Oh, I am the sterilized heiress,
The butt of all laughter of rubes.
I'm comely; I'm rich; I'm a bit of a bitch,
And my mother ran off with my tubes.

Chorus:
Fie on you, mater, you scoundrel,
For stealing my feminine joys.
Restore my abdomen, and make me a woman.
I want to go out with the boys.

The butler and second man scorn me.
No more do they use my door key.
The cook from Samoa has spermatozoa
For others, but never for me.

Imagine my stark consternation
On feeling the rude surgeon's hands.
Exploring my person was Surgeon McPherson
And fiddling around with my glands.

No action in court can repay me
For stealing the peas in my pod.
Oh, where are the yeggs who took all my eggs?
I'll cut off their bollocks, by God!

Last Chorus:
Fie on you, mater, you scoundrel,
For stealing my feminine joys.
I've nothing but anger for Margaret Sanger.
I want to go out with the boys.

82

The Woodpecker's Hole

Another sea song come ashore, the bawdy element of this camp and college song has all but vanished. Just why American singers persist in abusing the wood-pecker is not clear. The version sung by English sailors makes a good deal more sense, if you read through the obvious bowdlerization:

I put me fist in the mate's earhole,
The mate, he cried, "God bless me soul.
Take it out! Take it out! Take it out! Take it out!"
So I took me fist from the chief mate's ear.
The mate, he cried, "Why that's darn queer.
Put it back! Put it back! Put it back! Put it back!"*

In any event, clean or dirty, sense or nonsense, the words are invariably sung to "Dixie."

I stuck my finger in the woodpecker's hole,
And the woodpecker said, "God damn your soul!
Take it out, take it out, take it out, remove it!"

I removed my finger from the woodpecker's hole,
And the woodpecker said, "God damn your soul!
Put it back, put it back, put it back, replace it!"

I replaced my finger in the woodpecker's hole,
And the woodpecker said, "God damn your soul!
Wrong way, wrong way, wrong way, revolve it!"

I revolved my finger in the woodpecker's hole,
And the woodpecker said, "God damn your soul!
Wrong way, wrong way, wrong way, reverse it!"

I reversed my finger in the woodpecker's hole,
And the woodpecker said, "God damn your soul!
Take it out, take it out, take it out, remove it!"

I removed my finger from the woodpecker's hole,
And the woodpecker said, "God damn your soul!
Put it back, put it back, put it back, replace it!"

And so on, *ad infinitum*.

---

* Quoted from Hugill, *Shanties from the Seven Seas*, p. 424.

Caviar Comes from Virgin Sturgeon

Some years ago, Burl Ives recorded a song which he called "The Eddystone Lighthouse," happily caroling a fragment of one of the better-known bawdy songs in the English language. (According to folk song scholar John Greenway, this is not the first time that the general public has been guyed by a seemingly innocent song; "The Big Rock Candy Mountain" is so highly regarded as to be included in elementary school music books. Little do the moppets, teachers or parents know that the song was originally an overdrawn picture to lure young lads away from home in the company of those known colloquially as "dirty old men." One can easily imagine the horrified shock were parents and administrators to learn this grubby little fact of life.)

This is a more extensive version of the song which Ives introduced to the mass media. It's tune is "Reuben, Reuben, I've Been Thinking."

Caviar comes from virgin sturgeon;
Virgin sturgeon's a very fine dish.
Very few sturgeon are ever virgin,
That's why caviar's a very rare dish.

Caviar comes from virgin sturgeon;
Virgin sturgeon's a very fine fish.
Virgin sturgeon needs no urgin';
That's why caviar is my dish.

I fed caviar to my girl-friend;
She was a virgin tried and true.
Now my girl-friend needs no urgin',
There isn't anything she won't do.

I fed caviar to my grandpa;
He was a gent of ninety-three.
Shrieks and squeals revealed that grandpa
Had chased grandma up a tree.

Father was the keeper of the
    Eddystone light,
And he slept with a mermaid one
    fine night.
Results of this were off-spring three;
Two were fishes and the other
    was me.

The postman came on the first of
    May;
The policeman came on the very
    same day.
Nine months later there was hell
    to pay:
Who fired that first shot, the blue
    or the gray?

Little Mary went a-sledding,
And her sled turned upside down.
Now little Mary's singing,
"M'ass is in the cold, cold ground."

84

Other versions detail the procreative habits of various fish, crustaceans and other denizens of the deep:

Shad roe comes from scarlet shad fish
Shad fish have a very sorry fate.
Pregnant shad fish is a sad fish,
Got that way without a mate.

The green sea turtle's mate is happy
With her lover's winning ways.
First he grips her with his flippers,
Then he grips and flips for days.

Mrs. Clam is optimistic,
Shoots her eggs out in the sea,
Hopes her suitor is a shooter,
With the self-same shot as she.

Give a thought to the happy codfish,
Always there when duty calls.
Female codfish is an odd fish;
From them come codfish balls.

Oysters they are fleshy bivalves.
They have youngsters in their shell.
How they diddle is a riddle,
But they do, so what the hell.

Life Presents a Dismal Picture

This cry of Job, probably of English origin, circulates at times embedded in other, completely separate songs, and sometimes as a full-fleged ditty in its own right. When sung to the maudlin melody of "Scarlet Ribbons," the pitiable lamentation is all the more humorous; some listeners are especially amused by the unspoken comparison of the bathic lyrics of the original and these.

Life presents a dismal picture.
Life is full of tears and gloom.
Father has a penile stricture.
Mother has a fallen womb.
In the corner sits my sister,
Never laughs and never smiles.
What a dismal occupation:
Cracking ice for father's piles.

Brother Bill has been deported
For a homosexual crime.
Sister Sue has been aborted
For the sixth or seventh time.
Little Luke is slowly dying
For he's always having fits.
Every time he laughs, he vomits;
Everytime he farts, he shits.

A Garland of Parodies

There is simply no way of telling just how many parodies there are circulating in oral tradition at any given time. This is only a small sample.

Parody on "Beautiful Dreamer"

Born in a whorehouse, raised like a slave,
Drinking and fucking are all that I crave,
Smashing in windows, breaking down doors,
Calling old ladies chicken-shit whores.
Little old lady, bring me a toddy.
I want to go out and fuck everybody.

Parody on "Sunday, Monday, and Always"

Oh, won't you tell me, dear,
The size of your brassiere?
Twenty, thirty, forty?
If it's forty-two,
I'll be in love with you,
Sunday, Monday, and always.

Parody on "You Are My Sunshine"

The other night, dear, as we lay sleeping,
I could not help it; I lost control.
And now you wonder, just why I'm leaving;
You will find out in nine months or so.

Parody on "Let Me Call You Sweetheart"

Let me ball you, sweetheart; I'm in bed with you.
Let me hear you whisper that it's time to screw.
Make your body wiggle in the same old way,
And I'll be back to see you on my next pay day.

Parody on "Home on the Range"

Oh, give me a home, where the beer bottles foam,
Where with blondes and brunets I can play,
Where seldom is heard, a discouraging word,
'Cause my wife is out working all day.

86

Parody on "Sweet Adeline"

Sweet Antoinette,
Your pants are wet.
You say it's sweat.
It's piss, I'll bet.
In all my dreams,
Your bare ass gleams.
You're the wrecker
Of my pecker,
Antoinette.

Parody on "Baby Face"

Pubic hair, you've got the cutest little pubic hair.
There is no finer anywhere, pubic hair,
Penis or vagina, nothing could be finer.
Pubic hair. I'm in heaven when I'm in your underwear.
I don't need a shove; I got a taste of love
From your pretty pubic hair.

Parody on "Carolina in the Morning"

Anything would be finer
Than to see my Carolina
In the morning,
Falsies lying on the floor
Next to teeth bought in a store
At dawning.
She looks like Mischa Auer
When she splashes in the shower.
Masochists come by the score
Just to see her strip once more
At dawning.

Parody on "The Last Time I Saw Paris"

I'll ne'er forget that wedding night.
Her figure round and neat
Came off like icing on a cake
And landed at her feet.
The last time I saw cotton
Was on the floor that night.
It might look good in fancy clothes
But it's not much fun to bite.

Parody on "O Tannenbaum"

Foam rubber pads, foam rubber pads,
Now we can tell the girls from the lads.
You've made our girls so fully packed;
They now have curves where once they lacked.
You've given each and every one
A silhouette where they had none.
Now every girl can [look] like Jane
And rustle forth for fun and gain.

Parody on "When You Wore a Tulip"

Oh, John saw a tulip,
A big yellow tulip
When Mary took off her clothes.
She dared him to take it
As she lay stript naked
And he did as everyone knows.
Oh, she laid a-dreaming
While he laid a-creaming;
'Twas down where the black hairs grow.
His cock was stiffer than julep
When he saw her tulip
For it looked like a big red rose.

Parody on "St. Louis Woman"

St. Louis woman, she had a yen for men;
She went to bed with a fountain pen.
The rubber busted and the ink ran wild.
St. Louis woman, she had a blue-black child.

Parody on "Jada"

Scrotom. Scrotom.
S-C-R-O-T-O-M.
Mangy, scrungy,
S-C-R-O-T-O-M.
Scrotom, scrotom,
Covered with hair,
What would you do
If it wasn't there?
Scrotom, scrotom,
It's what we keep our gonads in!

88

Parody on "Secret Love"

Once I had a secret love,
That lived within the heart of me.
When I asked my love her fee,
She said for me the fee was free.
When I asked why it was free,
She said, "Seeley Mattress sponsors me.
Last night, we were on channel four."
Now my secret love's no secret anymore.

Parody on "Alice Blue Gown"

In that little pink nightie of mine,
When I wear it, I always feel fine.
I remember the night; I was too tight to fight.
He said that he loved me. He loved me all right.
It's been six months tonight since that night,
And that little pink nightie's too tight.
I wore it; he tore it; I'll always adore it,
That little pink nightie of mine.

Parody on "The Object of My Affection"

The object of my affection makes my erection
Turn from pink to rosy red.
Everytime she touches its head,
It points the way to bed.

And finally, a two-line fragment sung to the familiar first bars of the nostalgic
favorite, "The Anniversary Waltz":

Oh, how we danced on the night we were wed!
We danced and we danced 'til we fell out of bed.

The Pioneers

This is a far cry from the schoolboy's myth of the overlanders braving the savage
land, fighting off the marauding Indians, turning the wilderness into a veritable
Garden of Eden. Even if the facts of this song are not necessarily applicable to
all pioneers, one suspects the tone of the piece is a lot closer to the attitude of
the overlanders themselves than school books would have us believe.

The pioneers have hairy ears.
They piss through leather britches.
They wipe their ass on broken glass,
Those hardy sons-of-bitches.

When cunt is rare, they fuck a bear.
They knife him if he snitches.
They knock their cocks against the
    rocks,
Those hardy sons-of-bitches.

They take their ass upon the grass
In bushes or in ditches.
Their two-pound dinks are full of kinks,
Those hardy sons-of-bitches.

Without remorse, they fuck a horse,
And beat him if he twitches.
Their two-foot pricks are full of nicks,
Those hardy sons-of-bitches.

To make a mule stand for the tool,
They beat him with hickory switches.
They use their pricks for walking sticks,
Those hardy sons-of-bitches.

Great joy they reap from cornholing
    sheep
In barns, or bogs or ditches,
Nor give a damn if it be a ram,
Those hardy sons-of-bitches.

They walk around, prick to the ground,
And kick it if it itches,
And if it throbs, they scratch it with
    cobs,
Those hardy sons-of-bitches.

The Gay Caballero

The antic muse wanders on—this time against the stream. This song, under one or another title, was known on various college campuses before Ohio State University student Frank Crumit edited and then recorded it. The recording sold two million copies before it suffered the usual fate of the hit song—virtual oblivion. Meanwhile, the original bawdy song lives on.

Oh, I am a gay caballero,
Going from Rio de Janeiro
With an exceedingly long latraballee
And two fine latraballeros.

I went down to Tijuana,
Exceedingly fine Tijuana,
With my exceedingly long latraballee
And my two fine latraballeros.

I met a gay senorita,
Exceedingly gay senorita.
She wanted to play with my latraballee,
And with one of my latraballeros.

Oh, now I've got the clapito,
Exceedingly painful clapito,
Right on the end of my latraballee,
And on one of my latraballeros.

I went to see a medico,
Exceedingly fine medico.
He looked at the end of my latraballee
And at one of my latraballeros.

He took out a long stiletto,
Exceedingly long stiletto.
He cut off the end of my latraballee
And one of my latraballeros.

And now I'm a sad caballero,
Returning to Rio de Janiero,
Minus the end of my latraballee
And one of my latraballeros.

At night I lay on my pillow
Seeking to finger my willow.
All I find there is a handful of hair
And one dried-up latraballero.

Mother

There were hundreds of tear-jerking ballads of hearth and home published in the last half of the nineteenth century; none of them can pretend to very much worth as either poetry or music. But since nothing is sacred to the erotic muse, inevitably someone had to write a parody of the most famous of the "mother" songs.

M is for the many times you made me.
O is for the other times you've tried.
T is for the tourist cabin weekends.
H is for the hell you raised inside.
E is for the everlasting passion.
R is for the 'reck you made of me.
Put them all together, they spell "Mother,"
And that is what you made of me.

Teasing Songs

There are literally dozens of these songs, which stanza after stanza rush right up to the brink of the tabooed word, then do a hasty about-face. They are especially popular amongst children, although an occasional adult will remember one from his childhood and sing it. This is a small sampling of the genre.

Suzanne Was a Lady

Suzanne was a lady with plenty of class
Who knocked the boys dead when she wiggled her

Eyes at the fellows as girls sometimes do
To make it quite plain that she wanted to

Go for a walk or a stroll through the grass,
Then hurry back home for a nice piece of

Ice cream and cake and a piece of roast duck,
And after each meal she was ready to

Go for a walk or a stroll on the dock
With any young man with a sizeable

Roll of green bills and a pretty good front,
And if he talked fast enough, she would show him her

Little pet dog who's subject to fits,
And maybe let him grab hold of her

Little white hand with a movement so quick.
Then she'd lean over and tickle his

Chin while she showed what she once learned in France,
And asked the poor fellow to take off his

Coat while she sang "Off the Mandalay Shore,"
For whatever she was, Suzanne was no bore.

92

Another in the same vein, sung to the same tune as is "Suzanne Was a Lady,"
is this:

The Ship's in the Harbor

The ship's in the harbor; she lies by the dock
Like a young man with a stiff standing

Backbone to brace when he stands and salutes,
Backbone to brace when he stands and salutes.

And there was young Johnny, the pride of the crew,
Who liked to drink whiskey and also to

Water the garden when he was at home,
Water the garden when he was at home.

He could swim like a fish and could swim like a duck.
He could show the young ladies a new way to

Save their sweet souls if they should have a cramp,
Save their sweet souls if they should have a cramp.

But then we put in at a far northern port,
And he froze it one morning and broke it off

Half-way to Juneau and half-way to Nome,
Half-way to Juneau and half-way to Nome.

The ship's in the harbor; she lies by the dock,
But, alas for poor Johnny, he has no more

Yardarm to splice with or topmast to brace,
Yardarm to splice with or topmast to brace.

And a third song, to the same tune, this one ending in mid-air:

There once was a farmer who lived by the crick,
A dirty, old farmer who played with his

Marbles in the Springtime with the lady next door.
You could tell by her actions that she was a

Very nice lady who swam like a duck.
She taught all the children a new way to . . .

The most aggressive of these teasing songs, and perhaps the most popular, finally plunges over the brink.

Country Boy, Country Boy

Country boy, country boy
Sitting on a rock.
Along came a bumble bee
And stung him on the

Cocktail, ginger ale,
Five cents a glass.
If you don't like it,
You can shove it up your

Ask me no questions;
I'll tell you no lies.
A guy got hit with a bucket of shit
Right between the eyes.

Finally, two recitations by school children, the first a thumb-to-the-nose parody of Longfellow's *The Midnight Ride of Paul Revere*.

Listen, my children, and you shall hear
Of the midnight ride of Paul Revere.
He jumped in the car, stepped on the gas.
The bottom fell out and he fell on his

Now don't get excited and don't be alarmed.
I was going to say he fell on his arm.

And the second, a parody of a parody, no less:

Listen, my children, and you shall hear
Of the midnight ride of a glass of beer.
Out of the icebox and into a glass,
Down the stomach and out of your

94

Don't get excited and don't get sore.
Down the stomach and out to the floor.

Hot Vagina

"Hot Vagina" is seemingly the first parody of a singing commercial—the original
was used on the Tom Mix radio serial of the late 1930's—and as such deserves
special notice. Nowadays, these parodies are common amongst schoolchildren
who know dozens such as:

Pepsi Cola hits the spot,
Ties your belly in a knot,
Tastes like vinegar, looks like ink.
Pepsi Cola's a stinky drink.

or:

I hate Bosco; Bosco ain't for me.
My mommy put it in my milk to try and poison me.
But I fooled mommy; I put it in her tea,
And now there's no more mommy to try and poison me.

Only rarely are schoolyard parodies as basic as this though.

Hot vagina for your breakfast,
Hot vagina for your lunch,
Hot vagina for your dinner,
Just munch, munch, munch, munch, munch.
It's so speedy and nutritious,
Bite-size and ready to eat,
So take a tip from Tom, go eat your mom;
Hot vagina can't be beat.

Charlotte the Harlot I

Sung to one of the most frequently borrowed tunes in the Anglo-American stock, "Sweet Betsy from Pike" or "Villikins and His Dinah," this song commemorates one of the more hospitable whores in American literature. Her untimely demise is still lamented in college dormitories and neighborhood bars.

Down in cunt valley where gizzum does flow,
The cocksuckers work for a nickel a blow;
There lived pretty Charlotte, the girl I adore,
My free-fucking, cock-sucking cowpunchers' whore.

Chorus:

Charlotte the harlot, the girl I adore,
The pride of the prairie, the cowpunchers' whore.

She's easy, she's greasy, she works on the street,
And whenever you see her, she's always in heat.
She'll do it for a dollar, take less or take more,
She's Charlotte the harlot, the cowpunchers' whore.

One day on the prairie, while riding along,
My seat in the saddle, the reins on my dong,
Who should I meet but the girl I adore,
Charlotte the harlot, the cowpunchers' whore.

One day on the prairie, no pants on her quim,
A rattlesnake saw her and slipped right on in.
She wiggled, she giggled; it ticked down there.
She had a vagina with rattles and hair.

I got off my pony, I reached for her crack.
The damn thing was rattling and biting me back.
I took out my pistol; I aimed for its head.
I missed the damn rattler; I shot her instead.

Her funeral procession was forty miles long,
With a chorus of cowpunchers singing this song:
"Here lies a young maiden who'll screw us no more,
Young Charlotte the harlot, the cowpunchers' whore."

Charlotte the Harlot II

Charlotte's story is lost, and in its place is a paean in praise of the prostitute's promiscuity, sung to the tune of "Down in the Valley."

Down in Cunt Valley where the Red River flows,
Where cock-suckers flourish and maidenheads grow,
That's where I met Lupe, the girl I adore,
She's my hot-fucking, cock-sucking, Mexican whore.

Chorus:

She'll fuck you; she'll suck you; she'll gnaw at your nuts;
She'll wrap her legs 'round you, and squeeze out your guts.
She'll hug you and kiss you 'til you wish you could die.
I'd rather eat Lupe than sweet cherry pie.

She got her first piece as a girlie of eight,
While swinging like hell on the old Golden Gate.
The cross-member broke and the upright went in,
And ever since then, she's lived a life of sin.

Now Lupe is dead, and she lies in her tomb.
The maggots crawl out of her decomposed womb,
But the smile on her face seems to say, "Give me more."
She's my hot-fucking, cock-sucking, Mexican whore.

Charlotte the Harlot III

Originally from Australia, this version of "Charlotte the Harlot" forgets all about the lady's misadventures with the poisonous serpent. The abrupt ending is deliberate.

'Twas the first time I saw her.
She was all dressed in blue,
All in blue, all in blue,
I said, "How do you do?"
    Down in the valley where she followed me.
    She's easy; she's greasy; she works in the street.
    And each time I see her she's always in heat.
    She'll do it for a dollar, take less or take more.
    She's Charlotte the harlot, the cowpunchers' whore.

The next time I saw her
She was all dressed in black,
All in black, all in black,
I laid her on her back
    Down in the valley where she followed me. (Etc.)

Successive verses follow the same pattern, substituting:

Pink . . . oh, how my finger did stink
Green . . . I slipped it in between
Red . . . oh, how her hymen bled
White . . . oh, how her pussy was tight

The last stanza, in full, is:

'Twas the next time I saw her
She was all dressed in mauve,
All in mauve, all in mauve . . .

The Mother-Fuckers' Ball

A collegiate parody of "Darktown Strutters' Ball," this has apparently only a limited circulation.

Oh, there's going to be a ball at the mother-fuckers' hall.
The witches and the bitches gonna be there all.
Now, honey, don't be late,
'Cause they're passing out pussy 'bout half-past eight.
Oh, I've fucked in France and I've fucked in Spain,
I even got a piece on the coast of Maine,
But the best damned piece of all
Was when I got my mother-in-law
Last Saturday night at the mother-fuckers' ball.

Ditties

In the course of his field work, a folk song collector is certain to turn up any number of short songs, or fragments of longer songs. Frequently, these do not see print unless the fragment is a survival of a rare song or ballad. These ditties are not necessarily rare at all.

To the tune of "The Irish Washerwoman":

Oh, Binnie, Oh, Binnie, oh come ye qiuck
And see the wild Irishman handle his prick.
'Tis as long as your arm and as thick as your wrist
With a knob on the end as big as your fist.

To the much-used tune of "Sweet Betsy from Pike":

You can talk about fucking; well, fucking's all right.
I fucked with a whore twenty times in one night,
And each time I fucked her, I came out a quart.
If you don't think that's fucking, well, you fucking well ort.

The melody for the verse of the Civil War classic "Tramp, Tramp, Tramp" carries this burden:

He was sitting in the prison with his head between his hands,
And the shadow of his prick against the wall,
And the hairs grew thick from his knees up to his prick,
And the rats were playing billiards with his balls.

This borrows the tune of "Turkey in the Straw":

Oh, I had a girl friend; she like to sport and play,
Cutest little girl friend that ever hit the hay.
The skin on her belly was tight as a drum,
And every time we fucked it went rub-a-dum-dum.

This lullaby uses the same melody:

Shmendrick had a horse and he thought it was a cow,
And he went out to milk it and he didn't know how,
And the night was dark and dreary and Shmendrick
    couldn't see,
And the darned little horsey went a-wee, wee, wee.

100

A third fragment to the same tune:

She ripped and she tore, and she shit on the floor,
Wiped her ass on the knob on the door,
And the moon shone bright on the nipple of her teat.
Bluebird singing, "Sweet chicken shit."

A variant of this quatrain is somewhat more coherent:

Oh, the moon shone bright on the nipple of her teat
As she went to the outhouse to take a little shit,
But her ass gave a grunt and she shit on the floor,
And the smell of her farts drove the cat out the door.

To the melody of "Goodnight, Irene," a fashion note:

Sometimes Irene wears pajamas.
Sometimes Irene wears a gown.
Sometimes Irene wears nothing,
And shocks all the people in town.

The much-used melody of "The Girl I Left Behind Me" serves for these two songs:

The wind blew free and she couldn't see,
And the wind blew up her nightie.
You should have seen those great big teats,
Well, Jesus Christ almighty!
    Oh, I pumped her once and I pumped her twice,
    And I pumped her once too often,
    And I broke the mainspring in her back,
    And now she's in her coffin.

And:

Oh, there's hair on this and there's hair on that,
And there's hair on my dog, Fido.
But there's far more hair, and I won't say where,
On the girl I left behind me.

Humoresque

This is atypical of American bawdy song. First of all, the tune is borrowed from the concert piece by Anton Dvorák, the only classical composer so honored.

Second of all, it makes no real sense; the last two stanzas bear no relation to the first two. Not that that really matters.

Passengers will please refrain
From flushing toilets while the train
Is standing in the station. I love you.
We encourage constipation
While the train is in the station.
Moonlight always makes me think of you.

If you simply have to go
When other people are too slow,
There is only one thing you can do.
You'll just have to take a chance,
Be brave, and do it in your pants,
But I'll forgive you, darling. I love you.

Every evening after dark
We goose the statues in the park;
If Sherman's horse can stand it, so can you.
Washington was very firm
And Lincoln didn't even squirm.
Darling, that's why I'm in love with you.

Mabel, Mabel, strong and able,
Get your big ass off the table.
Don't you know the quarter is for beer?
You can always earn your pay,
But make your tips another way,
And I'll forgive you, darling. I love you.

I Used to Work in Chicago

The plays-upon-words in this product of urban America are either the best, or the worst, depending upon your point of view, in bawdy songlore. Because of the wordplay, the song is most popular with high school students. Its survival in such an officially hostile climate is proof of the hardihood of bawdy songs.

Chorus:

I used to work in Chicago
In a department store.
I used to work in Chicago.
I did but I don't anymore.

A lady came in for some gloves one day.
"What will you have?" I said.
"Rubber," she said, and rub her I did.
I did but I don't anymore.

A lady came in for a hat one day.
"What will you have?" I said.
"Felt," she said, and feel her I did.
I did but I don't anymore.

The following verses substitute in this framework these products and reactions:

Cake . . . layer . . . layer her I did
Dress . . . jumper . . . jump her I did
Shoe . . . pump . . . pump her I did
Poultry . . . goose . . . goose her I did
Meat . . . neck . . . neck her I did

103

Schnooglin'

In one or another form, this warning in rhyme form is known to hundreds of girls' schools and summer camps. This version happens to come from a California B'nai B'rith Girls' camp in Southern California. It could just as well—contrary to what the counselors will tell worried parents—come from a YWCA, a Girl Scout, or a Catholic Youth Organization camper. Such songs are no respecters of race, creed, color or place of national origin; they are ubiquitous.

"AZA" is the organization for Jewish boys, the parallel of the BBG.

Schnooglin' is the process
By which we do perform
The gentle art of necking
In order to keep warm.

There's schnooglin' on the beaches,
Schnooglin' in the park.
An AZA can teach you
How to schnoogle in the dark.

Now gather round me, girlies,
And listen to my plea:
Don't ever trust an AZA
An inch above the knee.

I know a girl who tried it,
And dearly did she pay.
The son-of-a-gun, he left her
With the son of an AZA.

This little AZA boy,
He grew up one day,
And met a BBG girl
In the same old-fashioned way.

This little BBG girl,
She did not hear our plea,
And now they have between them
Another BBG.

The moral of this story
Is very plain to see:
Don't ever trust an AZA
An inch above the knee.

I Went Downtown

These two couplets may have at one time been a part of "The Chisholm Trail,"
but are now sung as a separate song to that tune.

I went downtown to buy a pound of butter,
And I saw a little nigger pissing in the gutter.

Chorus:

Singing, ki-yi-yippy, yippy-yay, yippy-yay,
Singing, ki-yi-yippy, yippy-yay.

I picked up a rock and hit him on the cock,
And you should have seen the little bugger run around the block.

UNDERGRADUATES COARSE

Fraternity and sorority houses, dormitories and living groups are veritable hot beds of bawdy song. The college student who doesn't know at least one improper ditty is a rarity, and even the most unlikely people can lead the group in song. The largest repertoire of bawdy songs which the editor has encountered reposed in the head of a mild-mannered superman, a bookish Ph.D. candidate in organic chemistry who possessed, among other things, an uncanny capacity for beer. One night, sufficiently bribed, he began singing. Two six-packs and a quick dash to the bathroom later, he had sung twenty choice bawdy songs.

So the old songs are preserved and new ones created in academe.

Last Night I Stayed Up Late to Masturbate

Parodists usually stay away from songs with tricky rhythms or complex rhyme schemes; it makes their work too difficult. "Last Night I Stayed Up" is a happy exception. Set to the tune of "Funiculi, Funicula," it sports one of the most felicitous meldings of tune and lyrics in this collection.

Last night I stayed up late to masturbate.
It was so nice! I did it twice.
Last night I stayed up late to pull my pud.
It felt so good! I knew it would.
You should see me working on the short strokes;
I use my hand. It's simply grand.
You should see me working on the long strokes.

108

I use my feet. It's really neat.
Smash it! Bash it! Beat it on the floor.
Smite it! Bite it! Ram it through the door.
I have some friends who seem to think that a fuck
    is simply grand,
But for all around enjoyment I prefer it in the hand.

We Go to College

In recent years, there has been a spate of articles in the popular journals concerning the morals, or lack of same, of today's college student. They are usually written with a "Gee whiz, we weren't like that" tone about them. Nonsense. The younger generation has nothing on the older.

We go to college, to college go we.
We have not lost our virginity.
If we have lost it, somebody tossed it.
We are from College Hall.

And once a week at the college dance,
We don't wear bras and we don't wear pants.
We always give the freshmen a chance.
We are from College Hall.

We go to college. Don't we have fun?
We know exactly how it is done.
We saw the movies in Hygiene A-1.
We are from College Hall.

We go to college and we can be had.
Don't take our word for it; just ask dear old dad.
He brings his buddies for graduate studies.
We are from College Hall.

To Thee, Hershey Hall

Dedicated in this version to a women's dormitory at UCLA, this grimly resolute vow is known and sung—especially by women, it would seem—at a number of centers of higher learning. Its tune is the saccharine-strained wedding staple, "My Wonderful One."

To thee, Hershey Hall,
We pledge our abortions,
The loss of our virginity,
To the friends we have made
And to those who have made us.
We linger through our pregnancy.
If I have a daughter,
I'll send her to college
As far from this place as can be,
Where the men will be truer
And not try to screw her.
To thee, Hershey Hall, to thee.

Cats on the Rooftops

At one time, this song concerned itself with the idiosyncrasies, anatomical and amatory, of the animal kingdom. Its attention since has wandered to higher mammals.

Chorus:

Cats on the rooftops, cats on the tiles,
Cats with syphilis, cats with piles,
Cats with their assholes wreathed with smiles
As they revel in the joys of fornication.

110

The hippopotamus, so it seems,
Very seldom has wet dreams,
But when he does, he comes in streams
As he revels in the joys of fornication.

The elephant is a funny bloke
And very seldom gets a poke,
So when he does, he lets it soak
As he revels in the joys of fornication.

The ostrich has a funny dick,
And it isn't very often that he dips his wick,
So when he does, he dips it quick
As he revels in the joys of fornication.

Promiscuous girls live under a strain,
Waiting for their monthly pain,
And when it comes, they smile again
As they revel in the joys of fornication.

Oh, you revel in the morning with an upright stand
(It's urinary pressure on the prostrate gland),
And you haven't got a woman so you jerk it off by
    hand
As you revel in the joys of fornication.

The priest of the parish has very little fun.
He doesn't even know how it is done.
When it comes to fun, he gets nun
As he revels in the joys of fornication.

The cocksucker blows his friend in haste,
Then he licks it up so it won't go to waste.
Don't think it odd; it's a matter of taste
As he revels in the joys of fornication.

"Rats!" cried the captain as he thought,
These new ensigns are not so hot
And the admiral takes the best of the lot
As he revels in the joys of fornication.

Do you ken John Peel? Yes, I ken him weel.
He sleeps with his wife but he never gets a feel.
He sleeps by her side, but he never gets a ride
And he wakes up in the morning in frustration.

Roll Your Leg Over

This is the champion college song, sung the length and breadth of the land. Few who sing it, however, realize that the song is ultimately derived from an English ballad in which a male magician—technically, a warlock—pursues a female magician—a witch—with something less than honorable intentions. She successively changes herself into a dove, an eel, a duck, a hare, a mare, a hot griddle, a ship, and finally a silken blanket to escape his attentions. Nothing daunted, the warlock matches her dove for dove, trout for eel, drake for duck, hound for hare, saddle for mare, cake for griddle, and with neat euphemistic significance, a nail in the bow of the ship. In the last stanza

> Then she became a silken plaid,
> And stretched upon a bed,
> And he became a green covering,
> And gained her maidenhead.

In one or another form, the theme of the ballad is known throughout Europe.

In the United States, the story is gone. Singers now rack their memories only to see who can come up with the most clever hypotheses.

If all the young girls were like fish in the ocean,
I'd be a whale and I'd show them the motion.

Chorus:

Oh, roll your leg over, oh, roll your leg over,
Roll your leg over the man in the moon.

If all the young girls were like fish in a pool,
I'd be a shark with a waterproof tool.

If all the young girls were like fish in the brookie,
I'd be a trout and I'd get me some nookie.

If all the young girls were like winds on the sea,
I'd be a sail and I'd have them blow me.

If all the young girls were like cows in the pasture,
I'd be a bull and I'd fill them with rapture.

If all the young girls were like mares in the stable,
I'd be a stallion and show them I'm able.

If all the young girls were like bricks in a pile,
I'd be a mason and lay them in style.

If all little girls were like bells in a tower,
I'd be a clapper and bang them each hour.

If all little girls were like bats in a steeple,
And I were a bat, there'd be more bats than people.

If all little girls were like little red foxes,
And I were a hunter, I'd shoot up their boxes.

If all little girls were like little white rabbits,
And I were a hare, I would teach them bad habits.

If all the young girls were like trees in the forest,
And I were a woodsman, I'd split their clitoris.

If all the young girls were like telephone poles,
I'd be a squirrel and stuff nuts in their holes.

If all the young girls were like gals down in Sydney,
I ain't got much left but I still got one kidney.

If all the young girls were like B-29's,
I'd be a jet fighter and buzz their behinds.

If all the young girls were like diamonds and rubies,
I'd be a jeweler and polish their boobies.

If all the young girls were like coals in the stoker,
I'd be a fireman and shove in my poker.

I wish all the girls were like statues of Venus,
And I were equipped with a petrified penis.

If all the young girls were like Gypsy Rose Lee,
I'd be a G-string; oh, boy, what I'd see.

If all the young girls were like sheep in the clover,
I'd be a ram and I'd ram them all over.

If all the young girls were pancakes in Texas,
I'd be a Texan and eat them for breakfast.

If all the young girls were grapes on a vine,
I'd be a plucker and have me a time.

Christopher Columbo

A sea song come ashore, or a landlubber's ballad gone to sea—the evidence is contradictory—"Christopher Columbo" is a detailed, highly inaccurate account of the voyage of discovery in 1492. Columbo's adventures are limited only by the inventiveness or memory of the singer.

Chorus:

His balls were big and round, oh;
They nearly reached the ground, oh;
That fornicatin', masturbatin'*
Son-of-a-bitch Columbo.

Alternate chorus:

He knew the world was round, oh,
He knew it could be found, oh,
That mathematical, geographical
Son-of-a-bitch Columbo.

* Or: That masturbatin', navigatin'

114

In fourteen hundred and ninety-two,
A schoolboy from I-taly
Walked the streets of ancient Rome
And jacked-off in the alley.

Columbo went to the Queen of Spain
And asked for ships and cargo.
He said he'd kiss the royal ass
If he didn't bring back Chicago.

Now three slick ships set out to sea,
Each one a double-decker.
The queen she waved her handkerchief,
Columbo waved his pecker.

Columbo paced upon the deck.
He knew it was his duty.
He laid his whang into his hand
And said, "Ain't that a beauty."

A little girl walked up on deck
And peeked in through the keyhole,
He knocked her down upon her brown
And shoved it in her peehole.

She sprang aloft, her pants fell off,
Columbo still pursued her.
The white of an egg ran down her leg,
The son-of-a-bitch had screwed her.

Columbo came upon the deck,
His cock was like a flagpole.
He grabbed the bo'sun by the neck
And shoved it up his asshole.

Columbo had a first mate,
He loved him like a brother,
And every night they went to bed
And buggered one another.

Columbo had a cabin boy,
A dirty little nipper.
He stuffed his ass with broken glass
And circumcised the skipper.

Columbo had a stowaway,
A bonnie little lassie.
He took her down below the deck
And shove it up her ass-ie.

The sailors on Columbo's ship
Had each his private knothole,
But Columbo was a superman,
He used a padded porthole.

For forty days and forty nights
They sailed the broad Atlantic.
They saw a whore upon the shore,
By God, she drove them frantic.

All the men jumped overboard,
A-shedding coats and collars;
In fifteen minutes by the clock,
She made ten thousand dollars.

Those were the days of no clap cure;
The doctors were not many.
The only doc' that he could find
Was a son-of-a-bitch named Benny.

Columbo strode up to the doc',
His smile serene and placid.
The God damned doc' burned off his cock
With hydrochloric acid.

The Good Ship Venus

"The Good Ship Venus," sometimes known as "Frigging in the Rigging," got its start in merry old England. American doughboys returning from the First World War carried it to the United States where it quickly gravitated to the halls of ivy. Rarely has the much-abused poetic form of the limerick been so battered as here, but rarely has it been put to such long use.

The melody for the verse may seem familiar; it is an adaptation of "Yankee Doodle."

'Twas on the good ship Venus—
By Christ, you should have seen us—
The figurehead was a whore in bed,
And the mast was a rampant penis.

Chorus:

Friggin' in the riggin',
Friggin' in the riggin',
Friggin' in the riggin',
There was fuck all else to do.

The captain of this lugger,
He was a dirty bugger.
He wasn't fit to shovel shit
From one place to another.

The captain's name was Morgan.
By Christ, he was a gorgon.
Ten times a day sweet tunes he'd play
On his reproductive organ.

The first mate's name was Cooper.
By Christ, he was a trooper.
He jerked and jerked until he worked
Himself into a stupor.

The second mate's name was Andy.
By Christ, he had a dandy,
Till they crushed his cock with jagged rock
For coming in the brandy.

The captain's wife was Mable;
To fuck she wasn't able,
So the dirty shits, they nailed her teats
Across the bar-room table.

The cabin boy was chipper,
Pernicious little nipper.
He stuffed his ass with broken glass
And circumcised the skipper.

116

The captain's daughter Mable,
They laid her on the table,
And all the crew would come and screw
As oft as they were able.

The captain's daughter Mary
Had never lost her cherry.
The men grew bold and offered gold,
Now there's no Virgin Mary.

The captain's other daughter
Fell in the deep sea water.
Delighted squeals revealed that eels
Had found her sexual quarter.

Roll Me Over

No one will ever confuse this with great poetry. That isn't the point. The point
is that this song is easy to sing, easy to learn and has a chorus wherein all may
join at the appropriate moments. This is why it is one of the three or four most
popular songs on college campuses.

Oh, this is number one,
And the fun has just begun.
Roll me over, lay me down
And do it again.

Chorus:

Roll me over
In the clover,
Roll me over, lay me down
And do it again.

Oh, this is number two,
And my hand is on her shoe.
Roll me over, lay me down
And do it again.

Three . . . and my hand is on her knee.
Four . . . and I'm really hot for more.
Five . . . and my hand is on her thigh.
Six . . . and I'm really in a fix.
Seven . . . and I feel like I'm in heaven.
Eight . . . and the doctor's at the gate.
Nine . . . and the baby's doing fine.
Ten . . . and it's time to start again.

Drive It On

Like "Roll Me over," this can hardly be considered inspired poetry. Nor does the tune, "She'll Be Comin' 'Round the Mountain," merit any greater notice. Put the two together, however, and the result is a rollicking song for less inhibited groups.

I gave her inches one and drove it on.
I gave her inches one and drove it on.
I gave her inches one. She said, "Honey, this is fun!
Put your belly close to mine and drive it on."

I gave her inches two and drove it on.
I gave her inches two and drove it on.
I gave her inches two. She said, "Honey, I love you!
Put your belly close to mine and drive it on."

Three . . . "Honey, please fuck me!"
Four . . . "Honey, give me more!"
Five . . . "Honey, I'm alive!"
Six . . . "Honey, this is kicks!"
Seven . . . "Honey, this is heaven!"
Eight . . . "Honey, this is great!"
Nine . . . "Honey, this is fine!"
Ten . . . "Honey, come again!"

118

Do Your Balls Hang Low?

A companion piece or masculine counterpart to "Four Old Whores," "Do Your Balls Hang Low?" peters out in the end, stretched from the ridiculous to the absurd. It is sung either to the tune of "The Parade of the Wooden Soldiers" or the traditional fiddle tune, "Sailor's Hornpipe." (The tune here is "Sailor's Hornpipe.") If the words are fitted to "The Parade of the Wooden Soldiers," the last line is shortened to the question: "Do your balls hang low?"

Chorus:

Ting-a-ling, God damn, find a woman if you can.
If you can't find a woman, find a clean old man.
If you're ever in Gibraltar, take a flying fuck at Walter.
Can you do the double shuffle when your balls hang low?

Do your balls hang low? Do they swing to and fro?
Can you tie 'em in a knot? Can you tie 'em in a bow?
Can you throw 'em o'er your shoulder like a Continental soldier?
Can you do the double shuffle when your balls hang low?

Successive verses substitute for the third line of the first verse the following:

Do they make a lusty clamor when you hit them with a hammer?

Can you bounce 'em off the wall like an Indian rubber ball?

Do they have a hollow sound when you drag 'em on the ground?

Do they have a mellow tingle when you hit 'em with a shingle?

Do they have a salty taste when you wrap 'em 'round your waist?

Do they chime like a gong when you pull upon your dong?

119

The Rugby Song

No occupation worth its salt is without a bawdy song unique to the trade. This includes athletics, it would seem. "The Rugby Song" is said to be just that, *the* rugby song. It is not hard to understand why.

If I were the marrying kind,
Which, thank the Lord, I'm not, sir,
The kind of man that I would wed
Would be a rugby hooker.
    He'd hook balls and I'd hook balls
    And we'd hook balls together;
    There we'd be in the middle of the night,
    Hooking balls together.

If I were the marrying kind,
Which, thank the Lord, I'm not, sir,
The kind of man that I would wed
Would be a rugby prop.
    For he'd hold it up and I'd hold it up
    And we'd hold it up together.
    There we'd be in the middle of the night
    Holding it up together.

Successive stanzas follow the same pattern, running through the entire team and its athletic responsibilities.

Rugby lock . . . screw the scrum
Break . . . breaking hard together

Scrum half . . . putting it in together
Standoff . . . feeding it out together
Wing . . . running hard together
Fullback . . . kicking hard together
Referee . . . blowing hard together
Spectator . . . coming again together

High Above a Theta's Garter

Poor Cornell. Never has a school's song suffered so much at the hands of so many as has that institution's "Alma Mater." This is just one of a number of parodies set to that famous melody.

High above a Theta's garter,
High above her knee,
Lies the key to Theta success,
Her virginity.
    Once she had it, now she's lost it.
    It is gone for good.
    She goes down for all the brothers,
    Like a Theta should.
    Lift her dress, oh, lift it gently;
    Lay her on the grass.
    Often are the times I've dreamed of
    A piece of Theta ass.

The Cardinals Be Damned

This bit of verbal violence upon the person of Stanford University's Cardinals originated at the University of California's Berkeley campus but is now sung up and down the Pacific Coast. With a few names changed, it has probably been applied to most of the colleges and universities in the country. "The Rambling Wreck from Georgia Tech" melody is once again pressed into service.

Oh, the Cardinals be damned, boys.
The Cardinals be damned.
The Cardinals be damed, boys.
The Cardinals be damned.
If any Stanford son-of-a-bitch
Don't like the Blue and Gold,
He can pucker up his rosy lips
And kiss the Bear's asshole.

Wellesley's run by Harvard,
And Harvard's run by Yale.
Yale is run by Vassar,
And Vassar's run by tail.
But Stanford is the only school
Entirely run by hand,
And those masturbating bastards
Are the blackest in the land.

Oh, I'm just a prostitute from Stanford
And I fuck for fifty cents.
I'll lay my ass upon the grass,
My pants upon the fence.
I'll lick your slimy belly;
I'll suck your cock with with glee,
But get off me you son-of-a-bitch,
If you're from USC.

Oh, here's to _____, boys,*
That Stanford son-of-a-bitch.
I hope he gets the syph and clap
And dies of the seven-year itch.
If you use his cock for a fulcrum,
And suspend his balls in space,
You can prove by the theory of limits
That his asshole is his face.

* The name of Stanford's football coach is generally inserted here.

Oh, listen, all you maidens,
Oh, listen here to me.
Never trust a Stanford man
An inch above your knee.
He'll take you down to Menlo,*
And he'll fill you full of fizz,
And in a half an hour
Your maidenhead is his.

If I had a little girl,
I'd dress her up in green,
And send her up to Stanford
Just to coach the Cardinal team.
If I had a little boy,
I'd dress him up in blue,
And he'd holler, "To hell with Stanford!"
Like his daddy used to do.

---

* Menlo Park, California, the location of the university.

Uncle Joe and Aunty Mabel

Much of the humor of parody comes from the use of the incongruous. In this case, the rather basic problems of Uncle Joe and Aunty Mabel are recounted to the festive tune of "Hark, the Herald Angels Sing," a grotesquely inappropriate match.

Uncle Joe and Aunty Mabel
Fainted at the breakfast table.
This should be sufficient warning:
Never do it in the morning.
Ovaltine has set them right;

Now they do it every night.
Uncle Joe is hoping soon
To do it in the afternoon.
Aunty Mabel will agree
It hits the spot at half-past three.

123

Seven Old Ladies

Inspired by, and sung to the tune of "Oh, Dear, What Can the Matter Be," this is another of the discreet "bawdy" songs. Aside from the subject matter, one would be hard put to find anything offensive about the seven old ladies; none-theless, it is as effectively proscribed as the more indecorous ditties in this collection.

Oh, dear, what can the matter be?
Seven old ladies were locked in the lavatory;
They were there from Monday 'til Saturday,
And nobody knew they were there.

The first old lady was Elizabeth Porter;
She was the deacon of Dorchester's daughter.
She went to relieve a slight pressure of water,
And nobody knew she was there.

The second old lady was Abigail Splatter;
She went there 'cause something was definitely the
    matter,
But when she got there, it was only her bladder,
And nobody knew she was there.

The third old lady was Amelia Garpickle;
Her urge was sincere, her reaction was fickle.
She hurdled the door; she'd forgotten her nickel,
And nobody knew she was there.

The fourth old maiden was Hildegard Foyle;
She hadn't been living according to Hoyle,
Was relieved when the swelling was only a boil,
And nobody knew she was there.

124

The fifth old lady was Emily Clancy;
She went there 'cause something tickled her fancy,
But when she got there it *was* ants in her pantsy,
And nobody knew she was there.

The sixth old lady was extremely fertile.
Her name was O'Connor, the boys called her Myrtle.
She went there to repair a slight hole in her girdle,
And nobody knew she was there.

The seventh old lady was Elizabeth Bender;
She went there to repair a broken suspender.
It snapped up and ruined her feminine gender,
And nobody knew she was there.

The janitor came in the early morning.
He opened the door without any warning,
The seven old ladies their seats were adorning,
And nobody knew they were there.

Next Thanksgiving

Obscenity is a broad term with no clear meaning, its definition largely subjective.
The obscene to one person may mean only the pornographic; to another, it may
include the profane. To some, it even includes the impudent, like this satire to the
familiar "Frère Jacques."

Next Thanksgiving, next Thanksgiving,
Don't eat bread. Don't eat bread.
Shove it up the turkey. Shove it up the turkey.
Eat the bird. Eat the bird.

125

Next Christmas, next Christmas,
Don't trim a tree. Don't trim a tree.
Shove it up the chimney. Shove it up the chimney.
Goose St. Nick. Goose St. Nick.

Next Easter, next Easter,
Don't color eggs. Don't color eggs.
Shove them up the rabbit. Shove them up the rabbit.
Eat the hare. Eat the hare.

My Girl's From USC

From USC or anywhere else. This is a small sampling of the verses to this commonly-sung parody of "My Best Girl's a New Yorker."

My girl's from USC.
She fights for chastity,
Fights everyone but me.
I love her so.

Chorus:

And in my future life,
She's going to be my wife.
How the hell do I know that?
She told me so.

My girl's from Vassar,
None can surpass her.
She is a stroke on the
Varsity crew.

126

My girl's from Bennington,
Bangs like a Remington.
She's got that slight-action
Finger control.

My girl's an Alpha Chi.
I feed her Spanish fly.
I am a horny guy.
I love her so.

My girl's a Kappa.
She chews tobacca,
Sits by the fireside and
Spits on the floor.

My girl's from Hollyoak.
She lives on rum and coke.
She tells me dirty jokes.
I tell them too.

My girl's a Tri-Delt.
She knows just how it's felt.
She tickles me below the belt.
I love her so.

My girl's from SMU.
There's nothing she won't do,
If I should ask her to.
I love her so.

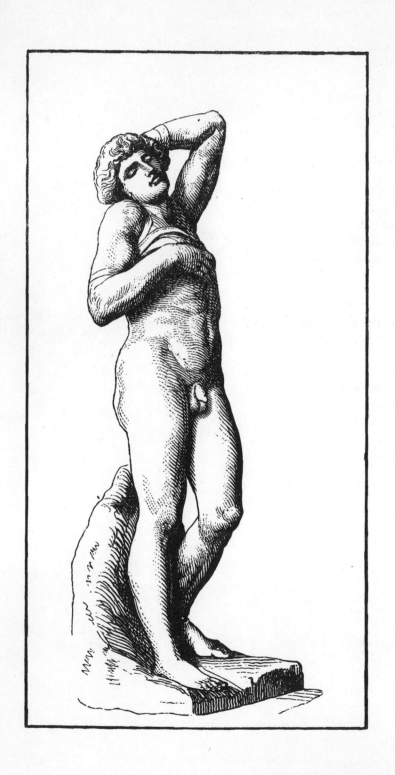

EYES RIGHT, FORESKINS TIGHT

After the first flush of patriotic enthusiasm, the foot soldier soon forgets the noble motives which sent him off to war. The militant songs of the home front are replaced with grousing ribaldry, the stirring sentiments of "The Marines' Hymn" turned to more personal matters:

> From the halls of Montezuma
> To the shores of Tripoli,
> We have fucked the whores and drunk the booze
> Just to prove virility.
> We have used pro kits and rubbers
> To keep our peckers clean,
> Still we have the highest V.D. rate.
> We're United States Marines.

The folks back home may think all those sons and husbands are caroling such artificial efforts as "The Caissons Go Rolling Along," but then the Pentagon isn't going to tell mothers and wives what the men are really singing.

In general, combat infantrymen have neither the time nor the inclination to write or sing songs, certainly not while they are on the line. This is a major factor in the content of the songs included here. Troops with more leisure who served in non-combatant or rear area, fliers fresh from colleges in the states who fought their war flying from secure bases far from the areas they bombed, boredom-ridden ensigns on routine watches, these men had time.

It would be hard even to imagine foot-soldiers singing this Marine aviators' adaptation of a World War II ballad. The "gung ho" enthusiasm the combat infantryman would consider little short of nonsense:

> Up in Korea midst high rocks and snow,
> The poor Chinese Commies [are] feeling quite low.
> For as the Corsairs roar by overhead,
> He knows that his buddies all soon will be dead.

> *Chorus:*

> Hinky di, dinky, dinky di, hinky di, dinky, dinky di,
> He knows that his buddies all soon will be dead.

> Lin Piao went way up to cold Koto-ri
> His prize Chinese army in action to see.
> He got there a half-hour after the U's,
> And all that he found was their hats and their shoes.

> Hinky di, dinky, dinky di, hinky di, dinky, dinky di,
> And all that he found was their hats and their shoes.

> Run, little Chinamen, save your ass, run.
> Three-twenty-three is out looking for fun.
> As the big white-nosed Corsairs come down in their dives,
> You'll know the "Death Rattlers" are after your lives.

130

Hinky di, dinky, dinky di, hinky di, dinky, dinky di,
You'll know the "Death Rattlers" are after your lives.

Uncle Joe Stalin, your stooges have found
It just doesn't pay to invade foreign ground.
For when they disturbed the serene morning calm,
They brought on the rockets, the bombs and napalm.

Hinky di, dinky, dinky di, hinky di, dinky, dinky di,
They brought on the rockets, the bombs and napalm.

Here's to the Twenty, the Vought people too,
And their well-known product, the blue Four F.U.,
To all Gyrene pilots and carriers at sea,
And the "Death Rattlers" Squadron, ol' Three-twenty-three.

Hinky di, dinky, dinky di, hinky di, dinky, dinky di,
And the "Death Rattlers" Squadron, ol' Three-twenty-three.

We fought at Pyongyang and at Hagaru,
At Kumhwa and Kaesong and Uijongbu.
So here's to our pilots and here's to our crew,
The target, the shake, and the blue Four F.U.

Hinky di, dinky, dinky di, hinky di, dinky, dinky di,
The target, the shake, and the blue Four F.U.*

There are, to be sure, combat soldiers who take pleasure in their
work and pride in their unit. But the songs they sing would seem

---

* "Hinky Di," taken from a mimeographed song collection, ca. 1951, entitled "Death Rattlers,"
and furnished to the editor by D. K. Wilgus. It was written sometime after November, 1950,
when the Fourth Field Army of the Chinese Peoples Republic overran United Nations Forces
around the Choisan Reservoir. Typographical and spelling mistakes have been corrected. "Shake,"
in the last stanza, is the rack of bombs or rockets the Vought F4U Corsair carried. The meaning of "the Twenty" in the fifth stanza is unclear. For an explanation of the super-enthusiasm
of the Marine pilots who wrote this, see Peter Thorpe, "Buying the Farm: Notes on the Folklore of the Modern Military Aviator," *Northwest Folklore,* II (1967), pp. 11–17, especially
pp. 13–14. But compare "Hinky Di" here to "Dinky Di," the Australian soldier's song to the
same tune, *infra.,* pp. 175–176.

to be shorter ditties, perhaps spur-of-the-moment efforts with a strong element of angry protest. In January, 1967, *The New Republic* carried a story by the late Bernard B. Fall, "You Can Tell 'Em, Buddy," with one such parody (the ellipsis is the magazine's):

Jingle Bells, mortar shells,
V. C. in the grass,
You can take your Merry Christmas
And shove it up your - - - - .

The combat infantryman would understand this sentiment only too well.

Lee's Hoochie

During the Second World War, a new phenomenon entered into the process of oral tradition: the mimeograph machine. Headquarters troops with time on their hands and mimeographs at the ready took advantage of the situation to turn out reams of copies of bawdy songs. At first, their efforts were confined to striking off single songs, but as the mimeographs and man-hours piled up, the troops turned to more ambitious projects. Some of the anthologies were quite extensive, running to 40 or more pages.

By the time of the Korean conflict, the mimeographs had been electrified and the headquarters complements beefed up. The natural result was that songs such as "Lee's Hoochie"—sung to the familiar "On Top of Old Smoky"—quickly circulated throughout the Far East Command.

Way down in Seoul City,
I met a Miss Lee.
She said, "For a short time,
You can sleep with me."

I went to her *hoochie*,
A room with hot floor.
We left our shoes outside,
And slid shut the door.

She took off her longjohns,
And unrolled the pad.
I gave her ten thousand;
'Twas all that I had.

Her breath smelled of *kimchi*.
Her bosom was flat.
No hair on her *poji*,
Now how about that?

I asked, "Where's the *benjo?*"
She lead me outside.
I reached for Old Smoky.
He crawled back inside.

I rushed to the medics,
Screamed, "What shall I do?"
The doc was dumbfounded;
Old Smoky was blue.

If you're ever in Seoul City
On a three-day pass,
Don't go to Lee's *hoochie*.
Sit flat on your ass.

Your ass may get tender,
And she may tempt you,
But better a red ass,
Than Old Smoky blue.

Moving On

This is certainly the most famous song to come out of the Korean conflict. It was written in 1950–51, after the disastrous retreat or "bug out" from the Yalu River (it's also known as "The Bug-Out Ballad") when Chinese Communist troops stormed over the border.

Its tone is unflattering and versions of the song sung by men of one unit invariably provoked fights with men in another.

The melody is Hank Snow's phenomenally successful song of the same name, then popular and now considered a "country classic."

Hear the patter of running feet,
It's the old First Cav in full retreat.

Chorus:

They're movin' on;
They'll soon be gone.
They're haulin' ass,
Not savin' gas.
They'll soon be gone.

Over on that hill there's a Russian tank;
A million Chinks are on my flank.

Chorus:

I'm movin' on;
I'll soon be gone.
With my M-1 broke,
It ain't no joke.
I'll soon be gone.

Million Chinks comin' through the pass
Playin' burp-gun boogie all over my ass.

Chorus:

I'm movin' on;
I'll soon be gone.
With my M-1 broke,
It ain't no joke.
I'll soon be gone.

Twenty thousand Chinks comin'
    through the pass.
I'm tellin' you, baby, I'm haulin' ass.

Chorus

Standin' in a rice paddy up to my belly,
From then on, they called me "Smelly."

Chorus

Here's papa-san comin' down the track,
Old A-frame strapped to his back.

Chorus:

He's movin' on;
He'll soon be gone.
He's haulin' ass,
Not savin' gas.
He'll soon be gone.

Here's mama-san comin' down the track,
Titty hangin' out, baby on her back.

Chorus:

She's movin' on;
She'll soon be gone.
From her teats to her toes,
She's damn near froze.
She'll soon be gone.

I sung this song for the very last time.
Gonna get Korea out of my mind.

Chorus:

I'm movin' on;
I'll soon be gone.
I done my time
In this shit and slime.
I'm movin' on.

134

Too Rally

The new recruit quickly learns the rules of the military game ("Don't volunteer for anything"; "If it moves, salute it; if it doesn't, paint it") and the traditions of the service, the most important of which is R.H.I.P.—Rank Has Its Privileges. "Too Rally" is a commentary, probably written by younger junior officers serving in the South Pacific during World War II.

The officers ride in a whaleboat.
The captain, he rides in a gig.
It don't go a fucking bit faster,
But it makes the old bastard feel big.

The officers ride in a whaleboat.
The admiral rides in a barge.
It don't go a fucking bit faster,
But it makes the old bastard feel large.

Chorus:

Sing too rally, oo rally, rally.
Sing too rally, oo rally, ay.
It don't go a fucking bit faster,
But it makes the old bastard feel large.

Oh, the officers eat in the wardroom.
The captain won't eat with the boys.
His chow ain't a fucking bit better,
But the bastard can't stand all the noise.

The officers go to the movies.
The skipper won't sit with the crowd.
He can't see a fucking bit better,
But it makes the old bastard feel proud.

Oh, we're always at general quarters.
The captain, he sits at his desk.
He issues the God damnedest orders
About how all the men should be dressed.

Oh, we may have lost one or two battles,
Or a sub in the midst of a storm,
But there's one thing that you can be
    sure of:
Our men were in full uniform.

Oh, the officers' head is communal.
The captain he has his commode,
But his bowels ain't a fucking bit looser,
But his pride swells up like a toad.

At the officers' club in Hollandea,
The captain won't drink with the gang.
He don't get a fucking bit drunker,
But it gives the old bastard a bang.

The Fucking Machine

This song began its career at the beginning of the First World War, probably with one or another of the allied navies. By the end of that conflagration, it was the property of every man in uniform. Unlike "Mademoiselle from Armentières," which became an unofficial anthem of the doughboys, there is no way to clean up "The Fucking Machine." So "Mademoiselle" went on to fame and glory while "The Fucking Machine" remained underground.

Except for nostalgic American Legionnaires, no one bothers with "Mademoiselle" anymore. But the big prick of steel continues to go in and out to the tune of the honored hymn "Old Hundred."

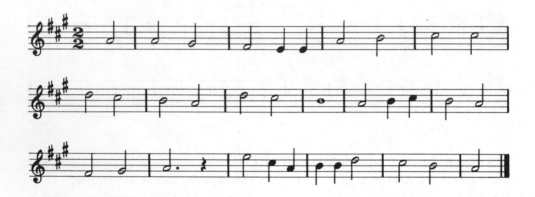

A sailor told me before he died—
I know not whether the bastard lied—
He had a wife with a twat so wide
That she could never be satisfied.

So he fashioned out a big fucking wheel,
Attached it to a big prick of steel,
Made two balls and filled them with cream,
And the whole fucking thing was run by steam.

'Round and 'round went the big fucking wheel,
In and out went the big prick of steel.
'Til at last the maiden cried,
"Enough, enough. I'm satisfied."

But here is a case of the biter bit:
There was no way of stopping it.
The maiden was torn from twat to teat,
And the whole fucking thing went up in shit.

The Flying Colonel

The Air Force of World War II produced more than its share of songs, most of them concerned with the problem of flying airplanes longer, harder, faster and higher than they were designed to fly. There was damn little the fliers could do about the occupational hazards; singing about them may have helped. The melody of this parody is appropriately "The Wreck of Old 97," a hillbilly ballad about a fatal train wreck.

We were on our way from Rangoonie to Shannon
And the flak was burstin' high,
And the P-51's and the P-47's
Were wingin' their way through the sky.

We were halfway between Rangoonie and Berlin,
Wingin' our way through the blue,
When the Jerries spotted us from five o'clock under,
And came up to see what they could do.

Now the first pass was made on the 497,
Colonel S - - - - - s was up ahead,
And he pissed and he moaned, and he shit and he groaned,
For he thought he would surely be dead.

The colonel called to his brave navigator,
"Give me a headin' home,"
But the brave navigator, with his hand on the ripcord,
Said, "Shit, boy, you're goin' home alone."

So the colonel he called to his brave bombardier,
Said, "Give me a headin' home."
But the brave bombardier had already scuttled;
There was silence on the colonel's interphone.

137

Well, at 24,000 he chewed on his candy,
And his balls drew up in their sack,
And he pissed and moaned, and shit and groaned,
For he thought he would never get back.

But with four engines feathered he glided into safety
On the runway of his own home base,
And it's with great pride that he tells this story
With a shit-eating grin on his face.

Sound Off

This goes under a variety of names; at one or another military installation, it is known as "Sound Off," "Swing Cadence," "The Airborne Chant," or "The Jody Song." There is no one version of the song; it adds and drops verses freely, depending upon who is singing it, how long the march is, and, sometimes, how many ladies are within earshot.

At Camp Chaffee, Arkansas, in 1952, the commanding general issued an order that the song was not to be sung on the post. (The orders of general officers are often ill-advised.) Such a drastic order might have destroyed morale had not the drill instructors continued to use it anyway—where women, children, commanding generals and staff officers couldn't hear it.

Leader: Sound off.
Chorus: One, two.
Leader: Sound off.
Chorus: Three, four.
Leader: Take it on down.
Chorus: One, two, three, four.
        One, two, three, four.

I don't know but I been told
Eskimo pussy is mighty cold.
   Sound off.
   Etc.

I don't know but I been told
Ass is worth its weight in gold.

I got a gal in Kansas City.
She's got a wart on her left titty.

I know a gal named Frisco Lil,
Touch her teat and get a thrill.

I know a gal from Jacksonville.
She won't do it but her sister will.

I got a gal in Mississippi.
She's got a pimple on her titty.

I got a gal named Sadie Kass.
She's got a face like the sergeant's ass.

I got a gal in San Antone.
She don't like to sleep alone.

If I die on the Russian front,
Box me up with a Russian cunt.

If I die in a combat zone,
Box me up and ship me home.

If I die in Tennessee,
Ship my ass home C.O.D.

I'm out to butcher the butcher's son,
But I'll give you some meat 'til the
    butcher comes.

I'm out to plumb the plumber's son,
But I'll fill your hole 'til the plumber
    comes.

I got a gal in Baltimore.
She's got a red light on her door.

I got a gal in Monterey.
She makes love the army way.

Every night before retreat,
Sergeant _____ beats his meat.
If Sergeant _____ didn't beat his meat,
Private _____ wouldn't eat.*

I got a gal all dressed in blue,
Man, oh man, she likes to screw.

I got a gal all dressed in yellow,
Out every night with a different fellow.

I got a gal all dressed in black,
Makes her living on her back.

I got a gal all dressed in red,
Makes her living in her bed.

The "Jody" verses tell the familiar story of the 4-F who steals the soldier's girl friend while the GI is defending family and country:

Ain't no use in writing home,
Jody's got your gal and gone.
Ain't no use in feeling blue,
'Cause he's got your Cadillac too.

Jody's got that gal and gone.
Left me here to sing this song.
Lost your car in a gamblin' game,
Left your gal for another dame.

Ain't no use to mourn and grieve,
Jody's gone, I do believe.
Left your gal in New Orleans
Sellin' pussy to earn her beans.

_____
* Fill in appropriate names.

139

Chamber Lye

According to the foremost annotator of bawdy songs, Gershon Legman, Von Hindenburg of the First World War and of "Chamber Lye" was formerly "John Haroldson" of the American Civil War. That worthy seems to have actually suggested that the flower of Southern womanhood do their bit for the Bonnie Blue Flag by saving urine. In no time at all, there was an unprintable song about it, sung to the then-popular tune known as "O Tannenbaum" or "Maryland, My Maryland."

During the First World War, someone made a few editorial changes and the song had a new lease on life.

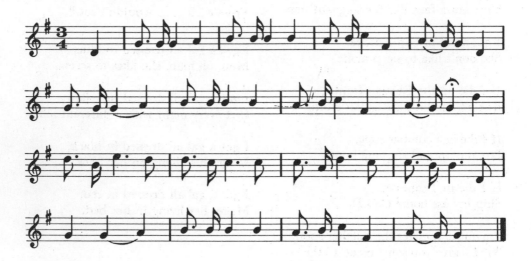

Von Hindenburg, Von Hindenburg,
You are a funny creature.
You've given the cruel war
A new and funny feature.
You'd have us think while every man
Is bound to be a fighter,
The women, bless their hearts,
Should save their pee for nitre.

Von Hindenburg, Von Hindenburg,
Where did you get the notion
Of sending barrels 'round the town
To gather up the lotion?
We thought a woman's duty was
Keeping house and diddling,
But now you've put the little dears
To patriotic piddling.

Von Hindenburg, Von Hindenburg,
Pray do invent a neater
And somewhat less immodest way
Of making your saltpetre.
For fraulein fair of golden hair
With whom we all are smitten
Must join the line and jerk her brine
To kill the bloomin' Briton.

Von Hindenburg, Von Hindenburg,
We read in song and story
How many tears in all the years
Have sprinkled fields of glory.
But ne'er before have women helped
Their braves in bloody slaughter,
'Til German beauties dried their tears
And went to making water.

140

No wonder, Von, your boys are brave!
Who wouldn't be a fighter,
If every time, he shot his gun
He used his sweetheart's nitre?
And vice versa, what would make
An Allied soldier sadder
Than dodging bullets fired from
A pretty woman's bladder?

And it is clear now why desertion
Is so common in your ranks.
An Artic nature's badly needed
To stand Dame Nature's pranks.
A German cannot stand the strain
When once he's had a smell.
He's got to have a piece or bust
The Fatherland to hell.

We've heard it said a subtle smell
Still lingers in the powder.
The battle-smoke grows thicker now
And the din of battle louder.
That there is found to this compound
A serious objection.
A soldier cannot take a whiff
Without having an erection.

Snapoo

Folk songs are no respecters of boundary lines and borders. With surprising ease
they will pass from one language into another. "Snapoo" started out in life either
as a German poem or a French song, no one can prove which. Then Prussian
officers, according to one authority, parodied the original poem or song to celebrate the fact that they had arrived in time to take part in the Battle of Waterloo
in 1815. From there it made its way to sea, and for a hundred years was sung by
crews of deep water sailing ships. Across the ocean then, Union soldiers during
the Civil War borrowed the tune and poetic form to create "When Johnny Comes
Marching Home." Finally, "Snapoo," the sea song, served as the model for the
original words and music of the song which was to all but drive it out of oral
currency, "Hinkey Dinkey Parlez-vous." "Snapoo" uses that tune, too.

Three Air Force officers crossed the Rhine.
Snapoo. Snapoo.
Three Air Force officers crossed the Rhine.
Snapoo. Snapoo.
Three Air Force officers crossed the Rhine
Looking for women and searching for wine.
A seven-inch peter and bollocks and all
And shake a snap peter snapoo.

The subsequent verses follow the same pattern:

"Oh landlady, have you a daughter fair
With lily-white teats and golden hair?"

"Oh sirs, my daughter is much too fine
To sleep with an airman from over the Rhine."

"Oh mother, oh mother, I'm not too fine
To sleep with an airman from over the Rhine.

"Oh mother, oh mother, he's teasin' me;
He's tickling the hole I use to pee.

"Oh mother, oh mother, he's up my bum
And if he don't stop, I will certainly come."

Eight months rolled by and the ninth did pass
And a little rear gunner marched out of her ass.

The little rear gunner grew and grew
And now he's chasing the chippies too.

The Little Red Train

Like "When Johnny Comes Marching Home," to which "Little Red Train" is
sung, this is a by-product of the fertile "Snapoo."

A little red train came down the track.
She blew. She blew.
A little red train came down the track.
She blew. She blew.
A little red train came down the track,
And I don't give a damn if she never comes back,
Away she blew, oh Jesus, how she blew.

Subsequent verses follow the same pattern, substituting:

The engineer was at the throttle
A-jacking off in a whiskey bottle.

The fireman he was shoveling coal
Right up the engineer's asshole.

The switchman he was at the switch
A-swishing away like a son-of-a-bitch.

A blonde was in the dining car
A-puffing away on a black cigar.

A porter was waiting in the car
To take the place of the black cigar.

The flagman he stood out in the grass,
The staff of the flag run up his ass.

Hobo Bill was riding the rods
When ninety-nine cars rolled over his cods.

The railroad cop was in the yard,
Holding his billy and making it hard.

143

The Yellow Rose of Taegu

A refurbished soldiers' song from World War II, this was localized to Korea in 1950. The original transplant was probably made by a Regular Army man, but verses of social protest were added by troops less enthused with the military and the police action in Frozen Chosen.

She's the yellow rose of Taegu, the girl that I adore.
Her cunt it smells like cock juice; she's a good two-dollar whore.
You may talk to me of Seoul girls or whores from Tokyo,
But the yellow rose of Taegu beats them all, I'd have you know.

Now I was shipped to Taegu; I didn't want to go,
But the Chinks came down from 'Chuko, and I left old Tokyo.
I landed from an LCT; I was left there all alone,
But the yellow rose of Taegu made me feel right at home.

I didn't want to shoot a gun and that is certain sure.
I didn't want to go on line; I'd rather stayed with her.
They handed me an M-1; it made me nervous more.
The only person I wanted to shoot was my little Taegu whore.

She was a young and charming girl; her age was scarce sixteen.
She took me in and she kicked out a sailor and marine.
She had no titties on her chest; that didn't bother me,
For what she had between her legs was big enough for three.

She liked to play the army way; she damn near broke my back.
My thoughts turn back to her each time I have to tote my pack.
My back she broke; my prick she bent; my balls were hollow too,
But I put calloses on the cunt of my rose from old Taegu.

I don't care much for GI food, the weather or the work.
I don't care much for the Chinks; up in those hills they lurk.
I don't care much for frozen ears, the colds, the flu, the shits.
I'd trade it all for a dose of clap from the girl without any teats.

I'm going back to see her some bright and sunny day.
I'll go a-wol or on sick-call; I'll get there any way.
I'm sure to get my balls shot off if I stay here on line,
But if my rose can fuck them off, well, that'll suit me fine.

The Sewing Machine

The girl who is sewn-up is pregnant, so it naturally follows that she must have a
sewing machine. This song, sung to the tune of "Down in the Valley" by GIs
during the occupation of Germany after World War II, is similar to the "Lee's
Hoochie" sung by comrades in arms in the Far East. The subject is universal.

Down in Cunt Valley, where the bullshit runs thick,
Where the soldier boys ramble, and babies come quick,
That's where she lives, the gal I adore,
That cock-sucking hussy, the Heidelberg whore.

She took me upstairs and she turned out the light,
And she said, "Big boy, you're here for the night."
So I took down my pants and I crawled in between,
And I started to sew on her sewing machine.

I sewed and I sewed until crack of dawn,
Then she said, "Big boy, you had better be gone.
Come back tomorrow night without being seen,
And you're welcome to sew on my sewing machine."

She gave me the clap and the blue-balls too.
The clap doesn't hurt, but the blue-balls do.
For seventeen days, she hasn't been seen.
I hope she's in Hell with her sewing machine.

Fuck 'Em All I

It was a poor unit during World War II that didn't have at least one version of this classic illustration of what the British army called "the Jack system," that non-Copernican approach to life epitomized by the motto, "I'm all right, Jack; fuck you."

They say there's a troopship just leavin' Bombay,
Bound for Old Blighty's shore,
Heavily laden with time-expired men
Bound for the land they adore.
There's many a soldier has finished his time;
There's many a twirp signin' on,
But they'll get no promotion this side of the ocean,
So cheer up, my lads, fuck 'em all.

Chorus:

Fuck 'em all, fuck 'em all,
The long and the short and the tall.
Fuck all the sergeants and their bleedin' sons,
Fuck all the corporals and W.O. ones,*
'Cause we're sayin' goodby to them all,
As back to the billet we crawl.
They'll get no promotion this side of the ocean,
So cheer up, my lads, fuck 'em all.

Fuck 'Em All II

Sung first during World War I, two wars and a number of international incidents
later the song was still in service as a gravel-scratcher's specific protest against the
indignities of war.

Fuck 'em all, fuck 'em all,
The long and the short and the tall.
Fuck all the blonde cunts and all the brunets.
Don't be too choosey, just fuck all you gets
'Cause we're saying good by to them all
As back to the barracks we crawl.
You'll get no erection at short-arm inspection,
So prick up, you men, fuck 'em all.

Fuck 'em all, fuck 'em all,
The long and the short and the tall,
Fuck all the cunts 'til you break it in two,
You'll get no lovin' where you're goin' to,
'Cause we're saying goodby to them all
As back to the barracks we crawl,
So get your big prick up and give it a stick up
The cunt or asshole; fuck 'em all.

---

* Warrant Officer First Class.

NOTES FOR THE RESEARCHER

In the annotation of this collection, the editor has used the more or less standard collections of American folk songs. Most were searched, but only a few were relied upon for bibliographic entry. This handful, cited in the bibliography, will open other anthologies to even the most indifferent of researchers.

More fully, musical variants are cited—in some cases extensively—largely because so little bibliographic work has been done in this area. Here the researches of Phillips Barry, Samuel Bayard, Bertrand Bronson, and George Pullen Jackson have proved both a beacon and a cross to bear. From nomenclature to methodology, their work is often at odds. In such cases, the present editor has silently chosen sides, sometimes with this proponent, sometimes with that critic.

In the most obvious cases, extended tune families have been identified, the editor harboring serious reservations about the *reductio ad minimum* of identifying only six, seven, or eight basic tunes from which the entire corpus of Anglo-American folk music springs. The nagging problem is that so many of these tune families are based largely upon subjective evaluations of given melodies; reduplication of results is difficult. (The best introduction to the problem—not unlike plunging into the middle of a rabbinical disquisition on the interpretation of Talmud and Torah—is in Bayard's "Prolegomena to a Study of the Principal Melodic Families of Folk Song," in MacEdward Leach and Tristram P. Coffin, *The Critics and the Ballad* [Carbondale, Ill.: Southern Illinois University Press, 1961], pp. 103–150.)

Finally, the editor has made no concerted effort to incorporate references to the many mimeographed collections of bawdy songs which steadily, if surreptitiously, issue from college dormitories. These are all but impossible to find, and are thus of little use to those who do not possess a copy. Those who do have copies will know well enough to check their ephemera for versions and variants. Nonetheless, two of these works—one from California Institute of Technology, circa 1960, the other from the University of Illinois, circa 1961—were especially large and especially helpful. They are cited.

Abdul the Bulbul Emir

This ballad is relatively rare in urban circles, and is perhaps dying. Despite inquiries, the editor was unable to collect any versions, nor did most correspondents know of it. The text printed here, sent without a tune, was furnished by a colleague who learned it while attending Harvard University in the 1940's. Its "pure" tradition may be questionable; the correspondent believes he had a hand in "filling out" or rewriting a then-current, shorter form of the ballad.

The text here, though longer and more detailed a narrative, is similar to an unpublished version collected by Mrs. Edith Fowke; and to the refurbished (?) variant in Christopher Logue's *Count Vicarion's Book of Bawdy Ballads.*

Tunes for the ballad and other texts, presentable in polite company, are in Sandburg, pp. 344–46; Spaeth, pp. 145–48; and Dick and Beth Best, *Song Fest* (New York, 1955), pp. 56–57.

Aimee McPherson

Few bawdy songs still in circulation are satirical, for satire must have a specific, identifiable subject. Pegged upon the topical, satirical songs generally have short life spans, the subject inevitably fading, it would seem, from popular memory.

"Aimee McPherson" is a topical satire only to those who know that there was actually an Aimee McPherson; for the others, it is simply a good song, one worth singing and remembering for its own sake, not because of an extrinsic relationship. "Aimee" may persist in oral tradition, as have other topical satires, but it will survive because the song is either inherently worthy, or because it can be attached to a currently familiar figure. (The localization or updating of a satirical song has taken place with "She Was Poor But She Was Honest," since hung on a Texas politician after it was first tagged to an Arkansas governor.)

For a concise recounting of Aimee Semple McPherson's fabulous career, see Carey McWilliams, *Southern California Country* (New York, c. 1946), pp. 259–62. Lately Thomas, *The Vanishing Evangelist* (New York, 1959) covers the woman's disappearance, reappearance and subsequent trial in detail. It is an excellent recounting of one of the most hilarious episodes in the annals of American jurisprudence.

Judging from internal evidence, the song was written sometime between August 3, 1926, and December 8 of the same year. More specifically, it may have been written between August 3, when the Grand Jury opened its inquiry into the case, and September 2, when the jury was dismissed, without having handed down indictments. Ormiston didn't turn up until the December 8 date, hence the reference to "Radio Ray" as a "goin' hound."

151

Three variants of the song are in the editor's files; they show almost no variation, either in text or tune. The melody is from the American folk song, "Willie the Weeper," which has more than a few bawdy verses of its own. Sandburg, p. 204; Spaeth, *Weep Some More, My Lady* (New York, 1927), pp. 123–26; Frank Shay, *More Pious Friends and Drunken Companions* (New York, 1928), pp. 76–77; and Randolph, III, pp. 272–73, all have "Willie the Weeper," less the ribaldry. The melody was borrowed, too, by Cab Calloway for a 1931 recording entitled "Minnie the Moocher."

The version of "Aimee McPherson" used here is from the singing of Phyllis Zasloff in Los Angeles, first in 1955, and again in 1964. She had learned it from a friend, "who learned it from someone, who learned it from someone. You know."

The Zasloff variant is virtually identical with that sung by Pete Seeger during a concert at Yellow Springs, Ohio, in the mid-1950's. (The editor has heard a tape recording of that concert through the courtesy of Joseph Lambert of Malibu, California.) Seeger has more recently recorded the song on *Songs of Struggle and Protest* (Folkways FH 5233).

Seeger includes that version in his *Bells of Rhymney* (New York, 1964), pp. 82–83, where he credits the song to John A. Lomax, Jr., who learned the ballad in California in the 1930's "from a hobo I think John said."

A-Roving

This sea song has survived largely on college campuses. The earliest reported versions—expurgated, to be sure—are frequent in turn-of-the-century collections of campus favorites.

In the late 1920's, Robert W. Gordon collected a seven-stanza version entitled "The Maid of Amsterdam." The last three stanzas of that text (No. 221 in the Gordon Collection of American Folk Song, University of Oregon) either influenced or borrowed from "The Monk of Great Renown":

> I laid my hand right on her quin [sic].
> Mark well what I do tell!
> When I laid my hand upon her quin,
> Said she, "For Christ's sake! shove it in!"
> I'll go no more a-rovin' with you, fair maid.
> A-rovin', a-rovin', since rovin's been my ru-in,
> I'll go no more a-rovin' with you, fair maid!
>
> I took her to her snow-white bed.
> Mark well what I do tell!
> I took her to her snow-white bed
> And I fucked her there till she was dead.

I'll go no more a-rovin' with you, fair maid. -
A-rovin', a-rovin', since rovin's been my ru-in,
I'll go no more a-rovin' with you, fair maid!

And when the bell tolled out "Amen."
    Mark well what I do tell!
And when the bell tolled out "Amen,"
I fucked her back to life again.
    I'll go no more a-rovin' with you, fair maid.
    A-rovin', a-rovin', since rovin's been my ru-in,
    I'll go no more a-rovin' with you, fair maid!

Other texts and tunes for the song are to be found in *Abelard Song Book,* Part II,
pp. 26–27; Hugill, pp. 48–52; Colcord, pp. 87–88; Shay, pp. 80–81; and Harlow, pp. 49–51, 70–71. The collegians' song is in *The Remick Favorite Collection
of College Songs* (New York and Detroit: Jerome H. Remick Co., 1909), p. 87,
among others.

The version included here is from a California college student, collected by the
editor in 1967.

The Ball of Kirriemuir

According to Legman, "It is very much to be doubted whether any male Scot
alive today, above the age of twelve, has not at least once heard 'The Ball o'
Kirriemuir' sung, and joined in *at least* on the chorus." Furthermore, he suggests
that the addition of at least one "outrageously obscene stanza" is *de rigueur* for
numerous cultivated persons in Scotland. (p. 228)

The song is one of the liveliest pieces in oral tradition; if it is not the most frequently encountered, it is certainly the longest. The editor has collected three
versions, the shortest of which is thirteen stanzas long; the total number of verses
which he has handled is more than thirty. No doubt those figures can be matched
easily by other collectors.

"The Ball of Kirriemuir" is a modern song, composed on the occasion of a particularly riotous wedding celebration. Legman, p. 227, suggests that the epic
epithalamium may owe something to "Blyth Will an' Bessie's Wedding," as
gathered by Robert Burns and printed in *The Merry Muses,* p. 131:

There was a weddin' o'er in Fife,
    An' mony ane frae Lothian at it;
Jean Vernor there maist lost hir life.
    For love o' Jamie Howden at it.

        Blyth Will an' Bessie's weddin',
        Blyth Will an' Bessie's weddin',

Had I been Will, Bess had been mine,
An' Bess an' I had made the weddin'.

Right sair she grat, an' wet her cheeks,
    An' naithing pleas'd that we cou'd gie her;
She tint her heart in Jeamie's breeks,
    It cam nae back to Lothian wi' her.

[Tam]mie Tamson too was there,
    Maggie Birnie was his dearie,
He pat it in amang the hair,
    An' puddled there till he was weary.

When e'enin' cam the town was thrang,
    An' beds were no to get for siller;
When e'er they fand a want o' room,
    They lay in pairs like bread an' butter.

Twa an' twa they made the bed,
    An' twa an' twa they lay the gither;
When they had na room enough,
    Ilk ane lap on aboon the tither.

Although the Burns song is a sketchy ballad and "The Ball" only a series of interconnected fornications in four lines; the first lines, the third stanza and the very meter of "Blyth Will" and company would award it paternity for "The Ball."

Withal, the tradition is seemingly older. As printed in Farmer, IV, pp. 48 ff., or *Pills to Purge Melancholy*, I, p. 276, the sixth stanza of "The Winchester Wedding" runs:

Pert Stephen was kind to Betty,
And blith as a Bird in the Spring;
And Tommy was so to Katy,
And wedded her with a Rush Ring:
Sukey that Danc'd with the Cushion,
An Hour from the Room had been gone;
And Barnaby knew by her Blushing,
That some other Dance had been done:
And thus of Fifty fair Maids,
That came to the Wedding with Men;
Scarce Five of the Fifty was left ye,
That so did return again.

Compare this with "The Ball's:

The village parson he came next day,
And was amazed to see
Four and twenty maidenheads
A-hanging from a tree.

Simpson, pp. 638–39, enters a number of these songs calling the roster of the wedding guests. Though he calls them "genuine Scotch piece[s]," the present editor is dubious.

"The Ball of Kirriemuir" has reached print or record no less than seven times. Brand has an ascetic version, pp. 88–89, which he also sings on Volume III of his recorded anthology. It appears as "Scotch Ballad" in *Songs of Raunch and Ill-Repute*, p. 28. *Unexpurgated Folk Songs of Men* has a version. Arthur Argo sings it on *A Wee Thread o' Blue* (Prestige International 13048). An expurgated version from Scots oral tradition is printed in *Kerr's "Cornkisters" as Sung and Recorded by Willie Kemp* (Glasgow: James E. Kerr, c. 1950), pp. 40–41. *Songs of Roving and Raking*, p. 114, has a twenty-stanza text with the usual tune. *Vicarion's Book*, No. XXI, has that tune also, but inexplicably omits the last four bars required by the words of the chorus. The text is a nineteen-stanza conflation of traditional verses and Logue's penmanship. *The Merry Muses of Caledonia*, pp. 23–25, offers a history of the song.

The version printed here is a conflation between a text sung by an anonymous male informant to Dean Burson in Los Angeles in 1960, and another collected by the editor from a male singer in that same city in 1963. All but stanzas 12, 15 and 19 are from Burson, though a number are common to both. The "king/queen/kitchen maid" verses circulate by themselves as a separate song or rhyme.

The melody is apparently wedded to the text; the editor has heard no other tune used for "The Ball." However, the melody is used to bear the unrelated "Lewiston Falls" by Frank Warner, *Our Singing Heritage* (Elektra 153).

Ball of Yarn

In its present version, "Ball of Yarn" is apparently a music-hall or buskers' rifacimento of an older Scots folk song. Legman, p. 225, accords parentage to "The Yellow, Yellow Yorlin," collected by Burns and printed in *The Merry Muses*, p. 138.

Hugill, pp. 533–34, has a sailors' version of "Ball of Yarn" sung to a melodic variant of "Blackbirds and Thrushes," borrowing for its chorus a stanza of that English country song. Gilbert, *Lost Chords*, pp. 74–75, dates "Ball of Yarn" to about 1870 in the United States, but gives no melody. By about 1887, according to Gates Thomas, the ballad was "widely distributed over Texas" in what Mack McCormick calls "Negro versions." (*American Folk Music Occasional*, No. 1 [1964], p. 10.)

155

Neither Hugill nor Gilbert are venturesome enough to print the last three verses of their texts, claiming them to be too bawdy. However, Gilbert's two stanzas correspond closely to Hugill's first and third, suggesting that Hugill's sea song is much the same as Gilbert's buskers' song. This would seemingly explain how the song came to the United States.

A bit more bold, Brand edits only the last stanza of his variant, pp. 56–57. The anonymous editors of *Songs of Roving and Raking,* p. 58; and *Songs of Raunch and Ill-Repute,* p. 4; print the song in full. A text dated to the 1930's by an internal reference to the "CCC" or Civilian Conservation Corps is in E. R. Linton, *The Dirty Song Book* (Los Angeles: Medco Books, 1965), p. 98. Abrahams gathered another version from "Kid" Mike in Philadelphia, inserting it in his doctoral dissertation, "Negro Folklore from South Philadelphia, A Collection and Analysis" (University of Pennsylvania, 1962), p. 251.

J. Barre Toelken has culled a text from the Robert W. Gordon Collection of American Folk Song at the University of Oregon (No. 135) which, though fragmentary, contains this bucolic metaphor:

> I took her by the waist, and I led her to the place.
>   Gently, gently I laid her down,
> And a jaybird and a thrush raised hell in the brush
>   While I wound up her little ball of yarn.

The tune presently in use is as new as are the words. It is typical of English music-hall material and the products of the popular music industry, circa 1870–80. It has a relatively wide ambit, a ninth, and there is the trademark stress upon the sub-mediant throughout.

The music for the verse, and the last stanza owe something to George F. Root's Civil War dirge, "Tramp, Tramp, Tramp," wildly popular just before "Ball of Yarn" ostensibly came across the sea. Professional singers, such as buskers were, audience-wise and ready to please, would happily borrow the Root song, expecting an added laugh from the deliberate parody of the last stanza.

The melody of the chorus is related to the post-Civil War cavalry song, "She Wore a Yellow Ribbon," the verse of which is also rhythmically similar to "Ball of Yarn." Though extant records will not support the hypothesis, it is possible that the troopers' song is a remnant of some earlier version of "Ball of Yarn."

The version of the song printed here is from the editor's collection, gathered in Los Angeles from a draftsman who learned it in college in the mid-1950's.

The Band Played On

Only the familiar chorus of the original song written in 1895 by John F. Palmer and Charles P. Ward is used in this parody. There are two versions in the editor's files, this through the courtesy of Roger Abrahams. It was current on American college campuses circa 1960.

The Bastard King of England

Two unexpurgated versions of this underground classic are recorded on *The Unexpurgated Folk Songs of Men,* and in *Songs of Roving and Raking,* pp. 58–59. The text in "Palmiro Vicarion's" horn book, No. XI, has been harshly served by the editor, though it retains its bawdry.

An edited version is sung by Oscar Brand on *Bawdy Songs and Backroom Ballads* (Audio Fidelity 1824). Leach, p. 79, and Dolph, pp. 140–42, print melodies and censored first stanzas only. Lynn, pp. 46–47, compromises; he includes a tune similar to those of Leach and Dolph, but completely rewrites the lyrics. Milburn's version, pp. 128–30, has been carefully edited also. So, too, the Niles-Moore-Wallgren text in *The Songs My Mother Never Taught Me* (New York, 1929), pp. 51–54.

Like so many of the other bawdy songs in the collection, "The Bastard King of England" clearly shows the marks of a literate creator at work: the story is involved, the meter is correct, the whole well-fitted to the tune.

The melody used here, from a version collected by the editor in Los Angeles in 1964, is a variant of the familiar "Irish Washerwoman," transforming a pure mixolydian tune to the major.

Three other versions of the ballad are in the editor's collection.

Bang Away, Lulu I

Published reports would hardly substantiate the claim, but this may well be one of the most frequently sung quatrain ballads in the repertoire of Southern Mountain singers. Brown, III, pp. 22–23, has a text with only the barest hint of bawdry in the last stanza. Some mildly suggestive texts are in Mellinger E. Henry, *Folk-Songs from the Southern Highlands* (Locust Valley, New York, 1938), pp. 436–37; and see John A. Lomax, *Cowboy Songs* (New York, 1938), pp. 263–64.

Sandburg's version, pp. 378–79, offers "nine of the nine hundred verses," some ribald. Dolph, pp. 93–94, has the tune and one expurgated stanza. Brand sings a version on *Bawdy Sea Chanties* (Audio Fidelity 1884), though the song has no special connection with the sea or with sailors. The Vicarion anthology, perhaps from British sources, has a text, and an idiosyncratic tune notation (the negative of the music was also stripped in upside down), numbered LXIV. The New Lost City Bang Boys (New Lost City Ramblers) sing a Southern Mountain version on *Earth is Earth* (Folkways 869 [that number is no accident]) which they credit to an older recording called "When Lulu's Gone," as sung by "The Bang Boys" (Roy Acuff and his band).

Songs of Raunch and Ill-Repute's "The Gruen Watch Song," p. 7, and Reuss' "Phi Delta Theta," pp. 88 ff., borrow the second stanza here. (Reuss also includes three college versions, pp. 264–68, sung to the tune, "Goodnight Ladies.") That second stanza printed here has a curious historical antecedent or parallel which appeared in a pioneering collection of folk epigraphy, *The Merry Thought,* subtitled *The Glass Window and Bog House Miscellany,* and published in 1731 in England. (Volumes I and II of this four-volume compendium are in the H. E. Huntington Library, San Marino, California, catalogued under call number 350019 in the Rare Book Room.) This stanza is dated to 1703:

Oh! that I were a turd, a turd,
Hid in this secret place,
That I might see my Betsy's arse
Though she shit in my face.

The first five stanzas here were sung by a Los Angeles attorney for the editor in 1964; he learned them in law school, some twenty years before. The next eight were gathered by the editor from a professional musician in Los Angeles in 1963; he had learned them while performing in a dance band from another musician. The last was sung by an insurance agent in Los Angeles in 1964.

The third and fourth stanzas circulate by themselves as an urban, children's street song and jump-rope rhyme.

The melody of "Bang Away, Lulu" used here is a set of the "Goodnight Ladies" —"Bell Bottom Trousers" tune family. The relative familiarity of these tunes is underscored by the fact that singers with faltering memories apparently refurbish their tunes by relying on the melody they know which is closest to the one they can only imperfectly recall. Miss Barbara Rogers, for example, sang a fragment in Los Angeles in 1967 as she remembered it from college in Salinas, California, in 1951—to the "Bell Bottom Trousers" tune:

Lulu had a boy friend.
He drives big red truck,
Takes her down an alley
And teaches her how to—
Flang dang, Lulu . . .

To the extent this occurs, it can be argued that popular records—it was such a recording from whence Miss Rogers, or her informant, learned the melody to "Bell Bottom Trousers"—actually aid oral tradition. See, too, the editor's article, "Barbara Allen in America: Cheap Print and Reprint," *Folklore International* (Hatboro, Pa., 1967), pp. 41–50.

J. Barre Toelken has forwarded an undated version of "Lulu" from the Robert W. Gordon Collection of American Folk Song housed at the University of Oregon (No. 3144) which contains these choice stanzas:

My Lulu she went fishing.
She caught a string of bass.
She hung them over her shoulder
And they still stink in her ass.

I wish I was a piss pot
Beneath my Lulu's bed,
And every time she took a crap,
I'd see her maidenhead.

I wish I was a diamond ring
Upon my Lulu's hand,
And every time she scratched her ass,
I'd see the promised land.

I wish I was a diamond pin
Upon my Lulu's breast.
I'd get between my Lulu's teats
And sink right down to rest.

The rich girl's pants are made of lace.
The poor girl's are chambray.
My Lulu wears no pants at all;
She claims they're in the way.

The rich girl's watch is made of gold.
The poor girl's is of brass.
My Lulu needs no watch at all;
There's movement in her ass.

The rich girl uses vaseline.
The poor girl uses lard.
My Lulu uses neither
But she gets there [it?] just as hard.

I took her to the circus,
The circus for to see,
But she got stuck on the elephant's cock
And had no use for me.

The three "rich girl-poor girl-Lulu" comparisons, along with the "white girl-black girl-my girl" analogues common in Negro songlore, deserve serious attention from some worker. The class and status dichotomies fall just short of verbal rebellion. They may also be poignant commentaries. In 1964, a 14-year-old

Negro youth from Tucson, Arizona, sang this fragment for the editor:

> Rich girl uses cold cream.
> Poor girl uses lard.
> My girl, uses axle-grease,
> But she gets there just the same.

Bang Away, Lulu II

This may be the first song ever collected through the services of the Bell Telephone system. Al Levy, a transplanted North Carolinian, sang it over the telephone at the editor's request in Los Angeles in 1964. Levy fitted it to the melody printed for "Bang Away, Lulu I" by dropping the eighth bar of the tune for the verse.

Reuss, p. 268, has a version of this which borrows the tune of a teasing song; this textual type of "Lulu" is, of course, one of that group.

A third version of "Bang Away, Lulu," sent to the editor by Miss Debbie Bonetti of Los Angeles in 1967, is something of a compromise between the uninhibited and the "teasing" forms.

> Lulu gave a party.
> Lulu gave a tea.
> Then she left the table
> To watch her chicken peck.

> *Chorus:*

> Bang, bang, Lulu.
> Bang away all day.
> Who we gonna bang on
> When Lulu goes away?

> Lulu was astonished,
> Lulu gave a start,
> For right upon the table
> She watched her ducky fly.

> Lulu had a chicken.
> Lulu had a duck.
> She'd put 'em on the table
> And then she'd watch 'em fight.

Bell Bottom Trousers

In both its older form, "Home, Dearie, Home," and the younger, frequently

160

bowdlerized "Bell Bottom Trousers," this ballad is well-known. See Laws, p. 163, for references, to which may be added the following: Leach, p. 113; Hugill, p. 498; Brand, pp. 41 ff. (two versions); and unexpurgated variants in *Songs of Raunch and Ill-Repute*, p. 26; *Songs of Roving and Raking,* p. 103; and Logue-Vicarion, No. XXII. Wallrich, pp. 60, 63, has two songs set to the familiar tune, but otherwise unrelated. Abrahams reports it, in a letter to the editor, from the West Indies.

UCLA college student Dean Burson collected in 1960 a formula song sung to the first eight bars of the melody printed here:

Walkin' down Canal Street, knock on any door;
God damn son-of-a-bitch, couldn't find a whore.

Finally found a whore and she was tall and thin;
God damn son-of-a-bitch, couldn't get it in.

Finally got it in and wiggled it about;
God damn son-of-a-bitch, couldn't get it out.

Finally got it out and it was red and sore.
The moral of this story is: Never fuck a whore.

Reuss, pp. 114–15, records a Marine Corps version of this "Walkin' Down Canal Street," dated to 1963. The Reuss song borrows its introductory verse from "In Bohunkus, Tennessee," its chorus from "The Frigging Fusillers," and the tune for these from "Tramp, Tramp, Tramp." The formulaic portion is sung to "Bell Bottom Trousers." *Songs of Raunch and Ill-Repute,* p. 30, has the formula version too, but with no tune indicated.

The Robert W. Gordon Collection of American Folk Song at the University of Oregon contains a text of "Bollochy Bill the Sailor" (No. 480) which melds the framework of that song with the words of this. As forwarded by J. Barre Toelken, that song runs:

"Oh, who's that knocking at my door?"
    Says the fair young maiden.
"Oh, who's that knocking at my door?"
    Says the fair young maiden.

"Oh, this is me and no one else,"
    Says Bolakee Bill the sailor.

"I'll open the door and let you in,"
    Says the fair young maiden.

"Now I am here; I'll stay till dawn,"
    Says Bolakee Bill the sailor.

At the point, the typewritten copy in the Gordon collection has a broken rule, indicating that the informant has omitted verses. The song continues after the obvious lapse:

"But a babe now I shall have,"
　　Says the fair young maiden.

"But it will never see its daddy,"
　　Says Bolakee Bill the sailor.

"And if it be a lass?"
　　Says the fair young maiden.

"Strangle it as soon as it's born,"
　　Says Bolakee Bill the sailor.

"But if it be a laddie?"
　　Says the fair young maiden.

"Send him out to sea,"
　　Says Bolakee Bill the sailor.

"I'll make him bell bottom trousers,"
　　Says the fair young maiden.

"Get him a suit of navy blue,"
　　Says Bolakee Bill the sailor.

"And he will climb the riggings,"
　　Says the fair young maiden.

"Like his daddy used to do,"
　　Says Bolakee Bill the sailor.

There are four versions of "Bell Bottom Trousers" in the editor's files. This was collected by Charles Marshall from Thorsten Gunther who learned the song in Pomona, California, while attending college there in 1936.

Big Black Bull

This is a college song of some popularity, and in laundered versions is frequently sung as a camp and hiking song by Boy Scouts and such.

Sandburg, p. 164, has a version which he dates to pre-Civil War years. It is possible, if not probable, that Negro chanteymen shipping out of Southern ports on the great sailing ships refashioned the song into the shanty, "A Long Time Ago." For a text of that shanty, see Colcord, pp. 65 ff., and the related "Leave Her,

Johnny, Leave Her" in Hugill, pp. 239 ff., which has both rhythmic and textual similarities. In a letter to the editor, Abrahams has suggested "Leave Her, Johnny, Leave Her" merits temporal primacy and that "Big Black Bull" is *its* descendant. In either case, the interpreting agents would apparently be Negro chanteymen. If, however, Sandburg's date is to be credited, "Big Black Bull" is the prime, for Negro sailors did not take to sea in great numbers until after Emancipation.

Peggy Seeger sings a version of "Big Black Bull" called "Great Big Dog" as a lullaby on *The Three Sisters* (Prestige 13029). Pete Seeger has recorded a sea variant as "Hoosen Johnny" on *Beasts, Birds, Bugs and Bigger Fishes* (Folkways FP711).

One of three in the editor's collection, this variant is from Stuart Grayboyse, an insurance salesman, who learned the song in Los Angeles prior to 1952. It was collected by the editor in 1964. The sixth stanza here is borrowed from a variant sung by attorney Alvin Tenner in Los Angeles in 1967.

Grayboyse's tune owes much to "The Old Gray Mare."

Blinded by Turds

This was given to the editor by a Hollywood record manufacturer whose version the editor suspects was strongly influenced by an Oscar Brand recording. That manufacturer was furiously rewriting the lyrics of Brand's recorded series of *Bawdy Songs and Backroom Ballads,* recording these hack works, and offering the resulting records for sale. The manufacturer readily conceded the "borrowing," but steadfastly denied that "Blinded by Turds" was anything but his own, in fact, the only bawdy song he knew. If it is easier to confess big sins than little ones, so be it. One should speak kindly of the dead; the record manufacturer was found murdered in his home a year after he gave copies of his "borrowed" songs to the editor in 1964; he had been executed—gangland fashion—with a bullet in the base of his skull.

In any event, "Blinded by Turds" may not be a native American ballad. J. Barre Toelken has forwarded from the Robert W. Gordon Collection of American Folk Songs a version entitled "Dirty Old Brown" with strong English traits (No. 385). It was given to Gordon on May 1, 1925; nothing more is known of it.

> There was an old lady
> I'd have you know
> Who went up to London
> A short time ago.
> She liked it quite well
> And she thought she would stay.
> The neighbors were tickled
> When she went away.

Singing Brown, Brown,
Dirty Old Brown.

Now when this old lady
Retired for the night,
She said, "Oh, gor blime,
I believe I must shit."
There's no use in talking
About things that have past.
So up went the window
And out went her ass.

There was an old watchman
Who chanced to pass by,
Looked up, got a chunk of shit
Right square in the eye.
He put up his hand
To see where he was hit.
He says, "Oh, gor blime,
I'm blinded with shit."

Now this poor watchman
Was blinded for life.
He had five healthy children
And a fine fucking wife.
On a London street corner
You may now see him sit
With a sign on his chest
Reading, "Blinded with shit."

Bollochy Bill the Sailor

A sea song come ashore, "Bollochy Bill" now appears to survive only on college campuses in the United States. Its progenitor, "Abel [Abram] Brown the Sailor," is even less well known, and may well be extinct.

Versions of "Abel Brown" so scarce in the literature or in tradition, it is worth reporting this text from the Robert W. Gordon Collection of American Folk Song, University of Oregon, forwarded by J. Barre Toelken. The undated text is numbered 1109 in that archive.

"Who's that knocking at my door?"
Said the fair young maiden.
"Who's that knocking at my door?"
Said the fair young maiden.

"It's me an' I wanna get in,"
Said Abram Brown the sailor.
"It's me an' I wanna get in,"
Said Abram Brown the sailor.

Successive stanzas follow the same pattern, each question and answer repeated.

"Open the door and walk in,"
Said the fair young maiden.

"There's only room in the bed for one,"
Said Abram Brown the sailor.

"You can sleep between my thighs,"
Said the fair young maiden.

"What is that hairy thing I see?"
Said Abram Brown the sailor.

"That is my pin cushion,"
Said the fair young maiden.

"I have the pin and it must go in,"
Said Abram Brown the sailor.

"What if we should have a child?"
Said the fair young maiden.

"I'd kill the dirty son of a bitch,"
Said Abram Brown the sailor.

Versions of "Bollochy Bill" are in Hugill, pp. 440–42; Colcord, pp. 112–13; Harlow, pp. 164–65; Shay, p. 204; and Elisabeth Bristol Greenleaf and Grace Yarrow Mansfield, *Ballads and Sea Songs of Newfoundland* (Cambridge, Mass., 1933), p. 105. Hugill also prints a variant of "Oh Aye Rio"—which has some bawdy stanzas of its own—that begins with the first verses of "Bollochy Bill," p. 96.

A variant credited to the singing of Oscar Brand is printed in *Songs of Roving and Raking*, p. 100, though Brand had not used it in his book or six-volume record series. *The Unexpurgated Folk Songs of Men* has it—as advertised. Lynn, pp. 54–55, carries an edited version. An Air Force parody is in Wallrich, p. 15. Reuss, pp. 240–43, has two texts from Indiana University as well as references to the appearance of the song in ephemeral collections of bawdy songs.

Shay's version in *More Pious Friends and Drunken Companions* (New York, 1928), p. 102, is the oldest in print, according to Fuld, *American Popular Music* (Philadelphia, 1955), p. 69. Shay says of that text that there are "many versions, all of them far better" than his, obviously alluding to the bawdry he excised. Frank Luther and Carson Robison copyrighted the song in 1929; Luther recorded it commercially (RCA Victor V–40043) that same year.

Abrahams has noted in a letter to the editor that "Bollochy Bill" is usually sung with alternating tempi—"Bill" rapidly, the girl slowly. This alternation was not indicated by the two former students who collected similar texts at UCLA in 1960.

Bye Bye Blackbird

The version here is from a manuscript collection made by the mother of one of Mrs. Hawes' former students. The manuscript dates from the years immediately preceding the Second World War, and contains the fullest version of the classic recitation, "The Diary of a French Stenographer," which the editor has seen. That collection rather amply refutes those who would argue that bawdry appeals only to the male.

Reuss, p. 255, notes the inclusion of this parody in "Dave E. Jones," *A Collection of Sea Songs and Ditties* (ca. 1928), pp. 22–23. The original song, published in 1926, was obviously parodied early on. Reuss also includes a text "quite similar" to that in "Jones," as it was collected in Chicago in 1951. Reuss' "A" version, like that printed here, is a conflation of the two-stanza Chicago-"Jones" effort:

Take off all your underwear,
I don't care if you're bare.
    Bye, bye blackbird.
You learned me how to dance and sing
And even how to shake that thing.
    Bye, bye, blackbird.
You took me to your bungalow in the wildwood,
And there you took advantage of my childhood.
You put your hand beneath my dress,
And there you found a blackbird nest.
    Boy friend, bye, bye.

Back your ass against the wall,
Here I come, balls and all.
    Bye, bye, blackbird.
I know I haven't got a lot,
But what I've got will fill you[r] twat.
    Bye, bye, blackbird.
Put your legs around me tighter, honey,
Now my prick is starting to feel funny.
Hoist your ass and wiggle your tits
Till the great big snapper spits.
    Cherry, bye, bye.

166

Reuss adds in a footnote that the only difference between the Chicago text and the "Jones" version is that the last three lines of the first verse of the "Jones" essay have it: ". . . He came once, I came twice,/Holy jumping Jesus Christ!/ Blackbird, goodbye."

Songs of Raunch and Ill-Repute, p. 24, has one incomplete stanza. Wallrich, p. 111, has an unrelated Air Force parody to this tune.

The Cardinals Be Damned

From texts in the New York State Historical Association Folklore Archives, Reuss dates this "at least as far as the mid-1930's" (p. 62). He footnotes one stanza, from a text in the Indiana University folklore archives, as sung at Renssclaer Polytechnic Institute, but gives nothing more of the song called here "The Cardinals Be Damned":

> R.P.I. was R.P.I. when Union was a pup.
> And R.P.I. will be R.P.I. when Union's busted up.
> And any Union son of a bitch we catch within our walls,
> We'll nail him up against the wall and castrate his balls.

A less-localized version of "The Cardinals" than that included here circulates as a camp song under the title of "Bill Braverman Be Damned." A version collected in Philadelphia and forwarded by Roger D. Abrahams contains these two verses:

> If we catch a Quebec man within these hallowed walls,
> We'll take him to the Rec Hall and amputate his balls.
> And if he cries for mercy, I'll tell you what we'll do,
> We'll stuff his ass with broken glass and seal it up with glue.
>
> I wish I had a prick of steel, two balls of solid brass.
> I'd find a marble statue and ram it up its ass.
> I'd breed a race of giants to roam around the land
> And to swell the mighty chorus of "Bill Braverman Be Damned."

There are four versions of "The Cardinals Be Damned" in the editor's collection; they vary only in length. This variant is from the singing of Stuart Grayboyse in Los Angeles in 1964. He learned it at UCLA in 1950.

The song is invariably sung to "The Son of a Gambolier," which has more than its share of bawdy songs to bear. See "The Tinker," "The Pioneers," and "Thais," *infra.* It has also served as a vehicle for "Fifty Thousand Lumberjacks," in *California Folklore Quarterly,* I (1942), p. 376; "The Riddle Song," Bronson, I, p. 379, No. 10; a marching song in praise of the 7th Infantry Regiment in Dolph, pp. 550–52; at least two Air Force songs in Wallrich, pp. 12, 84; and no less than seven not-unrelated songs cited by Reuss, p. 169. Oscar Brand uses it for a stage lampoon, "Dunderbecke," on *Laughing America* (Tradition 1014).

Joseph Hickerson, an assistant archivist in the Archives of American Folksong in the Library of Congress, provided Reuss with an extensive text of a song which Reuss dubbed "Godiva." Hickerson's offering was taken from the recently [?] issued, anonymous collection, probably compiled at M.I.T., "The *One* The *Only* Baker House Super-Duper Extra Crude Song Book." That omnibus song, to the "Gambolier" tune, runs:

Godiva was a lady who through Coventry did ride
To show the royal villagers her fine and pure white hide.
The most observant man of all, an engineer, of course,
Was the only man who noticed that Godiva rode a horse.

Chorus:
We are, we are, we are, we are, we are the engineers.
We can, we can, we can, we can demolish forty beers.
Drink rum, drink rum, drink rum, drink rum and come along with us,
For we don't give a damn for any damn man who don't give a damn
    for us.

She said, "I've come a long, long way and I will go as far
With the man who takes me from this horse and leads me to a bar."
The man who took her from her steed and led her to a bar [beer?]
Was a bleary-eyed survivor and a drunken engineer.

My father was a miner from the northern malamute [sic].
My mother was a mistress of a house of ill repute.
The last time that I saw them, these words rang in my ears,
"Go to MIT, you son of a bitch and join the engineers."

The Army and the Navy went out to have some fun.
They went down to the taverns where the fiery liquors run.
But all they found were empties, for the engineers had come
And traded all their instruments for gallon kegs of rum.

Sir Francis Drake and all his ships set out for Cazlais [sic] way.
They heard the Spanish rum fleet was headed out their way.
But the engineers had beat them by night and half a day
And though drunk as hooligans, you still could hear them say:

Venus was a statue made entirely of stone
Without a stitch upon here, she was naked as a bone.
On seeing that she had no clothes, an engineer discoursed,
"Why the damn thing's only concrete and should be reinforced."

Princeton's run by Wellesley, Wellesley's run by Yale,
Yale is run by Vassar, and Vassar's run by tail.
Harvard's run by stiff pricks, the kind you raise by hand,
But Tech is run by engineers, the finest in the land!!!!!

If we should find a Harvard man within our sacred walls,
We'll take him up to physics lab and amputate his balls.
And if he hollers "Uncle," I'll tell you what we'll do,
We'll stuff his ass with broken glass and seal it up with glue.

MIT was MIT when Harvard was a pup,
And MIT will be MIT when Harvard's busted up.
And any Harvard son of a bitch who thinks he's in our class
Can pucker up his rosy lips and kiss the beaver's ass.

A maid and an engineer were sitting in the park.
The engineer was working on some research after dark.
His scientific method was a marvel to observe:
While his right hand wrote the figures, his left hand traced the curves.

Texts of the original song, "The Son of a Gambolier," from which the melody is borrowed are in Sandburg, p. 44; Milburn, pp. 182–84; Leach, p. 115; Spaeth, pp. 88–90, who describes it as "probably the most popular of all those melodies that are at the service of the parodist . . ." He gives other songs set to the tune, pp. 90–91, then adds, "There are many other sets of words to this universal tune, some of them of an unprintable vulgarity, but widely circulated, nevertheless in the true folk-song style."

Whatever the origin of the song—Spaeth points to an "obvious" Irish source*— it was well known in the New World by the Civil War. Surprisingly, it has escaped significant notice by folklorists.

Casey Jones

Unlike "Frankie and Johnny" and "Stackolee," whose bawdy verses serve to elaborate upon a story essentially non-ribald, this version of "Casey Jones" has nothing to do with the native American ballad which usually chronicles the fatal last run of Luther Cayce Jones.

Commenting on the relationship of the tragic "Lord Randall" (Child 12) to the sprightly "Billy Boy," Bertrand Bronson has bemoaned this process of transformation in oral tradition:

Such, incidentally, appears to be the destined end of too many fine old tragic ballads: they are not to be permitted a dignified demise, but we

---

* On *The First Hurrah!* (Columbia CL2165), the Clancy Brothers and Tommy Makem sing "The Gallant Forty-Twa" which the liner notes by Robert Sherman assign to "19th Century Ulster." Sherman does not, however, recognize the "Son of a Gambolier" melody. He says the "cocky tune" sounds "like a bit of a cross between 'The Rising of the Moon' ['The Wearing of the Green'] and the American ditty 'Goober Peas.' "

must madly play with our forefathers' relics and make a mock of their calamities. The high seriousness of the parents is the children's favorite joke. So it has been with "Earl Brand," "Young Beichan," "Lord Lovel," "Lady Alice," "The Mermaid," "Bessie Bell and Mary Gray," "Queen Jane," and "The Three Ravens." (Bronson, I, p. 191.)

The present editor is less distressed than is Bronson. "Billy Boy" is, after all, as happy a bit of nonsense as is "Lord Randall" an interminable bore.

Mack McCormick, "The Damn Tinkers," *American Folk Music Occasional*, No. 1 (1964), p. 12, mentions an early version of the familiar train-wreck ballad, complaining that whites added an off-color stanza to the song:

> Casey said before he died,
> "There's two more women I'd like to try."
> "Tell me what can they be?"
> "A cross-eyed nigger and a Japanee."

Be that as it may, but Negro singers added a bawdy verse or two themselves before a pair of two-a-day vaudevillians, the Leighton Brothers, popularized Seibert and Newton's now "standard" version of the traditional ballad. Howard W. Odum and Guy B. Johnson, *The Negro and His Songs* (Chapel Hill, North Carolina, 1925), p. 207, include this stanza:

> Went on down to de depot track,
> Beggin' my honey to take me back,
> She turn 'roun' some two or three times:
> "Take you back when you learn to grind."

Judging from texts of the bawdy version which have come to the editor's attention, most texts of the ballad are little more than two-stanza jokes. This text and tune were notated by the editor from the singing of an insurance salesman and a bookseller as they swapped verses at a party in Los Angeles in 1964. Both men, approximately 30, had learned the song while in college, ten years before.

References to the classic American ballad may be found in Laws, *Native American Balladry*, p. 204; Brown, II, p. 510; Lomax, *Folk Songs of North America*, p. 564; to which may be added the version in Hubbard, p. 364.

Wallrich, pp. 31–33, 35, 71, 155, has other parodies to the same tune.

Cats on the Rooftop

This is another of the most commonly-heard bawdy songs, at least within West Coast collegiate circles. It has been printed, with some scrubbing or judicious selection of verses, by Brand, pp. 32–33, and in an 11-stanza variant in *New Locker Room Humor*, rev. ed. (Chicago: Burd Publishing Co., 1960), pp.

60–61. A third is in *Songs of Roving and Raking*, p. 101. Logue-Vicarion calls his version, No. XXXXVIII, for no apparent reason, "Nightfuck."

In the interest of presenting a fuller record of "Cats on the Rooftop," the text in *Songs of Raunch and Ill-Repute*, p. 5, is worth reprinting (typographical errors and orthography have been corrected):

The crocodile is a funny animal;
He rapes his mate only once a year,
But when he does he floods the Nile
As he revels in the throes of fornication.

Chorus:

Cats on the roof tops, cats on the tiles,
Cats with the clap and cats with the piles,
Cats with their butts all wreathed in smiles,
While they revel in the throes of fornication.

Now the hippo's rump is broad and round.
One of them weighs a thousand pounds.
Two of them will shake the ground
When they revel in the throes of fornication.

Now the camel has a lot of fun.
His height's ample when he has done [sic].
He always gets two humps for one
When he revels in the throes of fornication.

The clam is a model of chastity,
You can't tell a he from a she,
But she can tell, and so can he,
When they revel in the throes of fornication.

The queen bees fly out in the breezes,
And consorts with who she God damn pleases [sic],
And fills the world with sons of bees
As she revels in the throes of fornication.

The baboon's ass is an eerie sight,
It glows below like a neon light,
It waves like a flag in the jungle night,
As he revels in the throes of fornication.

The monkey's short and rather slow.
Erect he stands a foot or so—
And when he comes, it's time to go
As he revels in the throes of fornication.

171

Five hundred verses, all in rhyme,
To sing them all seems such a crime,
When he could better spend our time
Reveling in the throes of fornication.

There are five versions of this in the editor's collection. All but the last two stanzas were gathered from an anonymous informant who learned his version in college in New York about 1950. The last two stanzas are from Stuart Grayboyse, a Los Angeles insurance salesman, who learned them at UCLA in 1950.

The last verse here may be a clue to the song's ultimate origin. It is a mock of John Woodcock Graves' "John Peel," an 1820 art song set to a traditional tune, "Bonnie Annie," according to Spaeth, *History of Popular Music in America* (New York, 1948), p. 63. That melody has been borrowed for "Cats on the Rooftop," and at one time the bawdy song may have had verses, like the last here, closer in parody form to Graves' celebration of the huntsman.

Caviar Comes from Virgin Sturgeon

The content and vocabulary of this song would indicate its origins and development among a group not usually thought of as "folk"—educated urbanites. Its preservation in oral tradition since the First World War (it may well be older) indicates that, despite higher education and increasing urbanization, a substratum of oral currency persists. This, of course, is in direct opposition to the generally held view of folklorists that urbanization is the death knell of folklore.

"Caviar" is invariably sung to the tune, "Reuben, Reuben," the editor's collection indicates. That tune has been used, too, for other bawdy songs. Ed McCurdy sings one such, "Sally Brown," on his recording *Songs of the Sea* (Cambridge 11):

Sally Brown she had a baby.
Father said that he don't care.
It belongs to a fellow from Fortune
What was fishing up here last year.

Sally goes to church on Sunday,
Not to sing and pray, I fear,
But to see that fellow from Fortune
What was fishing up here last year.

Another Maritime province song, "Lots of Fish in Bonavist Harbor," uses the same melody and has ribald verses. Alan Mills sings a variant with a hint of this on *Songs, Fiddle Tunes and a Folktale from Canada* (Folkways FG 3532).

Reuss, pp. 200–01, has extensive citations to underground printings and offers three versions of "Caviar" from college sources. Other texts of the song may be

172

found in Leach, p. 118; Logue-Vicarion, No. XXV; Lynn, p. 33; *New Locker Room Humor* (Chicago: Burd Publishing Co., 1960), pp. 60–61; *Songs of Roving and Raking,* p. 79; and *Songs of Raunch and Ill-Repute,* p. 17. Other parodies to the same tune are in Wallrich, p. 184; and Dolph, pp. 17–18.

There are five versions of varying length and ingenuity—as well as zoological accuracy—in the editor's collection. The variant here is a compilation: the first seven stanzas are from Burson; the next four were collected by James W. Kellogg in 1963 in Texas and are used here through the courtesy of Roger D. Abrahams; the last stanza is from a shorter text collected by the editor in Santa Barbara in 1962 from an employee of the Center for the Study of Democratic Institutions.

Chamber Lye

Legman has traced this World War I satire to the Civil War song, "The Lay of John Haroldson," a copy of which is in the Harris Collection at Brown University. See Legman's *Horn Book*, p. 378.

The version here may ultimately derive from print. Apparently a post-World War II Japanese reprint of *Immortalia*—which the editor has not seen—contained the words. It was forwarded to the editor by Dale Koby who gathered it in Northern California in 1960. It is included here, despite a dubious oral currency, because the singer has apparently "re-created" the song from print by adding its original melody. *Immortalia* does not contain tunes, or references to tunes; Legman, who has worked through the collection, was pleased to learn from the editor that the song was sung to the melody of "Maryland, My Maryland" or "O Tannenbaum."

Charlotte the Harlot I

The Vance Randolph Collection of Erotic Ozark Folklore—publication rights to which Gershon Legman has secured—contains a tale, "The Half-Wit and the Eel" (No. 21), which Legman, p. 491, describes as "a *vagina dentata* story rationalized as of a serpent 'lost' in the woman's body . . ." The same motif is present here, though some may wish to question the *vagina dentata*-castration complex rationale laid to it.

There would seem to be two strains of the song called "Charlotte the Harlot" in oral tradition. One is a full-dress ballad, the other more a celebration of the lady's qualities. The ballad, of which the editor has handled four versions, is sung to the tune of "Villikins and His Dinah," or, as it is known in the United States, "Sweet Betsy from Pike." The other, for which three texts are at hand, runs to the melody of "Down in the Valley." The ballad generally identifies Charlotte as a "cowpunchers' whore," the lyric song styles her as a "Mexican whore."

The Villikins melody is one of the most used in Anglo-American balladry. A numbing profusion of songs travels on the tune and its variants, perhaps too many to encourage a full study of the tune family. Phillips Barry's short essay, "Notes on the Ways of Folk-Singers with Folk-Tunes," *Bulletin of the Folk-Song Society of the Northeast*, XII (1937), pp. 2 ff., is a firm beginning. Margaret Dean-Smith's index to the *Journal of the English Folk Dance and Song Society* enters this historical note under "William and Dinah":

> (Vulgarized as Villikins and his Dinah.) This tune, popular amongst folk singers, and to be seen in the Journal associated with The Blackberry Fold, George Keary, The Keepers and the Poachers, Peggy and the Soldier, etc. is found in the famous Skene Manuscript of airs for the lute, c. 1615, and can be seen in the transcription thereof, Dauney's Ancient Scottish Music, 1838, associated with the words "Peggie is over the sie wi' ye soldier."

Fuld, p. 493–94, dates "Villikins'" first printing, in London, to 1853, but suggests it may be a bit older. He also questions the relationship between that tune and the melody in the Skene Ms. Simpson, p. 572, reprints "Peggie," but makes no reference to the later "Villikins."

References to appearances of the song and tune are in Laws, *American Balladry from British Broadsides*, where it is entered as M 31B. For some flavor of the song as performed on stage, add Colyn Davies' singing on *Cockney Music Hall Songs and Recitations* (Tradition 1017).

In the frank hope that some student will muster enthusiasm enough to attempt a study of the tune family and/or the nature of song-making in oral tradition, the editor offers this farrago of references to the most used of "come-all-ye" melodies:

Ireland—"The Kerry Recruit" in O Lochlainn, *Irish Street Ballads*, p. 2; "The Old Orange Flute," *ibid.*, p. 100; "Master McGrath" on Patrick Galvin's *Irish Drinking Songs* (Riverside 12–604), the notes to which mention "Nottingham Fair" as being sung to "Villikins"; "The Mountjoy Hotel," written by Phil O'Neill in 1918, and sung by Patrick Galvin on *Irish Humor Songs* (Riverside 12–616); and see also the second part of "Buachaill an Chuil Dualaigh" in O'Sullivan, *Songs of the Irish* (Dublin, 1960), p. 54.

England—"Still I Love Him" sung by Isla Cameron on *English and Scottish Love Songs* (Riverside 12–656); "The Dover Sailor" in Frank Kidson, *A Garland of English Folk-Songs* (London, 1926 [?]), p. 20; "The Bold Princess Royal" in Peggy Seeger and Ewan MacColl, eds., *The Singing Island* (London, 1960), p. 57; "The Liverpool Packet" in Hugill, pp. 466–469, where "The Jolly Herring," "The Jolly Ploughboy," "Still I Live Him," "The Old Orange Flute," "Ratcliffe Highway," and "The Towrope Girls" ("The Liverpool Judies") are mentioned as using the melody; "The Ballad of Wadi Maktilla" in Hamish Henderson, *Ballads of World War II* (Lili Marleen Club of Glasgow, [1947]).

Australia—"Bluey Brink" as sung by A. L. Lloyd on *Australian Bush Songs* (Riverside 12–606), and printed in Long and Jenkin, pp. 83–84; "Bold Tommy Payne," *ibid.*, pp. 139–40; "A Nautical Yarn," *ibid.*, pp. 143–44; "Weston and His Clerk" in Hugh Anderson, *Colonial Ballads* (Victoria, 1955), pp. 51–52; "Sold," *ibid.*, pp. 89–90. Australian troops used the tune about 1940, judging from the text itself, to carry this classic example of a soldiers' song, "Dinky Die." As learned by Pete Seeger while serving in the South Pacific during World War II, and reported in an open letter dated September 16, 1945, it is reprinted here so that it might gain deserved attention from other workers:

He went up to London and straightaway strode
To army headquarters on Horse Ferry Road
To see all the blodgers who dodge all the straff
By getting soft jobs on the headquarters staff.

Chorus:

Dinky die! dinky dinky die,
Dinky die! dinky dinky die,
By getting soft jobs on the headquarters staff.

The lousy lance corporal said, "Pardon me, please,
You've mud on your tunic and blood on your sleeve.
You look so disgraceful that people will laugh,"
Said the lousy lance corporal on the headquarters staff.

Dinky die! dinky dinky die,
Dinky die! dinky dinky die,
Said the lousy lance corporal on the headquarters staff.

The digger just shot him a murderous glance.
He said, "We're just back from the shambles in France
Where whizzbangs are flying and comforts are few
[*Slowly*] And brave men are dying [*In tempo*] for bastards
   like you."

Dinky die! dinky dinky die,
Dinky die! dinky dinky die,
[*Slowly*] And brave men are dying [*In tempo*] for bastards
   like you.

"We're shelled on the left and we're shelled on the right.
We're bombed all the day and we're bombed all the night.
If something don't happen and that mighty soon,
There'll be nobody left in the bloody platoon."

(Chorus as in other verses)

The story soon got to the ears of Lord Gort
Who gave the whole matter a great deal of thought.
He awarded the digger a V.C. and two bars
For giving that corporal a kick in the arse.

(Chorus as before)

Seeger notated this melody for the unusual chorus:

Canada and the United States—"Lord Lovel" in Helen Hartness Flanders, *Ancient Ballads Traditionally Sung in New England* (Philadelphia, 1961), II, p. 150, the "A" version; "One Morning in May," Brown, V, pp. 11 ff., versions "A," "Al," and "C"; "Bonnie Annie" (Child 24), in *Bulletin of the Folk Song Society of the North-East*, X (1935), p. 11, and reprinted in Bronson, I, p. 304; "Henry Green and Mary Wyatt" in the *Bulletin*, XII (1937), p. 16; "The Crowd of Bold Sharemen" in Elisabeth Greenleaf and Grace Mansfield, *Ballads and Sea Songs of Newfoundland* (Cambridge, Mass., 1933), p. 240, citing also "The Dreadnought" melody as "Villikins" in the version in Colcord, *Roll and Go*, p. 90; "Burns' Log Camp" in William Main Doerflinger, *Shantymen and Shantyboys* (New York, 1951), pp. 217–18; "Clay Morgan" in Cecil J. Sharp, *English Folk Songs from the Southern Appalachians*, edited by Maud Karpeles (London, 1952), II, p. 274; "Kelly the Pirate" in Helen Creighton, *Maritime Folk Songs* (Toronto, 1961), p. 151; "Squarin' up Time" in Edith Fulton Fowke and Richard Johnston, *Folk Songs of Canada, Choral Edition* (Waterloo, Ontario, 1954), p. 88; and "Blooming Wilderness," according to Samuel Bayard's note in Jackson, *Another Sheaf*, p. 164; "Tourelay" in Lynn, p. 114. See, too, Spaeth, *Weep Some More, My Lady* (New York, 1927), pp. 174–75, for a stage song using the tune. Stephen Foster lifted the tune for his lampoon of the Abolitionists, "The Great Baby Show." Lincoln boosters pressed the melody into service for "There Was an Old Abraham."

The extent of the tune family, and the relationship of "Villikins" to the melody for some versions of "Lord Randall," is explored in Phillips Barry, Fannie H. Eckstorm, and Mary Winslow Smyth, *British Ballads from Maine* (New Haven, Conn., 1929), pp. 67–69, where the north-woods ballad, "The Prince Edward Island Boys," is mentioned as being sung to "Villikins"; and in Bronson, I, pp. 204–12, "Lord Randall" (Child 12), Nos. 35–61. See also Bronson, I, p. 378, for "The Riddle Song" (Child 46), No. 4; and "Bonnie James Campbell"

(Child 210), No. 3, in III, p. 291.

Schinhan has two versions of the tune and eight additional references in Brown, IV, pp. 263–64.

Members of the "Villikins" tune family are most easily identified by the outline of the major triad in the first bar(s) and the repeated fifth which follows immediately. For an example of the use of that trademark, and little else, in a "Villikins"-derived tune, see "The Sheepwasher's Lament" in Long and Jenkin, p. 103; or "The Bold 'Princess Royal' " in Kidson, *A Garland of English Folk-Songs*, pp. 34–35. "High Germany," *ibid.*, pp. 82–83, embroiders that formula in its first and last phrases. "The Red Light Saloon" in Brand, p. 50, on the other hand, is sung to "Villikins" with a slight modification of that trademark first phrase.

"Sweet Betsy from Pike" references are opened up in Ethel and Chauncey Moore, *Ballads and Folk Songs of the Southwest* (Norman, Okla., 1964), pp. 319–21.

"Charlotte the Harlot," in this version, appears on Brand's *Bawdy Western Songs* (Audio Fidelity 1920). Logue-Vicarion, No. XXXXIV, has an incomplete text.

The text and tune used here were furnished by the politician who contributed "Five Nights Drunk."

Charlotte the Harlot II

The editor has handled three versions of this short celebration. The variant in *Songs of Roving and Raking*, p. 123, borrowed from *Raunch and Ill-Repute*, p. 31, calls the girl "Lulu" and begins with the first verse here. Its second, and last, runs:

> She's dirty, she's filthy, she'll fuck in the street,
> Whenever you meet her, she's always in heat.
> She'll fuck for a quarter, take less, take more,
> She's a hard-fucking, cocksucking Mexican whore.

The text printed here is a conflation, chorus and tune from a variant given the editor by a draftsman in Los Angeles in 1966, the verses from a collection submitted by a young lady to Mrs. Hawes in 1964.

For references to the familiar melody, see Brown, V, p. 200. Textual references to "Down in the Valley" are opened up by Brown, III, p. 330; and Lomax, p. 289. The words of "Down in the Valley" have had some influence on this second version of "Charlotte the Harlot," especially in the chorus.

Charlotte the Harlot III

This unusual version of the ballad was contributed by Michael Higer at UCLA in 1959 as learned from an Australian. According to that gentleman, "Charlotte" is sung Down Under as a drinking song.

The melody is a thoroughly confused set of "Sweet Betsy from Pike" or "Villikins."

The Chisholm Trail

This odyssey has long had bawdy verses interwoven, though none have appeared in print. Except for John A. Lomax' quotation of a cowboy in *Adventures of a Ballad Hunter* (New York, 1947), pp. 41–42, who averred that some of the verses would "burn up" the horn of the recording machine, one might suspect that the song were asexual.

The editor has handled only three ribald versions of "The Chisholm Trail." *Songs of Roving and Raking*, p. 118, has an uncensored text. J. Barre Toelken has culled a second, unpublished, from the Robert W. Gordon Collection of American Folk Song at the University of Oregon; Gordon probably collected it in the late 1920's.

The third text, that is used here, was gathered by a former student in 1960 from a patron of a Los Angeles saddle shop. The informant, according to the student, was a rodeo cowboy with whom he had worked on a ranch in Colorado.

For references to other, non-bawdy texts, see Brown, III, p. 248; and Randolph, II, p. 174; to which may be added those in Lomax, *Folk Songs of North America*, pp. 370–71; and Moore, p. 285.

Fragments of the ballad have broken off and circulate among high school students, at least in Southern California. Ed Ulman, a Los Angeles attorney, in 1967 contributed this two-stanza version which he dated to his high school days in the early 1950's:

> Chorus:
> Tie my pecker to my leg.
> Tie my pecker to my leg.
>
> The last time I seen her
> And I haven't seen her since,
> She was jackin' off a nigger
> Through a barbed wire fence.
>
> The last time I seen her,
> She was sittin' on the stern.
> She was holdin' his'n,
> And he was holdin' her'n.

The chorus of Ulman's version, and the "saddle shop" variant printed here, sometimes appears—as in *Roving and Raking*—as:

> Gonna tie my pecker to a tree, to a tree,
> Gonna tie my pecker to a tree.

Christopher Columbo

Harlow, pp. 55–58, dates the bawdy version to 1876 when it was sung on board a sailing ship as a fo'c'sle song and chanty. Harlow's version, however, is expurgated and much of it dwells upon the contrived adventures of a larcenous monkey.

According to Leach, pp. 80–81, both words and music are by one Francis J. Bryant. Leach gives no date, but is at pains to note only his arrangement is copyrighted. This would suggest that Bryant secured his original copyright sometime after 1877 since Leach's work, published in 1933, respects Bryant's earlier copyright. (The maximum copyright is for 28 years to which may be added a 28-year renewal.) The priority of Harlow's version remains; more logically, the Bryant "original" is patterned after a bawdy song already in oral tradition; his text, at any rate, is a series of heavy-handed plays-upon-words, none of which are even remotely suggestive.

Legman's unpublished bibliography, "Unexpurgated Folk-Balladry," Part II, p. 6, cites Walter Klinefelter's *Preface to an Unprintable Opus* which traces the origin of "Columbo" to the Columbian Exhibition of 1892 in Chicago. Klinefelter says the bawdy song was deliberately modeled on Gilbert and Sullivan's song, "In Enterprise of Martial Kind," sung by the Duke of Plaza Toro in *The Gondoliers*.

The Gondoliers was first presented on Dec. 7, 1889, fully twelve years after Harlow dates the song. If Harlow's memory is to be trusted, his date would seemingly cast some doubt upon Klinefelter's account. However, it is possible that an older version (Harlow's) was recast (Klinefelter's) at the Exposition, or even more titillating, that W. S. Gilbert *deliberately used a then-current bawdy song as his model for the words of the famous song of the Duke of Plaza Toro.*

Gilbert was a Rabelaisian fellow, constantly feuding with the more restrained Sullivan, the composer of that model of Victorian romanticism, "The Lost Chord," and "Onward Christian Soldiers." It would not be impossible that Gilbert could succumb to the delicious joke of sending his antagonist-collaborator a poem deliberately modeled upon a bawdy song in oral tradition. (Sullivan did write the melodies after Gilbert presented him with the poems. For some years, they rarely met and barely spoke, their only tie a mutual appreciation of the financial success of their joint works.) Gilbert's joke would have been a more or less private one since hymn-writing Sullivan probably would not have known the bawdy song.

(Sullivan's nature, by the way, completely discounts the rumored joint authorship of a parody of their own popular musical comedies, *The Sod's Opera.*

According to David Loth, this epic featured, among others, the brothers Bollox, "a pair of hangers-on," and Scrotum, "a wrinkled old retainer." Legman, p. 96, states flatly enough, "There is no such work in existence as *The Sod's Opera*, and never was . . ." The present editor is not prepared to go that far.)

At any rate, Klinefelter's theory may be subsumed in this speculation. At the Columbian Exposition, matters turned full circle: the older bawdy song was reset to the tune the unwary Sullivan had composed for Gilbert's "parody" of that bawdy song.

There are three tunes used currently for the song: Sullivan's; a duple time similar to Harlow's; and the more frequently encountered triple-time melody such as in Brand, pp. 70–71, or here. The triple-time tune often appears as a dotted duple. A set of this has also served as a vehicle for the unrelated "No More Booze," on Oscar Brand, *American Drinking Songs* (Riverside 12–630).

Six other reports of the song have appeared. The anonymous editors of *Songs of Roving and Raking*, pp. 112–13, intersperse "Columbo" verses with stanzas from "The Good Ship Venus." The equally anonymous editors of *Songs of Raunch and Ill-Repute*, pp. 22–23, do likewise. Ewan MacColl, *Bless 'Em All* (Riverside 12–642) and *Unexpurgated Folk Songs of Men* have recorded versions. Additionally, two bowdlerized texts may be found in Shay, *American Sea Songs*, pp. 207 ff.; and in John J. Niles, Douglas S. Moore, A. A. Wallgren, *The Songs My Mother Never Taught Me* (New York, 1929), pp. 106–07. The latter also has another song to the "Columbo" tune, pp. 107–08.

Cod Fish Song

This unusual variant of "The Sea Crab" was given to the editor by D. K. Wilgus, curator of the Western Kentucky Folklore Archives at UCLA. It was collected, from an anonymous informant at Campbellsville College, Campbellsville, Kentucky, by two of Wilgus' former students in the Fall of 1964. The text was not accompanied with a melody as it was submitted to the archive; the chorus, however, suggests the proper tune. In the interest of making the narrative a bit more coherent, the tenth and eleventh stanzas have been transposed here.

The Darby Ram

Child's unannounced rule that the heroes and heroines of popular balladry had to be of the genus *homo sapiens* was enough to exclude "The Darby Ram" and the equally likely candidate, "The Frog and the Mouse," from his multivolume canon. This is unfortunate since neither ballad has yet to find a biographer. Roger Abrahams has begun a study of "The Darby Ram" (it was he who urged the song's inclusion in this anthology), and the editor has threatened for some years to apply himself to the chronicle of "ye weddinge of Mr. Frogge and Misses Mouse." Neither of us is as good as our resolution.

180

Despite the reference to a garbage truck in this version of "The Darby Ram," collected by Sidney Robertson Cowell in 1940 in California (and used with her kind permission), the ballad is an old one. Its roots lie somewhere in English pre-history, and the ballad is commonly thought to be a remnant of the winter luck-visits of masked and costumed dancers once common in England.

Exaggerations involving tremendous animals are widely known, and figure extensively in folktales. The Old Testament, borrowing from an even older tale, tells the story of David's climb up the side of a monstrous animal, the reem (ram?). When the animal stands up, the young David finds himself in stratospheric peril. Praying for aid, he offers to build a temple as high as the animal's horns if he is saved. That mythical reem sounds much like the Darby monster. Variants of the ballad sometimes note:

> The horns upon this ram, sir,
> They reached up to the sky,
> And eagles built their nests up there
> For I heard the young ones cry.

According to Legman, the ballad "has never yet been published in unexpurgated form." (See *The Horn Book*, pp. 424–425.) This is not altogether true. A. L. Lloyd sings a moderately robust stanza—which seems to hint of more—on *English Drinking Songs* (Riverside 12–618):

> Took all the boys of Darby to carry away his bones.
> Took all the gals of Darby to roll away his—That's a lie!

Reuss, p. 58, footnotes a single stanza from a Pine Bluff, Arkansas, informant, ca. 1957:

> There was a cow in barber town
> Who had two horns of brass.
> One grew out her upper lip,
> The other grew out her
>> Hinky dinky, tiddly winky,
>> You may think I lie,
>> But if you go down to barber town,
>> You'll see the same as I.

This "teasing" or intermediate form of the song Abrahams considers "the most common." Brand sings a variant of this verse on Vol. II of his record series (Audio Fidelity 1806).

More fully, Logue, under the Palmiro Vicarion pseudonym, prints this text (No. XXIII):

> There was a ram of Derbyshire
>> That had two horns of brass,

The one grew out of its head, sir,
    The other grew out of its arse.

Chorus:

If you don't believe me
    Or if you think I lie,
So [Go?] ask the girls of Derbyshire,
    They'll tell you the same as I.

When the ram was young, sir,
    It had a nasty trick .
Of jumping over a five-barred gate
    And landing on its prick.

When the ram was old, sir,
    They put it in a truck
And all the girls of Derbyshire
    Came out to have a fuck.

When the ram was dead, sir,
    They buried it in St. Paul's,
It took twelve men and a donkey-cart
    To carry away its balls.

For references to inoffensive versions and variants, see Dean-Smith, p. 63; Brown, II, p. 439; Hudson, p. 273; and Belden, p. 224. Add to those, Cazden, *Book of Nonsense Songs* (New York, 1961), p. 87; Hubbard, p. 390; and Hugill, pp. 437–38, who says of his version: "I have had to camouflage quite a lot as the sailors' version was markedly obscene."

The song has also been assigned the motif number X1243.1.

Abrahams has forwarded the following references to the use of the ballad in mummers' plays, describing those plays as "licentious," since in the course of things, the masked ram is ritually goosed: S. O. Addy, *Household Tales and Traditional Remains* (1895), p. xxi; S. O. Addy, "Local Pamphlets" (Sheffield Public Library, Vol. XC, n.d. [circa 1900]); Ivor Gatty, "The Old Tup and Its Ritual," *JEFDSS*, V (1946), pp. 23–30; *Folk*, I (Oct., 1962), pp. 9–10; and Reginald Nettel, *Sing a Song of England* (London, 1954), pp. 32–34.

Ditties

"Oh Binnie" was sung to the editor by management consultant Robert Leventhal in Los Angeles in 1955. Abrahams forwarded "You Can Talk About Fucking" with the comment that it was a personal favorite. "Shmendrick" served as a lullaby for Donald Naftulin, M.D., when his grandmother sang him to sleep in Toledo, Ohio, in the middle 1930's; Naftulin sang it for the editor in Los Angeles in 1964.

Off-color lullabies turn up now and again. Southern Mountain children, the editor has been told, were lulled to sleep with:

Daddy shot a bear, daddy shot a bear,
Shot him through the asshole, never touched a hair.

(A tune for this is in Ruth Crawford Seeger, *Animal Folk Songs for Children* [New York, 1950], p. 78, where the expurgated [?] words are credited to Miss Annie Brewer as collected by John A. and Alan Lomax.)

Eminger Stewart of San Francisco reported this sly lullaby from Eastern Oregon as current about 1932:

Today is the day they give babies away
With every pound of tea.
If you know any ladies who want any babies,
Just send them around to me.

Mrs. Rosalie Sorrels has collected a variant from Utah singers; she has recorded it on *Rosalie's Songbag* (Prestige 13025). Reuss, p. 90, has it from Indiana's folklore archives as sung by college students, and Abrahams, in a letter to the editor, has identified it as "part of a farcical circus routine which was common in my adolesence."

The balance of the fragments included here are from Bess Lomax Hawes who furnished the "Goodnight, Irene" mock and the first of the quatrains sung to the melody of "The Girl I Left Behind Me." The second is from Abrahams, who also furnished "She Ripped and She Tore" as collected by a former student. "Oh, I Had a Girl Friend" is from the editor's imperfectly remembered boyhood in Los Angeles, about 1945. Lynn, p. 141, has a similar song, "I Had a Little Duck," less the bawdry. "He Was Sitting in the Prison" is from the editor's youth also.

Doodle-De-Doo

This parody was sent to the editor after a radio appeal for bawdy songs. The anonymous listener unfortunately did not indicate where the song was learned, or when. A close variant, however, contributed by a former student in 1960 was reportedly current in Southern California high schools about 1955.

Songs of Raunch and Ill-Repute, p. 23, has this variant as sung at Calteach in 1960:

Now won't you do it to me like you did to Marie
Last Saturday night, Saturday night?
First you caressed her and then you undressed her
Last Saturday night, Saturday night.

Cherries are ripe and ready for plucking,
A girl sixteen is ready for high school,
Oh, won't you do it to me like you did to Marie
Late last Saturday night?

Now won't you do it to me like you did to Marie
Last Saturday night, Saturday [night]?
I know it's real because I heard her squeal
Last Saturday night, Saturday night.

It's really easy; there's nothing to it,
A dollar down and the rest when you do it.
Oh, do it to me like you did to Marie,
Late last Saturday night.

Do Your Balls Hang Low?

This inquiry is sung either to the tune of Leon Jessel's "The Parade of the Wooden Soldiers," written in 1910, or the first part of the traditional fiddle tune, "Sailors' Hornpipe" (known also as "College Hornpipe"). Copies of that fiddle tune are in most standard collections of jigs and reels, including [Ira] Ford's *Old Time Fiddle Music*, No. 1 (Los Angeles: Ford's Publications, c. 1931), p. 26, from which it is reprinted in his *Traditional Music in America* (New York, 1940), p. 46. Apparently the fiddle tune's second part, or turn, is derived from, or the inspiration of the seventeenth-century ballad air, "A-Begging We Will Go." See Simpson, p. 41; and p. 291, for the phrases used again in "Have at Thy Coat, Old Woman." "Sailor's Hornpipe" also carries the unrelated "Mother Rackett's," as sung by Oscar Brand on *American Drinking Songs* (Riverside 12–630).

There are five versions of this in the editor's collection, including a variant sung at children's camps in Southern California which substitutes "ears" for "balls." A text of that camp song is also in Frank Lynn, *Songs for Swinging House-mothers*, new enlarged ed. (San Francisco, 1963), p. 30, with the indicium that it is to be sung to the melody of "Turkey in the Straw."

Songs of Raunch and Ill-Repute, p. 25, and *Songs of Roving and Raking*, p. 65, have four-stanza variants of the "balls" text.

The text and tune here are from Peter Jaffee as he learned it at Los Angeles City College in 1956. Burson had the same from his Carnegie Tech informant.

Drive It On

This is descended from a pumping chanty given by Hugill, p. 508, as "Put Your Shoulder Next to Mine and Pump Away," and itself is undoubtedly the forerunner or progenitor of the more popular "Roll Me Over."

Songs of Roving and Raking, p. 118, has a version entitled "Shove It Home" credited to Gershon Legman. The stanzaic pattern is:

> I gave her inches one, shove it home, shove it home.
> I gave her inches one, shove it home.
> I gave her inches one; she said, "Johnny, ain't it fun?
> Put your belly close to mine and shove it home."

The melody of the Legman version is a compressed set of Hugill's, lacking the repetitious, formulaic responses of the crew to the chantyman's lead.

There are three versions of the song in the editor's files. A Texas variant forwarded by Abrahams furnished the tune. (That worthy reports in a letter to the editor that he has also gathered an as-yet-unpublished text from the West Indies.) The text here, all but identical to the Texas variant, is from a housewife living in New York City who reported she learned it while attending Antioch College in the early 1950's. She could not, however, recall the melody clearly.

The tune here is a member of the very extended family of which "I Was Born about Ten Thousand Years Ago" and "She'll Be Comin' 'Round the Mountain" are a part.

Expurgated versions of this circulate as "I Gave Her Kisses One," a version of which is sung by Mrs. Hartley Minifie on *Ontario Ballads and Folksongs*, collected by Edith Fowke (Prestige 25014). Mrs. Minifie's tune is a set of the melody various used for "They Had to Carry Harry to the Ferry" or "There's a Hole in the Bottom of the Sea," among others.

The Fire Ship

Although this song is quite well-known now—due to the popular recording of the 1950's which still occasionally is played on the radio—bawdy versions do not turn up too frequently. Hugill, pp. 171–2, had one, but chose to omit the two indelicate stanzas of his text.

The version here was forwarded by unsigned letter to the editor after he broadcast a radio appeal in Los Angeles and San Francisco for "bawdy or dirty" songs. The letter was postmarked "San Francisco" and contained this note:

> I learned this from my father who worked on the docks here when he
> was a boy about 1900. I suppose he learned it there. I am not sure if the

melody is the way my father sang the song. I picked it out on the piano the way I sing it.

The editor has corrected two minor errors in the musical transcription forwarded with the text.

A similar version of the song is in Shay, pp. 205 ff; and in Niles, Moore and Wallgren, *The Songs My Mother Never Taught Me* (New York, 1929), pp. 152–55.

Ultimately, the modern bawdy song may be traced to a far more extended metaphor-in-verse. David Loth, *The Erotic in Literature* (New York, 1961), pp. 77–78, credits his broadside to "Elizabethan yoemanry."

As I cam up to Arpendeen
And straight to Wattentown
And there I met a pretty wench
That looked like lay me down..

Chorus:

At Watten Towns end,
At Watten Towns end,
At every door there stands a whore
At Watten Towns end.

The Frigat's name was Thunder-bolt,
Her sails were all of Silk;
Her tacklen was of silver twist
Her colour like the Milk.

Her planks were all of ivory
Her bottom beaten-gold
Her deck was alabaster pure
She looked brisk and bold.

Her keep was guilded o'er and o'er
Her wanton flay did flye
And I was mad to be on board
So much a fool was I.

She seemed a stately pleasure-boat
With tempting good attire
But little knew that (under deck)
Her gun room was in fire.

I lodged with her, I laid her down,
I slept with her all night,

I supped upon a Coney fatt
Whose Gravey was delight.

She gave to me a Syrrup sweet
Was in her placket box
But o'er three minutes went about
It proved the French-pox.

The fire-ship she did blow me up
As my effigies shows
And all may read upon my face
The loss of teeth and nose.

Now as I walk along the streets
They gaze upon my face
And every one that looks at me
Salutes me with disgrace.

By me beware then Gentlemen
From King to country clown,
And when you see a pretty Wench
Remember lay me down.

Simpson, p. 461, puts this "in print very early in the Seventeenth Century," sung to a tune he gives as "London Is a Fine Town."

Legman, *The Horn Book*, pp. 189–190, cites other analogues to the modern bawdy song. One of these, known variously as "While Cruising 'Round Yarmouth," or "Ratcliffe Highway," or "The Gun Tackle Fall" in this version, was collected by Robert W. Gordon in the late 1920's.

Just listen to me and a story I'll tell
All about an adventure that did me befall.
As I was out cruising the town for to spree,
I met a fair lass goin' wing and wing free,
　　Singin' Fal-diddle-laddidie, fal-diddle-laddidie,
　　Folderol-day, di-doodle-die-day.

Now the country she came from I couldn't tell which,
But judged by her appearance I think she was Dutch,
For she flew the tricolor; her masts they were low;
She was round in the counter and bluff on the bow.
　　Singing etc.

"Oh, what is your cargo, fair maiden," I cried.
"I'm sailing in ballast, kind sir," she replied,
"And I'm as fast-going clipper as ever was seen,
And I'm just fit for you for my hold is swept clean."
　　Singing etc.

So I handed me hawser and took her in tow,
And yardarm in yardarm away we did go.
We chaffed on so lightly, so frisky and gay
Till we came to an anchor down Ratcliffe Highway.
    Singing etc.

She took me upstairs into a snug room,
And into her parlor I run my jib boom.
She took down her topsails, her staysails and all,
Clapped her lilywhite hand on me gun-tackle fall.
    Singing etc.

Then I fired away at her all to me desire,
And all the night long I kept up a sharp fire.
My shot-locker got empty and me powder was spent
And me gun it wanted spongin' for 'twas choked in
        the vent.
    Singing etc.

Says, I, "Me fair lass, now it's time to give o'er.
For between wind and water I've sculled you ashore,
And I never before saw shots fired so well
But she had a hole in her counter to sink her to—
        Jerusalem.
    Singing etc.

Culled from the Gordon Collection of American Folk Song at the University of Oregon by J. Barre Toelken, this song has seemingly seen the light of day rarely. A variant entitled "While Cruising Round Yarmouth"—learned from an English traditional singer—is recorded on A. L. Lloyd and Ewan MacColl, *Blow Boys Blow* (Tradition 1026). Hugill has it as "Ratcliffe Highway," pp. 200–01, with two verses deliberately omitted; and Doerflinger, *Shantymen and Shantyboys*, pp. 114–16, carries it as "As I Was A-Walking Down Ratcliffe Highway" in fragmentary form. The melodies for the refrains of all three variants have some points of similarity; the tunes for the stanzas are less clearly related.

As a curiosity piece, it is perhaps worth reprinting a mock letter from *The Pearl, A Journal of Facetiae and Voluptuous Reading*, Vol. II, No. 1 (January, 1880), p. 15:

"A Copy of a Letter

"Was given mee by my cozen SC of Kempston, and written in a Tarpaulin style,

"Madame,—
"Premising you are safe returned to Towne, I made bold to acquaint you that Mr. F— is lately arriv'd att ye haven of matrimony; He had been long in ye

middle state of Purgatory between ye Church & ye Ladyes Chamber; ere she with ye advice of her mother, and some other experienced Ladyes, was lanced forth into ye marriage bed. The Vessell had been 14 years & three months on Building, that it is though she will care well under Sail. It is a fine smooth ship, I will promise you, & one of ye first-rate; and likely to doe ye King good service if ably and well man'd. The only fault there is (if any) she is too narrow in ye Poope. She hath a fine large shroud, & all difficulty soone vanish'd saving only ye maine yard may prove too burly for the midle Deck. The Capt. it is thought this night will goe on board of her; hee is bound for ye Straites Mouth, and cannot come off without bloodshed: Nay worse; 'tis fear'd if opposition be made, hee may be forced to spend his provision in ye channel, & soe returne without doeing ye Kingdome a penny worth of service."

The possibilities of nautical wordplay are endless.

Five Nights Drunk I, II

Joseph Hickerson, who is making an extended study of this ballad, suggests that "Our Goodman" (Child 274) may well be the most popular of the English and Scottish popular ballads in oral tradition. According to Hickerson, were not informants and collectors both handicapped by modesty, printed texts and tunes would surpass in number the acknowledged leader, "Barbara Allen" (Child 84).

Collectors and editors have found themselves in an awkward position in handling bawdy versions of the ballad. Duly certified by Child, "Five [Four] Nights Drunk," as it is known generally in the United States, is, *ipso facto*, a nugget in the tailings of oral tradition. But how handle those embarrassingly common verses?

Discrete mention sufficed for some. H. M. Belden, *Ballads and Songs Collected by the Missouri Folk-Lore Society*, 2nd ed., p. 90, noted a two-stanza version sent to the editor by a student with the appended comment that "there are some twenty verses of it, each one 'rottener' than the one before. It is often sung by the older generation of miners." The wife responds in the song: " 'You old fool, you damn fool, you son of a b——,' says she."

Eloise Hubbard Linscott was a bit more bold in her *Folk Songs of Old New England* (New York, 1939):

> When he thought no one could overhear him, a certain young man of North Irish extraction sang this naughty song to his little sister. Since this little sister is today too much of a gentlewoman, she could not sing the last verse; but she finally consented to write it.

> Oh, the old man he came home one night,
> As drunk as he could be,

He saw a face between the sheets,
Where no face ought to be.

*   *   *   *   *

"It's nothing but a little kid
My uncle sent to me." (pp. 259–62)

Significantly, that gentle woman remembered the three-stanza version from puberty to adulthood before modestly writing it down for Mrs. Linscott.

John Harrington Cox, *Folk-Songs of the South* (Cambridge, Mass., 1926), p. 154, also reported that "by variation or extension several vulgar stanzas are current in West Virginia and elsewhere." A. P. Hudson elected to print only "a fragment of a ribald version of the old English and Scottish ballad, said to be well known among students of the University of Mississippi" in his *Folk Songs of Mississippi* (Chapel Hill, North Carolina, 1936), p. 122.

Arthur Kyle Davis, *More Traditional Ballads of Virginia* (Chapel Hill, 1960), p. 301, concludes, "If ribald versions were collected and printed, no doubt every state would be represented!"

For references to reported versions, expurgated or otherwise, see Belden, p. 90; and Brown, II, p. 181. Add to them Arthur Argo's singing of "Hame Drunk Came I" on *A Wee Thread o' Blue* (Prestige International 13048); Brand, pp. 76–77; Shay, *More Pious Friends and Drunken Companions* (New York, 1928), p. 31, and p. 104; Lynn, *Housemothers*, p. 138; Davis, *More Traditional Ballads from Virginia* (Chapel Hill, North Carolina, 1960), pp. 300 ff. The texts in Helen H. Flanders, *Ancient Ballads Traditionally Sung in New England*, Vol. IV (Philadelphia, 1965), pp. 63–71, are prefaced with this comment on the gap between informant and collector: "Many informants refuse to sing this ballad on moral grounds. . . ." Quite obviously, the informants learned the "usually bawdy" (Mrs. Flanders' description) verses though. John Greenway sings another on *The Cat Came Back* (Prestige 13011). An English version is sung by Jack Elliott on *The Elliots* [sic] *of Birtley* (Folkways FG 3565).

Songs of Roving and Raking, p. 80, credits its version to the underground Parisian publication, *Count Vicarion's Book of Bawdy Ballads*, where it is No. LII. That text has a hat upon the rack, chamber pot with head band; head upon the bed, baby's bum with whiskers; a nob betwixt her legs, rolling pin with balls attached; a mess on her nightdress, clotted cream that smelt of fish.

On the recording *The Unexpurgated Folk Songs of Men*, "The Merry Cuckold" has pants on the chair, blanket with fly hole; head upon the bed, turnip with whiskers; ass upon the bed, an asshole on a pumpkin; a thing within the thing, a foreskin on a carrot.

The editor collected the first version here in one of those legendary smoke-filled rooms at a political convention from a legislator from an urban district who

190

prefers to remain nameless. His constituency, he says, is not yet ready for this form of campaign song.

The second was forwarded by Roger D. Abrahams as learned by a student in Amarillo, Texas, about 1964. The editor has adjusted the notation of Abrahams' former student in bars 12, 25 and 26 to relieve two unnatural stresses placed on unaccented words.

The Foggy Dew

This version, as is the case with most, only hints delicately at the bawdy. It was collected by the editor from John Terrence O'Neil, an advertising artist who remembered it from the singing of his father, a New York City construction worker. O'Neil's melody, in the mixolydian (with the sixth of the scale added), is one of the handful of clearly modal tunes in the collection. The addition of the sixth in this tune suggests that it, too, will eventually shift from the modal to the major, conforming as it were to more modern tastes. (The deliberate use of modal tunes, especially those in the mixolydian and dorian, by contemporary songwriters such as the Beatles is atypical recidivism.)

Other American texts of this widely known song are cited in Laws, pp. 227–28, to which may be added Hubbard, p. 115; Brand, p. 55; and Fowke, pp. 108–09, who gives additional references at p. 186. Lomax, pp. 89–90, has an English version; Pinto and Rodway, *The Common Muse*, offer two: a five-stanza variant, p. 370, and a shorter version, p. 393.

Four Old Whores

This was collected by Dean Burson from an anonymous informant who learned the song at Carnegie Tech, Pittsburgh, Pennsylvania, prior to 1959.

A close parallel is recorded by Arthur Argo on his collection of Scots bawdy songs, *A Wee Thread o' Blue*. John Greenway's notes to that album say this is "probably the oldest indecent song in the English language, going back to 'A Talk of Ten Wives on Their Husbands'" which dates from about 1460. That ballad deals with the size of the husband's equipment.

The theme, of course, is probably older. Thompson's motif index lists only two entries, both from the oral tales of India, under the entries F 547.3.1, long penis; and F 547.5.2, enormous vagina. This would not seem to reflect the international distribution of the theme in oral tradition, however; most collectors and editors have felt constrained in the presentation of this sort of folklore. Aleksandr Afanasyev was an anonymous exception; see his *Stories from the Folk-lore of Russia*, pp. 112 ff. This includes three versions of a tale called "The Enchanted Ring," the ring possessing the power to make the wearer's penis grow to impractical lengths.

Legman, *The Horn Book*, pp. 414–15, is more certain than Greenway, considering "Four Old Whores" to be a "version of the oldest surviving erotic folksong in English." The Scots song, "Our John's Brak Yestreen," in Burns, *The Merry Muses of Caledonia*, p. 84, Legman judges to be a mid-point between the older form of the ballad and the newer. This is the Burns text:

> Twa neebor wives sat i' the sun,
> A twynin' at their rocks, [spinning thread]
> An' they an argument began
> An' a' the plea was c - - ks.

> 'Twas whether they were sinnens [sinews] strang,
> Or whether they were bane? [bone]
> An' how they row'd about your thumb,
> And how they stan't themlane?

The meaning of these two lines is unclear. If "row'd" means "rolled," then the second line may be: "And how they stood them long." ("Themlane" would be a typographical error for "them lang.")

> First, Raichie gae her rock a rug,
> An' syne she claw'd her tail;
> "When our Tam draws on his breeks,
> It waigles like a flail."

> Says Bess, "They're bane I will maintain,
> And proof on han' I'll gie;
> For our John's it brak yestreen,
> And the margh [marrow] ran down my thie."

Another variant of the American song, the boasts of "Three Whores of Winnipeg," is in *Songs of Roving and Raking*, p. 117. The text in *Vicarion's Book*, No. XXXII, is to be sung to the tune of "My Love Lies Dying."

The last stanza here is probably influenced by, or influences "The Darby Ram." At any rate, they share the motif of the extraordinary long absence. The melody for this version is a set of "The Lincolnshire Poacher" which frequently carries the words of another bawdy song, "The Chandler's Wife." (See Brand, pp. 24–25, for a text and tune.) Chappell considered the melody, about 1859, "rather *too* well known among the peasantry."

The comparisons the four old whores make are more or less constant from version to version. The ships sail in, the birds fly about, men get lost for a while, all with predictable regularity. A soldiers' variant dated to 1914 in the Robert W. Gordon Collection of American Folk Song, University of Oregon (No. 2432), does offer these anatomical curiosities:

192

"You're a liar!" said the third one,
"For mine is as big as the air,
The sun could set in the crack of my ass
And never singe a hair."

"You're a liar!" said the fourth one,
"For mine is the biggest of all.
I have the flowers twice a month
As big as Niagara Falls!"

"Oh, feel o' my slimy belly,
Fondle my fat old can,
Rattle your nuts against my guts,
I belong to an infantryman!"

The Flying Colonel

This was collected by Dean Burson from his Carnegie Tech informant in Los Angeles in 1959. For other parodies to the same tune, see Wallrich, pp. 23, 54, 75, 104 and 128. The tunes for the latter two are said to be "Casey Jones," but the stanzas are modeled upon "The Wreck of Old 97."

Wallrich, *passim,* and his "United States Air Force Parodies Based upon 'The Dying Hobo,'" *Western Folklore,* XIII (1954), well cover the printable Air Force songs. The bawdy remain to be anthologized.

For a history of the popular recording by Vernon Dalhart, to whom credit must go for the wide currency of the melody and stanzaic model, see Brown, II, pp. 512 ff. Sandburg, p. 146, has the song upon which the railroad song is ultimately based, "The Ship That Never Returned," written by Henry C. Work after the Civil War.

Frankie and Johnny

This is one of a handful of American ballads still thriving in oral tradition, and one of the most frequently collected prior to this generation. For some estimate of the song's popularity, see Belden, pp. 330 ff. To the references there, add those in Brown, II, pp. 589 ff.; and Fuld, *American Popular Music* (Philadelphia, 1955), pp. 20–21. See also Spaeth, pp. 34 ff.; and Mellinger E. Henry, *Folk-Songs from the Southern Highlands* (Locust Valley, N.Y., 1938), p. 338.

For all the prior reports of the song, "Frankie and Johnny" has not been publicly printed before this in all its flaming glory. It was well-known among scholars that the song did have bawdy stanzas, indeed, any number of them. Robert W. Gordon, for example, had two bawdy versions, one from Wisconsin collected on a field trip in the Summer of 1924, and this unnumbered text from a California student, dated 1921 in the Gordon Collection of American Folk Song, University of Oregon:

Frankie and Johnie were lovers,
Lawdy, oh God, how they loved,
Swore to be true to each other,
As true as the blue sky above.
    He was her man,
    But he was doin' her wrong.

Frankie she worked in a hump-house,
A hump-house with only two doors,
Gave all her money to Johnie
Who spent it on the parlor-house whores.
    Damn his soul,
    For he was doin' her wrong.

One night when Frankie was lonely,
Nobody came out to call.
Frankie put on her kimonie
And went out to the nickel crawl*
    Lookin' for the man
    That was doin' her wrong.

Frankie blew down to the corner,
Ordered herself up some beer,
Said to the gentle bartender,
"Have you seen my lovin' Johnie here?
    For he's my man,
    But he's doin' me wrong."

"I don't want to tell you no story.
I don't want to tell you no lie,
But Johnie was here about an hour ago
With that fat bitch Nellie Bly.
    He's your man,
    But he's doin' you wrong."

Frankie blew back to the hump-house.
This time 'twasn't for fun.
Under her dirty kimona,
She packed a big 44 gun,
    Lookin' for the man
    That was doin' her wrong.

---

* Presumably a taxi-dance charging a nickel a dance.

Frankie blew into the hump-house,
Didn't even ring the bell,
Said, "Look out, all you pimps and whores
Or I'll blow you all straight to hell.
    I'm lookin' for the man
    That's doin' me wrong."

She went on back through the hallway,
Looked over a transom so high.
There she saw her lovin' boy
Finger-fucking Nellie Bly,
    God damn her soul.
    But he was doin' her wrong.

Johnie saw Frankie a-comin',
Said, "My God, Frankie, don't shoot!"
But Frankie pulled out her big 44 gun
And the gun went root-i-toot-toot.
    She shot the man
    That was doin' her wrong.

"Bring on your rubber-tired hearses,
Fill 'em up plumb full of maques [sic]
For they're taking my Johnie to the cemetery,
And they'll never bring his penis back,
    Best part of the man
    That was doin' me wrong."

At the end of the song, either Gordon or his informant (who was probably white) noted: "This song is pure Negro. I got it from a man that has played in cafés, and he said that it is universal among the Negroes. I have heard it before myself. There are probably more verses to it than are here."

The version here is from a hand-written copy sent at the editor's request by a radio listener. The unsigned note, in a woman's hand, said only that the song was learned in Cleveland, Ohio, prior to 1940. A second version, gathered in Northern California about 1960 by Dale Koby, is similar but less lengthy.

The editor has "corrected" what appear to be errors in the barring of the tune sent by the radio listener.

Fuck 'Em All I

As Ewan MacColl has noted, this has been *the* anthem of British fighting men since World War I. A version suited for popular consumption was copyright in 1940 by Jimmie Hughes and Frank Lake, with additional lyrics copyrighted by Al Stillman the next year, but this has only served to teach civilians the proper tune for the many improper verses which circulate. "Bless 'Em All" has been thankfully forgotten; "Fuck 'Em All" goes right on.

Lynn, p. 55, has a sickly parody, "Kiss 'Em All," as well as the copyright version, pp. 80–81. Wallrich has two sanitary Air Force adaptations, pp. 28 and 88. For a recording of a British Army version, see Ewan MacColl, *Bless 'Em All* (Riverside 12–642).

There are five variants or versions of the song in the editor's files. The first version here was collected in 1961 by a former student of Mrs. Hawes' whose informant presumably learned it while serving in His or Her Majesty's armed services.

Fuck 'Em All II

There is an endless number of adaptations of "Fuck 'Em All," localized variants and songs of protest. In 1953, the editor learned one stanza of a United States Marine Corps version current in Korea two years before, that verse topically concerned with the then raging police action:

> Fuck 'em all; fuck 'em all,
> The commies, the U.N. and all.
> Those slant-eyed Chink soldiers hit Hagaru-ri
> And now know the meaning of U.S.M.C.,
> But we're saying goodbye to them all.
> We're Harry's police force on call.
> So put your pack back on,
> The next stop is Saigon,
> And cheer up, my lads, fuck 'em all.

(The reference to Saigon is a reflection of the not-so-idle rumors then current in Korea that U.S. troops would leave Korea at the end of the police action to aid the failing French in Viet Nam. The rumors were not false, strictly speaking— only ten years premature.)

A Korean War Air Force version grouses about the dangers of breaking the sonic barrier in the first operational jet fighters. As collected by James W. Kellogg in 1963 in Austin, Texas, from a Korean War veteran, the song has it:

> Bless 'em all; bless 'em all.
> Bless tiptanks and tailpipes and all.
> Bless old man Lockheed for building this jet,
> But I know a guy who is cussing him yet,
> 'Cause he tried to go over the wall
> With tiptanks and tailpipes and all.
> The needles did cross and the wings did come off
> With tiptanks and tailpipes and all.

196

Through the wall, through the wall,
That bloody, invisible wall,
That transonic journey is nothing but rough,
As bad as a ride on the local base bus.
So I'm staying away from the wall,
Subsonic for me and that's all.
If you're hot, you might make it,
But you'll probably break it,
Your butt or your neck, not the wall.

Wallrich, p. 70, has this "tiptanks" version also.

A slim collection of jokes, limericks and songs, "Super Stag Treasury," rev. ed. (Los Angeles, Mada Distributing Co., 1964), contains a Marine Corps version from World War II lampooning the other services. The first and fifth verses of the song—possibly borrowed from a recording by Oscar Brand—are:

Well, we sent for the army to come to Tulagi,
But General MacArthur said, "No,"
And this is the reason: "This isn't the season;
Besides you've got no U.S.O."

Then we sent for the nurses to come to Tulagi,
The nurses they made it with ease,
Their arse on the table, each bearing this label,
"Reserved for the officers, please."

In an open letter from the Marianas, dated September 16, 1945, Peter Seeger reports that U.S. troops in the Pacific at that time learned the song from the Australians. The text he gives, three verses long, includes the U.S.O. stanza printed above; Seeger described the song as "widely known, especially among Marines."

Evidence that the song continues in circulation, Los Angeles attorney Alvin Tenner in 1967 sang for the editor a version he had learned in the Marine Corps in 1958 or '59:

Bless 'em all; bless 'em all,
The long and the short and the tall.
Bless all the sergeants and W.O. ones,
Bless all the corporals and their bastard sons,
'Cause we're going back to the front.
There'll be no more wine, women or cunt.
We'll lay in our trenches and dream of fine wenches,
And beat off our meat with a grunt.

A second verse Tenner could not recall, though it contained a choice threat to gunnery sergeants in general: ". . . And just to be funny, we'll gang bang the gunny . . ."

197

Finally, the men of Ricketts Hall at Caltech, about 1960, adapted it to the college setting, according to the text in *Songs of Raunch and Ill-Repute,* p. 16.

The version numbered "II" here was given to the editor by a former student in 1959 who said he had learned it while on a Sierra Club outing in Yosemite a few years before.

The Fucking Machine

A psychological study of the theme of the great fucking wheel or machine would fill a sizeable volume. For some suggestion of the recurrent popularity of the subject, see Legman's notes to limerick 1325, pp. 447–8. That limerick, which Legman identified as the most frequently collected in his research, runs:

> There was a young man from Racine
> Who invented a fucking machine.
> > Concave or convex,
> > It would fit either sex,
> With attachments for those in between.

There are seven versions of the ballad in the author's collection, remarkable for their similarity. This variant is from New Jersey, ca. 1955, and was sung to the author by an engineer living in Los Angeles in 1964.

While the singers frequently mention the solemn quality of the melody, most do not recognize one of the oldest hymn tunes still in use. It is generally credited to Guilliaume Franc, Kapelmeister in Geneva at the time of the Reformation. The tune dates from sometime before 1554 when it appeared in the *Geneva Psalter* as a setting for the 134th Psalm. Knox's *Anglo-Genevan Psalter* used the melody for the 3rd Psalm two years later. In 1562, it first appeared—in Sternhold and Hopkins' *Psalter*—as a setting for the 100th Psalm. Henry Ainsworth borrowed the song from Sternhold and Hopkins in 1612 for the hymn book which would be taken to the New World by Governor Bradford's Puritan colonists. In 1661, Bishop Ken added new words to the older tune: "Come loud anthems let us sing/Loud thanks to our almighty King." Despite the fact that these are now the most frequently encountered words to the tune, the melody retains the title, "Old Hundred," deferring to the 100th Psalm once sung to the stately tune.

That melody has also been borrowed to carry a version of "On Springfield Mountain," J. Barre Toelken has informed the editor; A. P. Hudson has reported its use in "the South" to carry the quatrain: "I'll eat when I'm hungry./I'll drink when I'm dry./If the Yankees don't get me,/I'll live till I die." A set of "Old Hundred," seemingly bearing a secular text is called "Franklin Is Fled Away" in Simpson, p. 233.

"The Fucking Machine" has seen semi-public light in *Songs of Roving and Raking,* p. 111, where the tune, p. 119, is identified by contributor Legman as "O Master, Let Me Walk with Thee," that melody presumably Robert Schumann's 1838 composition which some hymn books name "Canonbury." The Vicarion anthology, No. I, also cites that tune, but the source may be ultimately Legman. *Songs of Raunch and Ill-Repute,* p. 27, sports the song, too, but indicates no tune.

Reuss, pp. 206–210, lists additional references to the song and gives two versions. The one tune which, Reuss says, is "seemingly familiar," but which he does not identify, is a set of "Old Hundred."

An unrelated poem, "The New Patent Fucking Machine," is included in *The Pearl, A Journal of Facetiae and Voluptuous Reading,* Vol. II, No. 12 (June, 1880), pp. 199–200. It includes these four lines describing an inevitable —it would seem—result from using such devices:

> It beats fingers by far too—a long way, its shape is just like a tool,
> The girls who owns its [sic] good natured, she has fucked, I believe, the
>   whole school;
> She has it herself much too often, and is getting most awfully lean,
> And her pussy's quite tender with using the patent new Fucking Machine.

A Garland of Parodies

These parodies were selected from more than twenty-five in the editor's collection, chosen solely on the basis of personal favoritism. Dan Burson collected three in Los Angeles from college students in 1960: "Beautiful Dreamer," "Sweet Adeline," and "St. Louis Woman." Miss Anne Smith gathered "Secret Love" from sorority sisters at the same time. Miss Barbara Rogers sang the mock on "Alice Blue Gown" to the editor in 1967; she learned it attending college in Salinas, California, in 1951. "You Are My Sunshine" was contributed by Dale Koby, who learned it in Northern California in 1961. Robert Easton notated the parodies on "Home on the Range," "Carolina in the Morning," "The Last Time I Saw Paris," "Sunday, Monday and Always," "Foam Rubber Pads" (the reference there is to Jane Russell, a well-endowed actress) and "The Anniversary Song," all from fellow professionals in the motion picture industry in Los Angeles in 1960. "Let Me Call You Sweetheart" is from Miss Bethel Morgan, who sang it to the editor in Los Angeles in 1964. "The Object of My Affection" is from the singing of the editor's brother-in-law in Oakland, California, in 1964. "Baby Face" and "Jada," sung by San Fernando Valley State College students, were collected by a former student of Mrs. Hawes in 1965. J. Barre Toelken furnished the parody of "When You Wore a Tulip" as it is archived in the Robert W. Gordon Collection of American Folk Song, University of Oregon (No. 2377). Gordon's informant learned the song about 1915.

The Gatesville Cannonball

A singular text, sung to the frequently used tune of "The Wabash Cannonball" made popular during the 1920's by hillbilly singers, this was given to the editor by Marilyn Eisenberg Herzog. Mrs. Herzog had it from a girl friend who, in turn, had learned it in Newport Beach, California, at a beach party in 1961 from unidentified boys who had reluctantly sojourned at Gatesville.

In the editor's opinion, this is one of the most significant songs in the collection. The shift from the female narrator in "When I Was Young" to the male transforms the ballad from a lament to an overt song of defiance, indeed, a song of social protest.

The narrator's pride in his appearance is a hallmark of the song's authenticity. A variety of anti- and not-so-anti-social groups place great stress upon outward appearance. Frequently, the exquisitely impeccable dress or a specific item of clothing serve as a kind of uniform, a symbol of peer group identification. This is especially true if the members of the group cannot afford other, more costly status symbols such as automobiles. The narrator's claim of neatly polished "stomps" or boots and neatly combed hair reinforces the feeling of pride in the group (Gatesville graduates) even as it explains why a fair young maiden would go home with a defiant social outcast.

The song can be dated approximately to the 1950's, when "ducks" or "ducktail" hair styles were common among teenage boys. If the song is older, then "ducks" could be presumed to have replaced "hair."

"The Wabash Cannonball" has been parodied elsewhere. Wallrich, pp. 80 ff., has an Air Force adaptation. Greenway, pp. 291 ff., has Woody Guthrie's "Grand Coulee Dam," modeled in part upon, and using the melody of the hillbilly song. A set of the melody carries "The Bootlegger's Song" on Oscar Brand, *American Drinking Songs* (Riverside 12–630).

The original song, traditional despite the copyright issued to one William Kindt in 1904, is in Milburn, pp. 188–191. (That copyright reference was furnished by D. K. Wilgus.)

The Gay Caballero

J. Barre Toelken found a text of this song in the Robert W. Gordon Collection of American Folk Song, University of Oregon (No. 448), which Gordon dated "December, 1927." That find confirmed a suspicion the editor nurtured that the song was traditional, and the copyright version credited to Lou Klein and Frank Crumit was an adaptation, *not* the original.

The Gordon text is incomplete, but is obviously "The Gay Caballero."

200

There once was a gay Don d'Ilio,
Who lived in a high white castilio
And he played with his trototoilio
And the works of his raggle de bam, bam! bam!

One day to that high white castilio
There came a gay young senorio [sic]
And she played with his trototoilio
And the works of his raggle de bam, bam! bam!

Next day that gay Don d'Ilio
Laid her down on a soft sofailio
And he eased in his trototoilio
And the works of his raggle de bam, bam! bam!

Nine days later that gay Don d'Ilio
Gnashed his teeth with rage at the senorio [sic]
And gazed with sorrow on his trototoilio
And the works of his raggle de bam, bam! bam!

He went to see Dr. Gonzalio
Who told him he had the clapilio
And he gave him a bottle of castorio
For the works of his raggle de bam, bam! bam!

The college song inspired not only Crumit's recording (RCA Victor V–21735) but may also be responsible for this limerick:

There once was a Spanish nobilio
Who lived in a Spanish castilio.
His *cojones* grew hot
More often than not
At the thought of a Spanish jazzilio.

(It is possible, too, that the limerick gave rise to the college song for the limericks are sung to the tune used for "The Gay Caballero.") In any event, the record seems incomplete.

The version of "The Gay Caballero" used here, one of three in the editor's files, was gathered by Burson from his fertile Carnegie Tech informant. Legman, *The Horn Book,* p. 228, has one stanza of a close variant. Reuss, pp. 261–62, has a seven-stanza variant, from Michigan State University, collected in 1953. Wallrich, p. 132, has another set of words to the same tune.

The editor remembers from his youth a similar parody sung to the melody of "Alla en el Rancho Grande," a 1934 Mexican import which also achieved great popularity in the United States:

201

My name is Pancho Villa.
I got the gonorrhea.
I got it from Maria,
She gave it to me free-a.
  Ha-ha-ha-ha.

I took her to my castle,
And laid her for a peso.
I fucked her in the asshole,
And fucked her in the face-o.
  Ha-ha-ha-ha.

If there ever was more to the song, memory has failed. Reuss, p. 263, could come up with only a four-line fragment from Phoenix, Arizona, circa 1959.

The Good Ship Venus

There are five closely-related versions of this in the editor's files; the longest has nine stanzas, though Legman describes the British form of the ballad in limerick form as "absolutely endless." He prints one version of seven stanzas in his limerick anthology, pp. 107–08.

The version here, sung to a set of "Yankee Doodle," was lifted from an unidentified military songbook, mimeographed in Japan about 1950, but lacking a title page.

Brand sings a desalinated version on *Bawdy Sea Songs* (Audio Fidelity 1884). Stanzas 3, 9, 10, 11, 12, and 13 of "Columbo" in *Songs of Roving and Raking,* pp. 112–13, are more properly a variant of "The Good Ship Venus." The editors of *Songs of Raunch and Ill-Repute,* pp. 22–23, offer a pastiche of "Columbo" and "The Good Ship," and give their entry *both* titles. Verses 3, 6, 7, 8, 10 and 11 of that version belong to "The Good Ship Venus." The balance is "Columbo's" responsibility. The text in Vicarion's book, No. XVIII, has been doctored, not skillfully, by an editor who apparently had no tune.

Hallelujah, I'm A Bum

Harry McClintock's song, having been expropriated by the public, has acquired innumerable stanzas, erotic and otherwise. This version was collected by the editor from a retired postal worker in Los Angeles in 1966; he thought he might have learned the song during the late Depression while riding America's finest railroads *al fresco.*

The melody borrowed by McClintock for his song is the hymn tune, "Revive Us

Again." For a history of "Hallelujah, I'm a Bum," see Greenway, pp. 197 ff. To his textual references, add Sandburg, p. 183; Leach, p. 108; and John A. Lomax and Alan Lomax, *American Ballads and Folk Songs* (New York, 1934), pp. 26–28. Milburn, pp. 97–101, gives two versions.

The last stanza of the version here, the only text in the editor's collection, may be a snide allusion to the widespread homosexual intercourse practiced by those not-so-romantic Knights of the Road.

The Hermit

This is from Koby's collection made in Northern California in 1961, and in all probability should be ultimately credited to Oscar Brand's recording *Bawdy Songs and Backroom Ballads*, II (Audio Fidelity 1806). That version is in Brand's book of the same name, pp. 74–75. Similarly, the text in *Songs of Roving and Raking*, p 78, is also credited to Brand.

Textual variations between the version here and Brand's are slight; changes in the melody—a variant of "Roll Your Leg Over"—are similarly minor.

The melody here and in Brand is, as he notes, borrowed from "Roll Your Leg Over."

High Above a Theta's Garter

One of the two full versions in the editor's collection, this is from a sorority girl not a member of the organization named—as it was sung in Los Angeles in 1955.

At Michigan State and Indiana Universities, the sorority is usually the Pi Phi's, Reuss notes, p. 76. He suggests that the attribution may be a result of that sorority's prestige, a prestige based in part upon the handsome physical endowments of the group's members. Reuss gives four versions, noting another eight from midwestern schools, pp. 76–80.

The editor learned another parody set to this tune, sung by men at Officers' Candidate School at Fort Benning, Ga., in the early 1950's to satirize the plight of the newly-commissioned infantry platoon leaders trained at that military post:

High above the Chattahoochie,
On the Upitoy,
Stands our noble alma mater,
Benning School for boys.
    Forward ever, backward never,
    Next of kin goodbye.
    To the port of embarkation,
    Follow me and did.

The last line is especially pointed in that "Follow Me" is the motto of the Benning OCS.

Reuss has still other parodies of the Cornell Alma Mater, pp. 153 ff.

Horse Shit

This third version of "The Monk of Great Renown" was included in a collection of bawdy songs sung by Air Force officers on Guam between 1956 and 1959. The collection, owned by Col. G.W.P., was transcribed by James W. Kellogg in 1963 as a project for a folklore class at the University of Texas where the colonel was then serving. No tune was indicated. It is included here through the courtesy of Roger D. Abrahams.

Hot Vagina

This was current at UCLA in 1960, Dean Burson reports. It appears to be unique. Because of possible copyright infringement, only the first four bars of the melody for the breakfast food's singing commercial are given.

Humoresque

This is another of the more frequently encountered bawdy songs, though most informants seem to know only one or two verses. The song is unusual in that it is one of a very few with a genuine oral currency set to melodies drawn from what is known as "art" or "classical" music. The most popular of these impertinent art songs is sung by children to the melody of Bizet's "Toreodor Song":

> Toreodor-a, don't spit on the floor-a,
> Use the cuspidor-a, that's what it's for-a.

Less well-known than this are two children's ditties to "The Soldier's Chorus" from Gounod's *Faust*:

> My father killed a kangaroo,*
> Gave me the grisily part to chew.
> Wasn't that a helluva thing to do,
> To give me to chew the grisily part of a dead kangaroo?

---

* Roger D. Abrahams, an impeccable poet, points out that, to scan, "killed" should be "murdered." It is in the text he sings.

204

Mrs. Marjorie Morris of Los Angeles remembered the second from her youth:

> Hey, Aunt Jemima, look at your Uncle Jim.
> He's in the bathtub learning how to swim.
> First he does the backstroke, then he does the crawl,
> Now he's under water doing nothing at all.

Christopher Logue, as Count Palmiro Vicarion, offers this to the tune of "La Dona E Mobile":

> Arseholes are cheap today,
> Cheaper than yesterday,
> Small boys are half-a-crown,
> Standing up or lying down,
> Big ones for bigger pricks,
> Biggest ones cost three-and-six,
> Get yours before they're gone,
> Come now and try one. (No. VL)

To these notices may be added Bronson's citation of a portion of a Gluck melody used to carry a Kentucky text of "The Two Brothers" (Child 49). See his first volume, p. 387.

Dvorak published his melody in 1894; it seems to have acquired these insensitive stanzas sometime later. Wallrich, p. 166, in presenting a World War II Air Force version in three verses, says that he first heard the song on college campuses in the early 1930's. Legman, *The Limerick*, p. 465, n. 1676, dates his version to 1944. Brand's text, pp. 18–19, is undated. *Songs of Roving and Raking*, pp. 64–65, has another—from Brand and a mimeographed collection compiled at Caltech in Pasadena in 1960, *Songs of Raunch and Ill-Repute*—centered entirely upon the problems of untimely elimination. The Pasadena offering is on p. 2 and has this unusual stanza:

> Prostitutes and pretty ladies
> Douche to keep from having babies.
> How do you like the way
> I part my hair?

The text here is a pastiche of three gathered by the editor in Los Angeles 1960–1964.

I Am Growing Old and Gray

One of two versions in the editor's collection, this last of the "Sam Hall" cycle was sung by a 50-year-old carpenter in Los Angeles in 1964. He had learned it, perhaps in 1945, while working in a shipyard in Seattle, Washington.

The melody is an adaptation of the familiar "She'll Be Comin' 'Round the Mountain When She Comes."

Abrahams, in a letter to the editor, has noted "the same point made, but castratorily, not masochistically," in Burn's "John Anderson, My Jo." Two other laments for a lost youth may also be mentioned, though whatever sexual connotations they might have are elliptical: "I'm One of the Has Beens" on John Greenway, *Australian Folk Songs* (Folkways FW 8718); and "Poor Old Horse" in Frank Kidson, *A Garland of English Folk-Songs* (London, 1926 [?]), p. 22. The latter is descended from "The Palphry" in *Pills to Purge Melancholy,* IV, pp. 10–12.

In Kansas

This is an American twig on the Irish branch of Sam Hall's family tree. Directly parodied upon "The Famine Song," a variant of which is in Galvin, *Irish Songs of Resistance,* p. 44, "In Kansas" itself has spawned a number of offspring. The closest is "In Mobile," for which see Legman, *The Limerick,* pp. 321–322, or Logue-Vicarion, No. X (with the editor's handiwork visible).

There are many others. See, for example, Dolph, pp. 64–65; Hudson, *Folk Songs of Mississippi,* pp. 216–17; and Lynn, *Songs for Singing,* p. 104. Spaeth, p. 33, has a popular redaction dated to 1844, placing it hard on the heels of the famines during which the undated song in Galvin was seemingly written. A number of citations to ephemeral prints are included by Reuss, pp. 190–191.

The editor has collected a one-stanza complaint from Lee Bluestone in Los Angeles in 1964, probably a fragment of a longer song ultimately traceable to "In Kansas." (Legman's *The Limerick,* p. 320, has a two-stanza version.)

> It's a helluva situation up at Yale.
> It's a helluva situation up at Yale.
> As a means of recreation,
> They rely on masturbation.
> It's a helluva situation up at Yale.

Many college campuses sport a second variation on the theme, like this forwarded by Mrs. Bess Hawes from San Fernando Valley State College:

> Oh, there are no Chi Omegas at Purdue.
> Oh, there are no Chi Omegas at Purdue.
> So the Betas and the Fijis
> Make do with frigid Dee Gees.
> Oh, there are no Chi Omegas at Purdue.

Reuss reports that at Indiana University rival fraternities append a hint of homosexuality in a second stanza (Beta Theta Pi and Sigma Chi are fraternities):

> Oh, we have some Chi Omegas at IU,
> Oh, we have some Chi Omegas at IU,

But the Beta Theta Pi's,
They still sleep with Sigma Chi's,
Even though we have some Chi O's at IU.

See Reuss' thesis, pp. 31 ff., noting the tune as "I Was Born About Ten Thousand Years Ago."

Roger Abrahams has forwarded a seven-stanza slander from the University of Texas related to this college-centered sub-group. Two stanzas of that, sung to the tune of "There's No Hiding Place Down There," are:

Oh, the Thetas they are a bunch of wrecks, a bunch of wrecks. (2)
Oh, the Thetas are a bunch of wrecks,
Turn out the lights, turn on the sex.
There's no hiding place down there.

Oh, the Chi O's they wear the low cut dress, the low cut dress. (2)
Oh, the Chi O's wear the low cut dress.
It's so low, I must confess,
There's no hiding place down there.

The first phrases of the melody of "In Kansas" printed here—collected by the editor from an informant who had learned it in his boyhood in Philadelphia in the 1930's—are a variant of "I Was Born About Ten Thousand Years Ago." (A version of that song is in Sandburg, pp. 330–31.) The tune used here is otherwise a derivative of the "Aikendrum" branch of "Sam Hall's" family tree.

In the Shade of the Old Apple Tree

Claire Biane, a former student, collected this from Eric Firth, who learned the song as a boy in Hull, England, about 1936. In spite of the English source for this version, the song bears a "Made in America" stamp; it was written by Harry Williams and Egbert Van Alstyne in 1905.

Reuss, pp. 252–54, includes five parodies of varying faithfulness to that printed here. Seemingly, traditional singers have been more free in remaking this song than they have with most parodies. Reuss also includes references to ephemeral collections housed in the library of the Kinsey Institute at Indiana University. Legman, *The Limerick,* p. 23, No. 110, has another version, as does Vicarion, No. IX, who may owe credit to Legman. Lynn, p. 5, has an inoffensive parody.

The editor's brother-in-law, living in Sonoma County, California, has a variant of the last stanza used here:

Oh, I took out my forty-foot pole,
And shoved it right down that dark hole.

I bounced once or twice;
It really felt nice
In the shade of the old apple tree.

I Used to Work in Chicago

The editor first heard this while in high school in 1948 in Los Angeles, California. Memory of that version coincides closely with the two collected by Miss Anne Smith in 1960 and Miss Sandra Stolz the following year. Memory serving —and such formula songs as this are hard to forget—the editor's vocal wild oats were scattered as:

Fruit . . . plums . . . plum[b] her I did
Cake . . . layer . . . lay her I did
Hardware . . . nails . . . nail her I did
Cinnamon . . . sticks . . . stick her I did
Pea soup . . . split . . . split her I did
Milk . . . cream . . . cream her I did
Booze . . . liquor . . . lick her I did
Covers . . . spread . . . spread her I did
Banana . . . peeled . . . peel her I did
Some rope . . . jump . . . jump her I did (or)
    Dress . . . jumper . . . jump her I did

There are a number of leads to the possible origin of the song. The last line of each verse, "I'll never go there anymore," and that portion of the melody are identical to the last line of the chorus of "The Bowery," the popular song written in 1892 by Percy Gaunt. There is no other similarity, either in tune or text. In the present form then, "I Used to Work in Chicago" would seem to postdate the popularity of "The Bowery."

The first phrases of the melody are those of the all-too-familiar "The Bear Went Over the Mountain" or "Marbrough s'en va-t-en guerre." B. A. Botkin's *The American Play Party* (Lincoln, Nebraska, 1937), p. 290, locates a one-stanza fragment of what may be the forerunner of "Pig in the Parlor," a fragment which hints, too, of the same Scots-Irish tinkers' song which gave rise to "My God, How the Money Rolls In." (For a summary of the appearances elsewhere of "Marbrough," see Spaeth, *A History of Popular Music in America* [New York, 1948], p. 31.)

Arthur Argo sings two stanzas of a variant of that Scots-Irish tinkers' song under the title, "Haben Aboo an' a Banner," on *A Wee Thread o' Blue* (Prestige 13048). These stanzas may well indicate that the American "I Used to Work in Chicago," like "My God, How the Money Rolls In," is a by-product of "My Father Was Hanged for Sheep Stealing" or some such title. Argo's song runs, in part:

Then I was a draper in London.
A lady cam' into my shop.
Oh, she asked for three yards o' my linen.
I gave her three yards o' my
    Haben aboo an' a banner,
    Haben aboo an' a bay,
    My haben aboo an' a banner
    Mish-a-toodle-i-oodle-i-ay.

(Argo's tune is unrelated, a set of "Mush Mush Mush Touraliady.)

If the history can be reconstructed from these potshards, the line of descent would apparently stem from the tinkers' song, this leading to an unrecovered version of a game or play-party song set to the tune of "Marbrough" and containing something close to the "store-shop" verses in some texts of the tinkers' song.

This game or play-party song would, in turn, spawn both "Pig in the Parlor," with its "Marbrough" tune, and "I Used to Work in Chicago," set to the same tune—until warped a bit by "The Bowery."

A pair of historical survivals-in-print suggest the origin of the "shop" verse in the tinkers' song, though the editor's reconstruction is speculative.

"The Jolly Tradesmen," from D'Urfey's *Pills to Purge Melancholy,* VI, pp. 91 ff., uses the same formulaic wordplay of "I Used to Work in Chicago" and the "shop" verse found in the tinkers' song. The second, fourth, and eighth stanzas of "The Jolly Tradesmen" are example enough of the *double entendre:*

Sometimes I am a Butcher,
And then I feel fat Ware, Sir;
And if the Flank be fleshed well,
I take no farther care, Sir;
But in I thrust my Slaughtering-Knife,
Up to the Haft with speed, Sir;
For all that ever I can do,
I cannot make it bleed, Sir.

Sometimes I am a Glover,
And can do passing well, Sir;
In dressing of a Doe-skin,
I know I do excel, Sir.
But if by chance a Flaw I find,
In dressing of the Leather;
I straightway whip my needle out,
And I tack 'em close together.

The Tanner's Trade I practice,
Sometimes amongst the rest, Sir;

Yet I could never get a Hair,
Of any Hide I dress'd, Sir;
For I have been tanning of a Hide,
This long seven Years and more, Sir;
And yet it is as hairy still,
As ever it was before, Sir.

Were the wordplay of "The Jolly Tradesmen" fitted to the satirical quatrains of "Have You Heard of a Frolicksome Ditty?", the result might well be something close to the "shop" stanza in the tinkers' song. As "Song CCXXXIX" in *The Vocal Miscellany*, 3rd ed. (London, 1738), I, pp. 214–15, the satirical stage song, "Have You Heard," runs:

1 Man. I once was a Poet at *London*,
        I kept my Heart still full of Glee;
        There's no Man can say that I'm undone,
        For begging's no new Trade to me.
            Tol derol, &c.

2 Man. I once was an Attorney at Law,
        And after a Knight of the Post:
        Give me a brisk Wench in clean Straw,
        And I value not who rules the Roast.
            Tol derol, &c.

3 Man. Make room for a Soldier in Buff,
        Who valiantly strutted about,
        Till he fancy'd the Peace breaking off,
        And then he most wisely—sold out.
            Tol derol, &c.

4 Man. Here comes a Courtier polite, Sir,
        Who flatter'd my Lord to his Face;
        Now railing is all his Delight, Sir,
        Because he miss'd getting a Place,
            Tol derol, &c.

5 Man. I still am a merry Gut-Scraper,
        My Heart never yet felt a Qualm;
        Tho' poor, I can frolick and vapour,
        And sing any Tune, but a Psalm.
            Tol derol, &c.

6 Man. I was a fanatical Preacher,
        I turn'd up my Eyes when I pray'd;
        But my Hearers half starved their Teacher,
        For they believ'd not one Word that I said.
            Tol derol, &c.

1 Man. Whoe'er would be merry and free,
          Let him list, and from us he may learn:
          In Palaces who shall you see,
          Half so happy as we in a Barn?
            Tol derol, &c.

          CHORUS of all.

          Whoe'er would be merry and free,
          Let him list, and from us he may learn,
          In Palaces who shall you see,
          Half so happy as we in a Barn?
            Tol derol, &c.

This song, too, is set to the tune of "Old Hewson the Cobbler," the "scurrilous and indecent" ditty which led eventually to "My God, How the Money Rolls In." Thus, early in its life—in 1731, according to James C. Dick, *The Songs of Robert Burns,* p. 415—when it was sung in the ballad opera *The Jovial Crew,* "Old Hewson" is carrying the stanzaic kernels of "I Used to Work in Chicago." From these would pop a version of the tinkers' song represented by Argo's "Haben Aboo an' a Banner." Then from that would come "Pig in the Parlor," "I Used to Work in Chicago" and "My God, How the Money Rolls In."

The version of "I Used to Work in Chicago" printed here is a conflation of the close variants the Misses Smith and Stolz contributed. Three other versions, varying only in length and, perhaps, in ingenuity, are also at hand.

Songs of Raunch and Ill-Repute, p. 14, has another.

I Went Downtown

This self-contained fragment of "The Chisholm Trail" was current in Los Angeles public schools circa 1950. It was written down for the editor by Clifford McCarthy in 1964. McCarthy, a bookseller, was reluctant to sing the song at all, not because of the words "pissing," "cock," or "bugger," but because of the word "nigger." Quite obviously, the definition of the vulgar is highly subjective.

I-Yi-Yi-Yi

Gershon Legman's comprehensive *The Limerick* establishes far beyond question that limericks are the product of the educated, and circulate largely in that group. Those included here—culled from approximately 100 in the editor's files—were collected by Burson in 1960, by Robert Easton in Los Angeles in 1960, by two of Abrahams' former students in 1963, and by the editor over a five-year period.

In order, the limericks here correspond to Legman's numbers 1325, 1073, 388, 1311, 468, not included, 195, 195, 1137, 622, 1601, 242, 417, 463, 313, 278, 782, 202, not included, 185, 1473, 909, 1186, 540, 1234, not included, 222,

982, 1070, 314, 582, 116, 339, 56, not included, not included, 935, cf. 237, and not included.

The first chorus, from the imported popular song, "Cielito Lindo," and the alternate are both current in Los Angeles. "Cielito Lindo" was printed first—credited to Quirino Mendoza y Cortéz—in Mexico City in 1919. *Grove's Dictionary* says, however, the song is traditional, and dates it to 1850; Mendoza y Cortéz merely arranged it. As well-known as the song is in the United States, it did not make its way to this country until 1923.

The second chorus is fashioned from the last three lines of the song, "Sweet Violets," by J. K. Emmet as it was sung in his now-forgotten play of 1882, *Fritz Among the Gypsies*. Those lines run:

Oh, sweet violets, sweeter than all the roses,
Zillah, darling one, I plucked them
And brought them to you.

Leach, p. 101, has a melody for a song he calls, appropriately enough, "Limericks." That tune is the same as that used for the verses here: "The Gay Caballero." He does not include a chorus.

Reuss, p. 219, says the tune his informants used for the verses was also "The Gay Caballero." He prints four texts, a tune, and 24 limericks.

The seemingly standard melody used here for the verses is another redaction of "Goodnight Irene" *et al.*

Kathusalem

This is a parody of a song which Sigmund Spaeth dates to 1866. Published in New York by Frederick Blume under the title "Kafoozelum," it is vaguely credited to one "S. Oxon." Whoever "S. Oxon" was—the abbreviation may stand for Bishop of Oxford or Son of Oxford—he intended his song to satirize the period's bathetic love songs as well as the then-current, pervasive influence in the popular arts of the exotic. For texts of the original song, see Spaeth, pp. 148–49; Leach, pp. 86–87; or Lynn, pp. 34–35.

By World War I, says Spaeth, *A History of Popular Music in America* (New York, 1948), p. 166, the song had been parodied by soldiers "who substituted the name of Jerusalem for that of the heroine in the refrain and touched up the words in general to conform with standards other than those of the drawing room."

Brand has a heavily-edited version of the ribald redaction on *Bawdy Songs and Backroom Ballads*, III (Audio Fidelity 1824); the same version is in his book, pp. 20–21. *Songs of Roving and Raking*, p. 113, and *Songs of Raunch and*

Ill-Repute, p. 26, are uninhibited. *Vicarion's Book,* No. XXXXIX, has apparently been doctored by the putative editor, Christopher Logue. Edith Fowke has collected a variant, yet unpublished, in the Northeast. The text here is a conflation of two. Stanzas 2, 4, 7, and 11, and the tune are from a variant collected by the editor in Los Angeles from an aerospace engineer who had learned it while attending CCNY, circa 1950. The balance is from the version collected by Burson as the song was sung at Carnegie Tech in 1959.

The melody used here is the children's song, "London Bridge Is Falling Down" disguised in triple time. The editor suspects that this melody was grafted to the song by British soldiers during World War I (Spaeth to be credited). The melody for the chorus in the popular song strongly suggested a triple-time variant of "London Bridge" already in tradition—used as early as 1715 for "Will Ye Go to Sheriffmuir?" as sung by Ewan MacColl on *Songs of Two Rebellions* (Folkways FW 8756). The traditional tune then may have replaced the popular melody. On *Laughing America* (Tradition 1014), Oscar Brand sings a variant of the *popular* song to the *traditional* tune, calling his text "without question, a laundered version of one of America's bawdiest ballads." In fact, his song appears to be an intermediate between popular and bawdy forms.

Mrs. Marjorie Cray used a variant of this tune for her version learned in San Diego about 1960.

Last Night I Stayed Up Late to Masturbate

Denza's "Funiculi Funicula" was written in 1880 to commemorate the opening of the Neapolitan funicular railway, but the parody is apparently of much more recent vintage.

There are two full variants in the editor's files, and two fragments. This is from Burson's Carnegie Tech informant. Reuss's "B" text, p. 214, is also from that school and little different from the Burson find.

Another is in *Songs of Roving and Raking,* p. 117, reprinted from *Songs of Raunch and Ill-Repute,* p. 20, which was compiled in 1960 at Caltech. This is the earliest the editor has been able to place the song, and it may not be much older than that. Reuss, pp. 211–214, also concludes the song is of recent, if choice, vintage. The version of the song given by Vicarion, No. XXXI, is unsingable in its present form, though it, too, is supposedly to the tune used here.

Lee's Hoochie

This is just one of a spate of parodies, inoffensive and otherwise, which popped up in the wake of the Weavers' recording in 1951 of the American folk song, "On Top of Old Smoky." One sung by children in Los Angeles which was collected by a number of the editor's former students runs:

On top of Old Smoky, all covered with snow,
I saw Georgie Jessel with Marilyn Monroe.
He took off his jacket. He took off his vest.
And when he saw Marilyn, he took off the rest.

Abrahams' thesis, *Negro Folklore from South Philadelphia,* p. 247, has the same with Betty Grable and Gene Autry as stand-ins. He also has forwarded:

On top of old Rachel, all covered with sweat,
I've been fucking two hours, and I haven't come yet.

Other parodies of "Smoky" collected by Mrs. Nancy Leventhal in Hawthorne, California, from school children are printed in *Western Folklore,* XXII (1963), p. 243.

On April 15, 1963, *Newsweek* magazine offered proof that the muse of parody is not yet dead with yet another song set to the same tune. According to *Newsweek*'s correspondent in South Viet-Nam, GIs in that embattled country had fashioned a griping song to the familiar tune. Written after the disastrous battle of Ap Bac on January 2, 1963, the song is sung when the helicopters fly into action.

"Lee's Hoochie" was second in popularity with troops in the Far East at the time of the Korean Conflict only to "Movin' On." It was current in Japan and Korea in 1951–52 when a mimeographed copy came into the editor's possession. "Hoochie" is, in the GI's trade language, a house; "kimchi" is a Korean dilled pickle recognizable by its noxious and pervasive odor. "Poji" is the vagina; "benjo" is the impolite word for toilet in Japanese, approximately the equal of "shit-house." The "ten thousand" (yen), by the way, is something of a humorous overstatement. The editor can report that 10,000 yen would be a bit steep— even in a war-inflated economy—except perhaps for an evening with a true geisha, who is not a prostitute.

The melody used by the Weavers in their recording of "On Top of Old Smoky" was widely borrowed for military parodies. Wallrich has four from the Korean War, pp. 72, 124, 131, and 183. The latter, "On Top of Old Fuji," is a parallel to "Lee's Hoochie," though it contains no censorable lines. "Super Stag Treasury," rev. ed. (Maga Distributing Co., Los Angeles, 1964), n.p., has "Lee's Hoochie" with these introductory lines:

I'll mention a name, please remember it well,
The name is Lee's Hoochie, God damn it to hell:
There's a sign at the door says, "All welcome in here,"
And each air force man gets a nice souvenir.

The Weavers' version of the original song is in Lomax, p. 221.

The text and tune here were learned by the editor while serving in the Far East in 1953. It is one of three close variants in the editor's collection.

The Lehigh Valley I

There are two versions of this in the editor's collection, including this from Marvin Gelfman who learned it in New York City in 1960.

John Greenway sings a necessarily-edited variant on *The Great American Bum* (Riverside 12–619). An unexpurgated variant is in *Songs of Roving and Raking*, p. 116. Differences between the three are minimal.

Randolph, IV, pp. 369–70, has the parlor song original. Milburn, pp. 41–58, gives a thirteen-stanza text, pp. 41–43, calling it "an original poem" (p. 48), a "pathetic recitation" (p. 52), seemingly unaware that the words were set to music. His second version, pp. 52–53, he considers "the most brilliant item the Lehigh Valley school has produced" (p. 54). The first and last of Milburn's verses are:

> Don't move over, stranger,
> I won't _____ on your seat,
> Nor _____ on the coat that's on your back,
> Nor the shoes that's on yer feet.

> Now, God be with you, stranger,
> And I'll be on my way.
> I'll hunt the runt that stole my _____
> If it takes till Judgment Day.

Logue, No. **XXXVIII** is "Poor Blind Nell" which might be a spin-off from "The Lehigh Valley." The texts differ, and Logue has no tune, but somehow "Nell" has a hint of the hobo ballad.

> The sun shone on the village green,
>   It shone on Poor blind Nell,
> But did she see the sun that shone?
>   Did she fucking 'ell!

> A sailor to the village came,
>   . The captain of a lugger,
> He captivated Poor Blind Nell,
>   The dirty, lousy bugger.

> One night he slept with Poor Blind Nell,
>   He knew it wasn't lawful,
> And though her tits were very sweet
>   Her feet smelt fucking awful.

> He took the girl out in a punt
>   And to the seat he lashed 'er,
> Then lacerated Poor Nell's cunt,
>   The dirty, lousy bastard.

And when he went to sea again
    He sent her [she sent him?] books and parcels,
But did he write and thank poor Nell?
    Did he fucking arseholes!

Another representative of the bathetic parlor-song style is the not-unrelated Charles K. Harris potboiler, "For Old Time's Sake," in Spaeth, *Weep Some More, My Lady* (New York, 1927), pp. 248–49.

The Lehigh Valley II

Starting with the same popular song, another parodist got off this little effort. It was collected by Dale Koby in Northern California, and is the only version in the editor's files. Koby had no tune for his version.

Life Presents A Dismal Picture

Legman terms this a recitation in his *Horn Book,* p. 422, perhaps unaware that it has acquired various melodies to which it may be sung, and is sometimes used as a two-stanza insertion in bawdy quatrain ballads.

Roger D. Abrahams has forwarded a text as sung by college students in Austin, Texas, in 1963; they used the vehicle ridden here, "Scarlet Ribbons," a 1949 composition copyright by Jack Segal and Evelyn Danzig.

That version differs only slightly from this, collected by the editor in 1965 while staying in the Detroit YMCA. A third text, without a tune, was gathered by Robert Easton in Los Angeles in 1960.

Vicarion's version, No. XVI, has two additional stanzas the present editor has not seen elsewhere, the product, one assumes, of Palmiro's pen. It is set to "Deutschland Über Alles."

The Little Red Train

Another of the "Snapoo" cycle, "The Little Red Train" is probably best-known now in college circles. There are three similar versions in the editor's collection, and a four-stanza variant in *Songs of Roving and Raking,* p. 117, all from a campus currency.

Sandburg, p. 379, has one stanza of "The Wind It Blew Up the Railroad Track," sung to "When Johnny Comes Marching Home." One suspects he had other, less presentable verses at hand. Milburn admits to such. " 'The Old 99' has a large number of stanzas too vigorous for pallid print." His tune, too, is "When Johnny."

216

The version offered here is a conflation. All but the last two stanzas are from Burson, as sung in Los Angeles in 1960. The additional verses the editor heard at a party in that city in 1961 as sung to the melody of "When Johnny Comes Marching Home Again." Burson's text runs to "Mademoiselle from Armentières."

Lydia Pinkham

Previous reports of this song indicate some currency in urban settings: Sandburg, p. 210; Leach, p. 106; Lynn, p. 49, all have it. The Lynn variant has stanzas similar to the second and third here. Additionally, Reuss mentions "some interesting documentation" for midwestern campus versions, p. 27, but prints no text or tune.

This is a good example of the sort of song—bawdy or otherwise—which folklorists have tended to overlook in the past. Certainly "Lydia Pinkham" can boast of no great antiquity; the melody dates the song to Tin Pan Alley of the late nineteenth and early twentieth centuries. Neither are the words particularly inspired; moreover, they are parodying a popular song written to spoof the patent medicine company's curative claims. The melody, barely strong enough to limp to the end, resembles nothing in American folk song tradition.

All of these "failings," and especially the popular origin of the song, tend to discredit it in the eyes of folklorists. Withal, it persists in oral tradition, its rather feeble existence kept alive in the singing of a dwindling number of people. As such, it is a folk song, for better or worse, and deserves at least passing mention.

The editor has handled three versions of this song with bawdy verses, one from the Koby collection made in Northern California in 1960, a second as furnished

by the mother of a former student. The latter was used here, with some confusions in the text straightened out by the Koby version.

The only other bawdy version of the song which the editor has handled is a three-verse fragment from the Robert W. Gordon Collection of American Folk Song, University of Oregon, forwarded by J. Barre Toelken. Collected in the late 1920's, it contains the "Widow Brown" verse, and these two stanzas:

> Gwendoline,
> She had a lover,
> And she couldn't make him ride
> Till she took, she gargled, she swallowed
> That vegetable compound.
> Now they have to keep him tied.
>> So we'll sing, we'll sing, we'll sing
>> Of Lydia Pinkham,
>> Savior of the human race.

How she makes, she bottles, she sells
The vegetable compound,
And the papers publish her face.

Once there was a man
Who had castritis,
Didn't have a single nut.
So he took, he drank, he swallowed
Some Lydia's compound.
Now they hang all 'round his butt. Etc.

Minnie the Mermaid

Tin Pan Alley did not exactly reach intellectual heights during the 1920's and '30's. "Minnie the Mermaid" was about par for the course.

This bawdy parody, with only a few lines of the original changed, was collected by Miss Anne Smith from a woman who learned it at Oregon State College in 1945.

Reuss, pp. 324–27, has an added variant, and references, including the information that the folklore archives at Indiana University contain no less than 88 versions from midwestern high schools and universities.

The Monk of Great Renown I, II

Tales of ecclesiastics who stray from the path of righteousness to diddle local girls are frequent in folklore and classic erotica. These fancies were a staple of the earliest tale collections such as Boccaccio's *Decameron* (first day, second and fourth stories; third day, first and eighth stories; fourth day, second story; seventh day, fifth story; eighth day, second story; ninth day, second story) or the earliest of the deliberate erotica like Pietro Aretino's *Ragionamenti* (1534 [?], reprinted North Hollywood, Calif., 1966).

The reputation of the various monkish orders was fearsome. Rabelais, himself a vicar, has Friar John warn the pilgrim Dogweary:

> Were your wife uglier than Prosperine, by God, she'd find herself jerkthumped as long as there was a monk within a thousand miles. Good carpenters use every kind of timber. The pox riddle me if you don't all find your wives pregnant on your return. They very shadow of an abbey spire is fecund!

For some indication of the currency of such stories in oral tradition—as distinguished from literary redactions—see Antti Aarne and Stith Thompson, *The*

218

Types of the Folktale, FFC 184 (Helsinki, 1961): MT 1726, 1730, 1775A, 1776, 1781 and 1825A. Add to those full tale references the motifs J 1211.1; K 1814.1; V 465 and the references there; T 401.1; and X 457.1. These are only a suggestion of the number of such tales in oral tradition. For example, Thompson did not index the heretofore scarce *Stories from the Folk-Lore of Russia*, an anthology of "secret" folktales which contains numerous accounts of the doings of covetous clerics. (This collection cannot be considered a fair sampling of *all* folklore, but it strongly suggests that the Ukrainian cossack, at least, had a good store of such stories.)

The anti-clerical is a recurrent element in erotic fiction. De Farniente's *Le Portier des Chartreux*, and the Marquis D'Argen's *Les Nonnes Galantes ou L'Amour Embeguine,* both recently reprinted, are but two of "that innumerable mass of atheistic-obscene works which literally flooded the French book-marts of the Eighteenth Century. In many cases the priests, themselves, were the authors of such scandalous products . . ." according to Iwan Bloch (Eugen Duhren), *Marquis de Sade's 120 Days of Sodom and the Sex Life of the French Age of Debauchery,* reprint edition (Los Angeles, 1967), p. 166.

Certainly by the end of the third decade of the nineteenth century, the libidinous monk was a stock player in underground literature. See, for examples, *The Lustful Turk* (ca. 1828; reprinted New York, 1967), *Autobiography of a Flea* (reprinted Atlanta, Georgia, 1967), and *Randiana* (1884 [?], reprinted North Hollywood, 1967). Olympia Press continued the tradition in the 1950's with at least "Henry Crannach's" *Flesh and Bone.*

The most extensive survey of anti-clerical erotica is in Pisanus Fraxi [Henry Spencer Ashbee], *Centuria Librorum Absconditorum* (London, 1879; New York, 1962), pp. 14–300.

The erotic cleric appears also in other art forms, witness the Rembrandt etching of a monk raping a peasant girl, entitled, pleasantly enough, "The Monk in the Cornfield." (This work was not atypical of his highly valued, though rarely hung efforts; at least one other drawing extant is a self-portrait of the artist servicing his wife.)

It is noteworthy that English obscenity law evolved from court actions against anti-clerical erotica. In 1739, Edmund Curll was receipted for the first fine for publishing an "obscene" book because fifteen years before he had issued *Venus in the Cloister or the Nun in Her Smock*. The first suppression of a book as an obscene work by English courts occurred in 1868 when "The Confessional Unmasked, Shewing the Depravity of the Romish Priesthood; the Inequity of the Confessional, and the Questions Put to Females in Confession" was banned.

Nor is the libidinous cleric a creation only of older erotic works. Terry Southern and Mason Hoffenberg worked a couple into their spoof of pornography, *Candy;* their "monks" were of the Eastern, not Western sort. During the 1960 presidential campaign, copies of mendacious Maria Monk's ghosted "autobiography," *Awful Disclosures*, were circulated. The character of this bit of authentic Americana, first published in 1836, may be judged by the fact that the putative author ended her life picking pockets in a New York whorehouse.

In spite of the prevalence of the theme of clerical incontinence in folktales and classic literature, there are few published folk songs dealing with the topic. In addition to "The Monk of Great Renown," a version of which is in Brand, pp. 84–85 (masked as a "Squire of Great Renown"), there are two others: The Priest and the Nuns," in Harlow, pp. 166 ff.; and "The Friar in the Well," Child 276. For possibly linked tunes, see Simpson, pp. 239, 242.

Of less certain oral currency are "The Tyranical Wife," Farmer, II, p. 47; "A Beggar Got a Beadle," Farmer, III, p. 141, both with an anti-clerical bent. The latter is sung to "The Friar and the Nun," according to Simpson, p. 239.

Limericks, deliberately piling shock upon shock, frequently center on the erotic inclinations of the priesthood. Legman's unsigned *The Limerick* devotes a chapter to "Abuses of the Clergy," pp. 109–17, containing forty-four limericks on that subject. The clergy and the prostitute are the only professions to which Legman felt called upon to devote an entire chapter.

There are five versions of "The Monk of Great Renown" in the editor's files. The first here was sung by an insurance salesman to the editor in Los Angeles in 1963. The second was collected by a former student of Mrs. Bess Lomax Hawes whose informant was at one time a member of Her Majesty's armed forces. It is included here with the kind consideration of Mrs. Hawes.

The "English" text may be compared with a version of the song printed in Pinto and Rodway's *Common Muse*, p. 439:

> There was an old monk of great reknown. (3)
> Who f - - - - d all the women of London town.
>
> > The old s - d, the dirty old s - d.
> > The b - - - - r deserves to die.
> > Glory, glory, hallelujah.
>
> The other monks cried out in shame,
> But he turned them over and did them again.
>
> The other monks to stop his folics
> They took a great knife and cut off his b - - - - - ks.
>
> And now deprived of all desire
> He sings soprano in the choir.

Mother

This is frequently heard on college campuses, though the parody of the sentimental mother-song-to-end-all-mother-songs—written in 1915 by Theodore Morse and Howard Johnson—seems to have had its origins elsewhere. A sequel on the word "father" is sometimes encountered in men's magazines and joke books, but the editor has not discovered it in oral tradition.

Lynn, p. 71, has both mother and father stanzas with the improper lines set to rights.

The version printed here is one of four in the editor's collection and was learned at UCLA, circa 1950.

The Mother-Fuckers' Ball

This parody was collected by Burson from his Carnegie Tech informant in 1960.

Abrahams, pp. 169–170, has a version of a recitation entitled "The Freak's Ball" modeled upon "Darktown Strutters' Ball." Other sung parodies of the original song, written in 1915 by Shelton Brooks, are in Dolph, pp. 160–61; and Wallrich, p. 11. Neither is bawdy.

Movin' On

This parody of Hank Snow's popular song was widely known in the Far East, usually under the title of "The Bug-Out Ballad." Additional stanzas, from T. R. Fehrenbach's *This Kind of War* (New York, 1963), include:

The Second Division sat on the hill,
Watchin' Old Joe Chink get set for the kill. (p. 324)

When the mortars started falling 'round the CP tent,
Everybody wondered where the high brass went.
They were buggin' out,
Just movin' on . . . (p. 339)

This version was learned by the author in Korea in 1953. Jacques Vidicam remembers hearing the song while serving at Fort Sam Houston, San Antonio, Texas, in 1964, where it was sung by Special Service Forces, many of whom are Korean veterans.

My Girl's from USC

This multi-stanza parody of John Stromberg's 1895 effort, "My Best Girl's a New Yorker," was current at UCLA in 1960. This version was collected by Miss Anne Smith from a male informant at that time. The last two stanzas were given to the editor four years later by Miss Bethel Morgan in Los Angeles; she said there were more verses, but couldn't recall them.

Frank Lynn, *Songs for Swingin' Housemothers*, p. 32, has another, perhaps expurgated parody of the original song. The last verse of that song, entitled "That's Where My Money Goes," hints of "My Girl's from USC":

> My gal's a hullabaloo,
> She goes to (college) U.
> She wears the colors, too,
> Love her, you bet I do.
> And in my later life,
> She's gonna be my wife.
> (*Shout:*) How in the hell did you get that way?
> She told me so.

"The Hygiene Song," *ibid.*, p. 17, has tagged on the end the second stanza of "My Girl's from USC" used here. See, too, Dick and Beth Best, *Song Fest* (New York, 1955), pp. 55–56, 69.

My God, How the Money Rolls In

This is a descendent twice, thrice removed from an English Commonwealth song, "Old Hewson the Cobbler," sung about a Cromwellian officer who eventually sat in judgment at the trial of Charles I. According to Dick's *The Songs of Robert Burns* (Hatboro, Pa., 1962), p. 415, "Hewson" is older than its first appearance in the *Vocal Miscellany,* I (Dublin, 1738), p. 338, and many "scurrilous and indecent verses" appeared in various Restoration song collections. The present editor failed to locate it in the extensive collection of drolleries in the Henry E. Huntington Library, San Marino, California, though the indicia "To the tune of Old Hewson the Cobbler" were not uncommon.

The tune of "Old Hewson the Cobbler," as printed in Chappell, II, p. 163, and *Popular Music of the Olden Time*, p. 451, helps to link the Commonwealth song with its descendants.

"Hewson" passed into oral tradition in the British Isles, notably with the tinkers. While no early version of this traditional text seems to have been recovered, a number of variants of a tinkers' redaction—Legman styles it "The Finest Fucking Family in the Land"—and a buskers'/broadside offspring survive.

"The Finest Fucking Family" seems to have been reduced to a scatological joke, its tune a tortured remnant of the music halls, if the version in *Songs of Roving and Raking*, pp. 42, 45, is representative.

> I've got a sister Lily,
> She's a whore in Picadilly,
> And my brother runs a brothel
> In the Strand.
> Me father cocks his asshole
> At the guards of Windsor Castle,
> We're a filthy, fucking family,
> But we're grand.
>
> Oh, please don't burn our shit-house down.
> Mother has promised to pay.
> Dad's laid up with the old D.T.'s
> And the cat's in the family way.
> Brother's been caught selling morphine,
> Sister's been hustling so hard,
> So if you burn our shit-house down,
> We'll have to make do with the yard.

Legman, p. 421, has an alternative second stanza, implying that his is the "correct" version. The Logue-Vicarion text, perhaps from British tradition, perhaps refashioned by the editor, is No. L.

The buskers' song, meanwhile, has had a lively currency, in print and in tradition as "Dick Darby [or somesuch] the Cobbler." Tommy Makem sings a version on *The Lark in the Morning* (Tradition 1004). The melody for the Makem song, a set of the music-hall mock, "Botany Bay," is printed in *Sing Out!*, XI, No. 2 (April—May, 1961). It is clearly related to the rudimentary strains of "Old Hewson" as given by Chappell.

Dick Darby the Cobbler

The first stanza of "Dick Darling" printed in Gilbert, *Lost Chords*, pp. 78–79, runs:

> Och! my name is Dick Darlin' the cobbler,
> My time I served down there in Kent.
> Some say I'm an old fornicator,
> But now I'm resolved to repent.

Makem's second even more clearly shows the paternity of the buskers' song to "My God."

> Now my father was hung for sheep-stealing,
> Me mother was burned for a witch,
> My sister's a dandy housekeeper,
> And I'm a mechanical switch.
>   With me ing-twing of an ing-thing of an i-day,
>   With me ing-twing of an ing-thing of an i-day,
>   With me roo-boo-boo roo-boo-boo randy,
>   And me lab stone keeps beating away.

Gilbert also cites a DeMarsan broadside, and it may be that the printing houses can take some credit for the song's wide currency in the United States. Lomax, *Folk Songs of North America*, pp. 134–35, reprints one of two variants gathered by Gardner and Chickering in southern Michigan. Flanders and Olney, pp. 176–77, comment of the probable paternity of their version. *The New Green Moun-*

224

tain Songster, p. 223; and Randolph, *Ozark Folk Songs*, I, pp. 385–86, are also from this broadside/buskers' strain. Harlow, p. 211, has a one-stanza fragment from sailors.

Grieg has another song—a maiden's lament of her uncourted state—that borrows its first stanza from the tinkers' tradition. (See No. XVIII.) A similar text, from Thomson's *Orpheus Caledonius* (London, 1733), p. 69, begins:

> My daddy's a delver of dykes,
> My minny can card and spin,
> And I'm a bonny young lass,
> And the siller comes linkin in.
> The siller comes linkin in,
> And it is fou [sic], fair to see,
> And it's wow, wow, wow,
> What ails the lads at me?

The chain of interrelationships does not stop here. Grieg's version of "My Daddy's a Delver of Dykes" is sung to the Scots tune of "The Muckin' o' Geordie's Byre." That same tune also carries a defiant girl's insistence that she "will not marry at all, at all." The sentiment of the song as printed in Linscott, *Folk Songs of Old New England*, p. 212, is the exact opposite of that in "My Daddy's a Delver of Dykes"—only the fact that both concern themselves with a girl speaking to the general questions of courting and marriage link the two texts.

Textually unrelated, "Lizie Lindsay" (Child 226) in a Scots version uses this tune, according to Bronson, IV, p. 365.

"My God, How the Money Rolls In" is certainly one of the most frequently encountered bawdy songs in the United States. Reuss reports 18 archived texts from Michigan State, Indiana University, and Western Kentucky State College, p. 186; adds a text he collected, p. 189; then gives ephemeral references, the earliest of which he dates to 1928. Brand, pp. 52–53, has a version as do Wallrich, p. 189; *Songs of Roving and Raking*, p. 64; and *Songs of Raunch and Ill-Repute*, p. 9. Sandburg, p. 381, and Leach, p. 89, each have one stanza of "My God" set to different—and well-worn—sets of the tune which Flanders and Olney, Gardner and Chickering, and Makem offer. This would suggest the strongest possible relationship between "My God" and the inoffensive derivatives of the older tinkers' song. "My God" is now generally sung to the nursery tune of "My Bonnie Lies Over the Ocean," which serves as a vehicle for the protest song "My Children Are Seven in Number" in Greenway, p. 166, and on Pete Seeger, *American Industrial Ballads* (Folkways FH5251).

The version of "My God" printed here is a conflation of four texts of this urban song. Stanzas two and three are from Sydney, Australia, and the University of Sydney. They were sung at a party in Los Angeles in 1962 by a young lady in her mid-twenties, lately come up from Down Under. The first stanza is from the editor's memory of a Los Angeles boyhood, circa 1945. The balance is from the singing of an anonymous male informant in Salt Lake City in 1960.

Next Thanksgiving

Songs of Raunch and Ill-Repute, p. 15, has a close variant ("Save the bread . . . tree . . . eggs") from Pasadena, circa 1960. It is reprinted in *Songs of Roving and Raking*, p. 65. Abrahams has forwarded a one-stanza version from Texas.

The text here is from the collection gathered at UCLA in 1960 by Dean Burson.

No Balls at All

This is a ribald member of a group of folk songs dealing with the mismatch in years of marriage partners. The sentiment of "No Balls at All" as well as the lack of sexual enthusiasm on the husband's part is shared by, among others, the sometimes erotic Scots-Irish-English folk song, "An Old Man He Courted Me."

For references to that song, see Edith Fowke, *Traditional Singers and Songs from Ontario*, pp. 32–33, 167; and her article "Bawdy Ballads in Print, Record and Tradition," *Sing and String*, II, No. 2 (Summer, 1963), pp. 3–9.

One suspects that Robert Burns had similar sentiments in mind when he fashioned "What Can a Young Lassie?" and this stanza:

> He's always compleenin' frae morin to e'enin;
>> He hoasts and he hirples the weary day lang:
> He's doylt and he's dozin; his blude it is frozen,
>> O, dreary's the night wi' a crazy auld man.

Dick, p. 417, credits the words to Burns, but it may be that the song, like so many others of the poet, was modeled upon, or suggested by, or an extension of a song in oral tradition. See also the original version of "John Anderson, My Jo," in *The Merry Muses,* pp. 114–15.

Two Irish members of the group, with the sexual longing discretely put, "Seanduine Chill Chocáin" ("The Old Man of Kilcockan"), and "An Seanduine" ("The Old Man"), are in Donal O'Sullivan, *Songs of the Irish* (Dublin, 1960), pp. 73–76. Songs such as these were the perhaps inevitable by-product of the traditional patterns of family structure and land ownership. As detailed in Conrad Arensberg's *The Irish Countryman* (New York, 1937), these social institutions tended to create "May-December" matches. The oldest son in a culture which followed the rule of primogeniture could marry only after his father retired and the land was passed on. Until then he was the "boy," no matter his age, unable to bring a wife home to his own farm, and not ready for

226

marriage until he could support a family with the produce of his own land. The theme is treated, too, in Brian Merriman's *Cúirt an Mheadhon Oidhche* (*The Midnight Court*). (Siobhan McKenna reads Frank Connor's translation on Spoken Arts 742, a recording which, in the editor's opinion, somehow captures the repressed sexual longing of the complainant.)

In the United States, the theme is implicit in "Get Away, Old Man, Get Away," as printed in Frank Shay, *More Pious Friends and Drunken Companions* (New York, 1928), pp. 132–33:

> Be sure to marry a young man no matter what the cost,
>> For an old man's like an apple when bitten by
>>> the frost.
> For an old man he is old, and an old man he is gray,
>> But a young man knows just how to love—
>>> Get away, old man, get away! (p. 133)

According to Legman, p. 377, "No Balls at All" dates from the American Civil War, and was modeled upon a then-topical song, "Nothing to Wear."

Brand has an expurgated version of "No Balls at All," pp. 30–31, with "hips" substituted for the codlings throughout. *Songs of Roving and Raking*, p. 60, borrows a version from a mimeographed song collection, circa 1960, "published" by students at Caltech in Pasadena, California, under the title of *Songs of Raunch and Ill-Repute*. Logue-Vicarion has it as No. LVI. A recorded version is on *Unexpurgated Songs of Men*.

There are four full versions, with virtually identical tunes, in the editor's files. This text and tune is from a recording made by a former student in Los Angeles in 1960. A variant of the melody carries the cowboy song "The Strawberry Roan."

The Old Gray Bustle

This was learned "sometime after adolescence and sometime before maturity," about 1950, according to the business man who sang it for the editor in 1963 in Los Angeles.

The text here is less than complete. Brand has a fuller parody on *Bawdy Western Songs* (Audio Fidelity 1920). Wallrich has another parody entirely, p. 157, as does Reuss, pp. 160 ff., from various midwestern colleges. The closest version in Reuss to that used here was collected by Merrill and Virginia Walker at Michigan State University in 1947:

> Put on your old gray bustle; get your fanny in a
>> tustle [sic]
> And we'll drink another glass of beer,

For it ain't for knowledge that I came to college
But to raise hell while I'm here.

See also Lynn, p. 135.

The original song, published in 1909, was written by Stanley Murphy and Percy Wenrich.

O'Reilly's Daughter

This is one of the songs which has most suffered from the voluntary and involuntary censorship of bawdy folk songs. The song is certainly old, and quite well-known nowadays among college students; but it has appeared in print infrequently. It does figure, however fleetingly, in the first act of T. S. Eliot's *The Cocktail Party*. See the appendix, p. 190, of the New York edition of the play for a tune and two stanzas Eliot himself knew.

Leach, p. 126, has one verse and a melody. Patrick Galvin sings a variant on *Irish Drinking Songs* (Riverside 12–604). Brand, pp. 22–23, says his version of the song is at least 100 years old, and the song is probably much older. The Brand version is reprinted in *Songs of Roving and Raking*, p. 115. *Songs of Raunch and Ill-Repute*, p. 27, has another.

"Shag" as a euphemism for sexual intercourse dates from the late eighteenth century. The reference to the necessary in the bedroom clearly dates the song to sometime prior to the invention or rise of indoor plumbing.

Suggestive of the interrelationship of bawdy song and folklore in general is the fact that Brand's version begins with an unusual first stanza, apparently a later accretion:

Oscar Brand is my name, America is my nation,
Drinking gin my claim to fame, shagging girls my
   occupation.

This is a portion of a well-known Scots book inscription. *Miscellanea of the Rymour Club*, Edinburgh, Vol. I, Part IV (February, 1909), p. 129, quotes a version written appropriately enough in a copy of *The Merry Muses of Caledonia* housed in the British Museum:

William Findlay is my name,
   And Scotland is my nation,
Crawford is my dwelling-place,
   A pleasant habitation.
When I am dead and in my grave,
   And a' my bones are rotten,
Tak' up this book and think of me
   When I am quite forgotten.

228

The version printed here, one of three full texts and three fragments in the editor's collection, was sung by Lee Bluestone, a legislative lobbyist, in Los Angeles in 1964.

The Pioneers

This is one of a group of parodies, generally sung to the tune of "Son of a Gambolier," which defame various occupations or branches of the military service. Leach, p. 115, has one entitled "The Infantry"; Dolph, p. 179, has "The M.P.s"; Wallrich's, p. 195, is "The A.P.s"; and Legman, *The Limerick*, p. 420, n. 752, cites one entitled "The Engineers." Niles, Moore and Wallgren, *The Songs My Mother Never Taught Me* (New York, 1929), pp. 29–42, have a spate of such slanders.

In his novel of pre-World War II China, *The Sand Pebbles*, Richard McKenna uses two verses of a song obviously from the same tradition:

> Us Hunaneers,* we got no fears,
> We do not stop at trifles;
> We hang our balls upon the walls
> And shoot at them with rifles. (p. 68 of the Fawcett
>   edition)

> Us Hunaneers, we shed no tears,
> We give no damn for riches;
> We prong our wives with butcher knives,
> Us hardy sons of bitches. (p. 70)

While these military satires are all sung to "Son of a Gambolier," the melody used here, however, is better known as "The Hearse Song." See Sandburg, p. 444, for a version.

The text and tune here was collected by Dale Koby in Northern California in 1961. *Songs of Roving and Raking*, p. 80, has another credited to Gershon Legman with slight variations; Legman's text may be from *Immortalia*, a collection of bawdy songs of World War I vintage, printed about 1927 in New York. The present editor has not seen a copy of that work, or its post-World War II Japanese reprint.

Red Wing

This ballad is well-known, or, at least, its first stanzas are frequently encountered. There are three variants in the editor's collection, and he heard it more than a few times before beginning the compilation of this anthology.

---

* From Hunan province.

The most extended text the editor has seen is in *Songs of Raunch and Ill-Repute*, p. 1; and *Songs of Roving and Raking*, p. 61, a version notable for its truly classic euphemism for a would-be rapist's emasculation:

> Now he was an Indian wise. He reached for Redwing's
>   thighs.
> With an old rubber boot on the end of his toot [root?],
> He made poor Redwing open up her eyes.
> But when she came to life, she grabbed her Bowie knife;
> It flashed in the sky as she let it fly,
> And shortened his love life.

For other versions, see Legman, *The Limerick*, p. 193, No. 939; and *Raunch and Ill-Repute*, p. 30. An Air Force parody (expurgated?) is in Wallrich, p. 164. Greenway, p. 299, notes that the original title faces the threat of displacement by a more recent creation: "I have seen at least a half-dozen union songs written to the tune of 'Red Wing,' but all of them have the notation, 'Sung to the tune of Union Maid.'" For those who know the bawdy lyrics to "Red Wing," Woody Guthrie's song in praise of the distaff union member is doubly funny. The editor suspects that Guthrie was aware of the bawdy lyrics when he wrote "Union Maid."

The popular song upon which Guthrie ostensibly modeled his parody is credited to Kerry Mills and Thurland Chattaway, and was published in 1907. Abrahams has noted in a letter to the editor that "in the late 'Nineties and early part of this century, there were reams of songs written in praise of Indian maidens, the progenitor—'Little Mohee.'"

The version printed here is from the singing of Norman Kaplan of New York City. He learned the song "in school" about 1940. He was then about eight years old.

The Ring-Dang-Doo

This ballad has two endings, one in which the owner of the ring-dang-doo passes on what is known as a social disease to all those who visit her, the other ending when her career is cut short by a soldier or sailor who gives her the pox.

Brand, pp. 80–81, has a variant of the former, only gently edited. Both *Songs of Raunch and Ill-Repute*, p. 19, and *Songs of Roving and Raking*, p. 111, have the latter. Those texts include this unusual last stanza:

> They tacked her teats to the courthouse wall;
> They pickled her pussy in alcohol.
> They buried it 'neath the avenue.
> Now the buses ride on her ring dang doo.

Abrahams, p. 171, reports the song in recitation form, and has collected un-published West Indies variants "from a number of women informants." The song is included also on *Unexpurgated Folk Songs of Men*.

There are four variants, notably similar, in the editor's collection. The first five verses here are from a written copy of the song contributed by Roy Torkington, who learned it in Rochester, New York, in 1956. The last two and the melody are from the editor's Los Angeles youth, learned perhaps in the late 1940's.

Roll Me Over

Ribald and scatological formula songs are found in about the same frequency as they appear in Anglo-American folk song in general. In a preliminary survey of Anglo-American formula songs, Mrs. Joan Ruman Perkal and the editor located about one hundred examples of the genre. Most were children's songs; more than a few were hymns or gospel songs.

Despite this relative scarcity, the formula song is of venerable lineage. The 1661 edition of *Merry Drollerie*—a copy is in the H. E. Huntington Library in San Marino, California—contains "There Were Three Birds," apparently a drinking song of traditional origin based upon *double entendres*. ("Birds" were men, then as now, and "wimble" is an older name for an auger.)

> There were three birds that built very low,
> The first and the second cry'd, "Have at her toe."
> The third went merrily in and in, in,
> And the third went merrily in.
>> Oh, never went wimble in timber more nimble
>> With so little screwing and knocking on 't in,
>> With so little knocking in.
>
> There were three birds that built on a pin.
> The first and the second cry'd, "Have at her shin."
> The third he went merrily in and in, in,
> The third he went merrily in.
>> Oh, never went wimble in timber more nimble (Etc.)
>
> There were three birds that built on a tree.
> The first and the second cry'd, "Have at her knee,"
> And the third he went merrily in and in, in
> And the third he went merrily in.
>> Oh, never went wimble in timber more nimble (Etc.)
>
> There were three birds that built very high.
> The first and the second cry'd, "Have at her thigh."
> The third he went merrily in and in, in,
> The third he went merrily in.
>> Oh, never went wimble in timber more nimble (Etc.)

There were three birds that built on a stump.
The first and the second cry'd, "Have at her rump."
The third he went merrily in and in, in,
And the third he went merrily in.
    Oh, never went wimble in timber more nimble (Etc.)

The formula in this song—aside from the rigid stanzaic structure—lies in the steady progression from toe to rump, an external, given arrangement to which the song is fitted. While most formula songs borrow some such external ordering or ranking—numbers, letters of the alphabet, playing card values, and so on—Mrs. Perkal and the editor have identified a second type of formula song, one which adopts an idiosyncratic, internal formula or chain of circumstances. The well-known lullaby "Hush, Little Baby" with its conditional offerings of gifts is one such. Another, forwarded by Rosalie Sorrels of Salt Lake City, Utah, as she collected it from children in 1963, is this scatological epistle:

Annie Morier peed in the fire.
The fire was so hot she peed in the pot.
The pot was so high she peed in the sky.
The sky was so blue she peed right through.

"Roll Me Over" may well be the most popular formula song in American oral tradition. There are six full versions in the editor's collection, and more might have been notated had they exhibited any variation from texts or tunes already in hand. In all, the editor has 22 reports of the song. The most radical is this variant from former Marine, now Los Angeles lawyer Alvin Tenner:

This is number one and the fun had just begun.
Nelly, put your belly close to mine.
    Roll me over in the clover,
    Roll me over, lay me down, and do it again.

This is number two, and my Nelly wants to screw. (Etc.)
This is number three, and it's time I had a pee. (Etc.)
This is number four, and I've got her on the floor. (Etc.)
This is number five; the bee is in the hive. (Etc.)
This is number six; the juices begin to mix. (Etc.)
This is number seven; Could this really be heaven? (Etc.)
This is number eight, and I'm still feeling great. (Etc.)
This is number nine; now I'm feeling mighty fine. (Etc.)
This is number ten; let's start over again. (Etc.)

Tenner is an indifferent singer, his tune a progression of doggedly rhythmic, indeterminate pitches over the compass of a fifth. For all its vagueness, it is clearly a set of the usual tune to which the song is sung, and for that reason, the song is classed here rather than under "Shove It Home." It remains, nonetheless, an obvious cross between the two songs, and well may be a milestone on the road from "Shove It Home" to "Roll Me Over."

Songs of Raunch and Ill-Repute, p. 20, adds "number 'leven, and it's just like number seven." Reuss, pp. 244–249, has three versions and references to appearances of the song in various manuscript holdings in the Kinsey Institute for Sex Research. The tune he gives, p. 247, is closer to "Put Your Shoulder/Belly Close to Mine and Pump Away" than is that used here. Randolph, III, pp. 89–91, has a modestly-phrased, traditional variant entitled "He Kept A-kissin' On," or "He Gave Her Kisses One." (See "Drive It Home," *supra*.) Oscar Brand's *G.I.—American Army Songs* (Riverside 12–639) sports a more robust variant.

Roll Your Leg Over

At least five workers—Kenneth S. Goldstein, Gershon Legman, Richard Reuss, D. K. Wilgus, and the editor—have independently come to the conclusion that the rowdy "Roll Your Leg Over" can be ultimately traced to a Child ballad, from which it thereby borrows a stout reputation for legitimacy. While "The Twa Magicians" (Child 44), the forebearer, has not persisted in oral tradition either in the British Isles or in the United States, its offspring are numerous.

The college song is seemingly derived from an English love song, "Hares on the Mountain," which, in turn, owes much to "Oh, Sally, My Dear," a descendent of the Child ballad. If there are intermediaries between "Oh, Sally, My Dear" and "The Twa Magicians," they do not seem to have survived.

Child's headnotes to the parent song suggest that the ballad is worth considerable study, embodying as it does a host of popular beliefs concerning witches and warlocks. The motif of successive transformations to aid flight from pursuers (D 671) is the core of MT 313, and occurs, too, in other tales. (See the references at the related motifs, D 615.3; 630; 641.1.2; 642.3; and elsewhere.) The theme of the transformation combat figures also in MT 325 in which a youth bests a magician. See Richard M. Dorson, *American Negro Folktales* (New York, 1967), p. 141, for notes supplementing those in Aarne-Thompson, *The Types of the Folktale*, FCC 184 (Helsinki, 1961), pp. 113–14. In all, the magical elements in tale and song are considerable.

For references to texts of both "Hares on the Mountain" and "Oh, Sally, My Dear," see Margaret Dean-Smith, *A Guide to English Folk Song Collections* (Liverpool, 1954). Add to those the entries in Bronson, I, pp. 348–53, which includes Andrew Rowan Summers' unique variant of "Hares on the Mountain" from Virginia. The Summers version is sung on *Seeds of Love* (Folkways FP 21). "Oh, Sally, My Dear" has been recorded by Pete Seeger on *Love Songs for Friends and Foes* (Folkways FA 2453) and by Ewan MacColl on *English and Scottish Love Songs* (Riverside 12–656).

The occupational punning in "Roll Your Leg Over" is suggestive of the similar wordplay in "The Jolly Tradesmen," as printed in *Pills to Purge Melancholy*, VI, pp. 91 ff. (See the endnote to "I Used to Work in Chicago," *supra*.)

Brand, pp. 72–73, has another text of "Roll Your Leg Over," included, too, on *Bawdy Songs and Backroom Ballads,* I (Audio Fidelity 906; or 1906). *Songs of Roving and Raking,* pp. 99–100, has a 22-stanza version, but that number is dwarfed by the impressive 49 in *Songs of Raunch and Ill-Repute,* pp. 10–12. A number of those, one imagines, were tossed off by the "Ricketts Rowdies" who compiled the collection.

> I wish all them ladies was linear spaces,
> And I were a vector aimed at their bases.
>
> I wish all them ladies was solutions to find,
> And I were a frosh, I'd plug in and grind.
>
> I wish all them ladies was dx/dt,
> And then I would integrate them d-me.

That Caltech chronicle ends with this assurance:

> I wish all them ladies was singing this song,
> It'd be twice as dirty and ten times as long.

Reuss, pp. 236–39, has three texts from college students in Ohio and Indiana. The one tune Reuss includes is a set of the melody used here. He adds, p. 234, a stanza which, he claims, "accurately analyzes the purpose and psychological outlet behind the singing of this and a great many other college songs":

> "We laugh and we sing and we joke all about it.
> It's only because we are doing without it."

The tune used here—generally the vehicle for the song—is apparently an elaboration of the last four bars of the melody collected by Cecil Sharp for "Oh, Sally, My Dear," and reprinted in Bronson, I, p. 352, No. 11. It is also borrowed, then simplified, for "The Sheep-Washer's Lament" in Anderson, p. 102.

There are eight variants of the college song in the editor's collection. The longest, gathered by Dean Burson in Los Angeles in 1960, runs 17 stanzas. This text was supplemented here with four additional verses collected by Miss Anne Smith in Los Angeles in 1960, and by the editor the following year.

The Rugby Song

This is a unique song in the editor's collection, an adaptation of an older college song which seems to have waned in popularity. D. K. Wilgus reports that he has not heard the song since his own college days, about 1940, when he learned and sang it. Twenty-seven years later, he could immediately recall only one stanza, "though given enough time and beer," he could "run through every occupation":

234

If I were a maiden fair,
Fairer than all the others,
I would marry a plumber
As quick as one of the others.
  We'd fix a pipe here.
  We'd fix a pipe there.
  We'd fix pipe together,
  But wouldn't we have a helluva time
  Laying pipe together?

Wilgus' tune is quite close to that used by Michael Higer for "The Rugby Song" here. Higer recorded it for the editor in Los Angeles in 1960. Apparently, this is the first time it has appeared in print.

Sam MacColl's Song

Another of the "Samuel Hall" family, this is more closely related to the head of the clan than most of the derivative songs and ballads. There are two versions of this in the author's collection, this from the singing of a woman in her mid-forties who learned it from her husband about 1940. It was collected in San Francisco by the editor in 1963.

The melody is a set of the tune usually associated with "I Was Born Almost Ten Thousand Years Ago," a version of which is in Sandburg, pp. 330–31.

Samuel Hall

It would be hard to find a more fertile source of traditional balladry than "Samuel Hall," or, more properly, "Jack Hall." Both its tune and its stanzaic form have had great influence in oral tradition. For some hint of this—and these articles barely begin to itemize all of the descendants of "Jack Hall," see Bertrand Bronson, "Samuel Hall's Family Tree," *California Folklore Quarterly,* I (1942), pp. 47 ff., and G. P. Jackson, "The 400-Year Odyssey of the 'Captain Kidd' Song Family," *Southern Folklore Quarterly,* XV (1951), pp. 239 ff.

To the references there, add "Remember O Thou Man" in Thomas Ravenscroft, *Melismata* (London, 1611; reprinted by the American Folklore Society, 1961), p. 144; "God Save Great King George" in William Chappell, *Popular Music of the Olden Time* (London, 1859), II, p. 45; "Ye Jacobites by Name" on Ewan MacColl, *Songs of Two Rebellions* (Folkways FW 8756); "Aikendrum" on Ewan MacColl, *Classic Scots Ballads* (Tradition 1013); "The Shan Van Vocht" in Patrick Galvin, *Irish Songs of Resistance,* p. 27; "The Famine Song," *ibid.,* p. 44; "Admiral Benbow" in Cecil Sharp, *Folk Songs from Somerset,* 3rd series (London, 1906), p. 5; "Benjamin Bowmaneer" in Ralph Vaughan

Williams and A. L. Lloyd, *The Penguin Book of English Folk Songs* (London, 1959), pp. 20–21; and "The Bold Benjamin," *ibid.*, p. 23. "Hurrah Lie" in Alan Lomax, *Folk Songs of North America* (New York: Doubleday, 1960), p. 260, and the references there introduce the nursery branch of the family. Silber, p. 189, has "Drink It Down," a Civil War drinking song.

Jackson has extensively documented the God-fearing members of the family. In addition to his article cited above, see *Spiritual Folk-Songs of Early America*, 2nd ed., (Locust Valley, New York, 1953), pp. 90, 114, 159, and 162; *Down-East Spirituals*, 2nd ed., (Locust Valley, New York, 1953), pp. 196, 241, 259–261 (text only), 267–68, and 271 (text only); and *Another Sheaf of White Spirituals* (Gainesville, Florida, 1952), pp. 27–28, 196.

Jackson credits the great popularity of the tune and stanzaic form to William Walker's *Southern Harmony* (Philadelphia, 1836, 1854; reprinted Los Angeles, 1966) which borrowed the text from *Mercer's Cluster*. The melodic grafting was Walker's.

Further references to the tune family are in Brown, V, p. 495; and Annabel Morris Buchanan, *Folk Hymns of America* (New York, 1938), pp. xv, 12–13. See too "The Freemason's Song" in Simpson, p. 234, which seems as if it were at any moment to break into "God Save the King"; and "Sound a Charge," p. 673.

Textual references for the "Jack Hall" ballad, and its congener, "Captain Kidd," are in G. Malcolm Laws, Jr., *American Balladry from British Broadsides* (Philadelphia, 1957), pp. 158–59, 167–68. W. Roy Mackenzie, *Ballads and Sea Songs from Nova Scotia* (Cambridge, Mass., 1928), pp. 278–79, has excellent notes on the ballad of the throttled pirate captain, as well as a parody dated to 1797. The assertion that Hall and Kidd are not related—made by Fannie Hardy Eckstorm and Mary Winslow Smyth in *Minstrelsy of Maine* (Boston, 1927), pp. 246–49—may be discounted.

Art songs set to traditional tunes have used the same stanzaic form. See."A Young Man and a Maid," in D'Urfey's *Pills to Purge Melancholy*, VI, p. 251. The tune there was borrowed by Burns for "Ye Jacobites by Name," according to James C. Dick, ed., *The Songs of Robert Burns* (Hatboro, Pa., 1962), pp. 264, 464.

Burns used a variant of the Kidd tune to bear the words of his poem "The Tailor." See James Johnson, *The Scots Musical Museum* (Edinburgh, 1853; reprinted Hatboro, Pa., 1962), I, p. 505; and Stenhouse's notes, II, p. 431.

The bawdy version of the original broadside is definitely dated to the middle of the Nineteenth Century. Defending the inclusion of Commonwealth and Elizabethan indelicacies in his edition of *Choyce Drollery*, J. W. Ebsworth gamely rationalized in 1876:

236

They are tokens of a debased taste that would be inconceivable, did we not remember that, not more than twenty years ago, crowds of M.P.s, Lawyers, and Baronets listened with applause and encored tumultuously, songs far more objectionable than these (if possible) in London Music Halls, and Supper Rooms. Those who recollect what R . . s sang (such as 'The Lock of Hair,' 'My Name It Is Sam Hall, Chimbley Sweep,' etc.) and what 'Judge N——' said to his Jury Court, need not be astonished at anything which was sung or written in the days of the Commonwealth and at the Restoration.

In a footnote to the version in his *Garland of English Folk-Song* (London, 1926[?]), p. 39, Frank Kidson identifies "R . . s" as G. W. Ross who "in the fifties of the last century . . . sang a version of the above named 'Sam Hall,' but with a very blasphemous chorus. This drew a big audience of a certain kind."

Wallrich, p. 171, has an Air Force version of "Sam Hall."

Schnooglin'

A unique text in the editor's collection furnished by Mrs. Marilyn Eisenberg Herzog who reported that it was sung by B'nai B'rith girls in Los Angeles about 1958. The tune is a flattened out set of "Soloman Levi."

The Sea Crab

This bawdy song is one of the few that have been accorded scholarly attention. Guthrie Meade, Jr., dealt with the song in an article in *Midwest Folklore,* VIII (1958), pp. 91–100. According to Meade, "In America, the song seems to have flourished over a large area," but he had only two versions from oral tradition and a report of a third.

Meade, and Legman, *The Horn Book,* p. 190, give tale references to this *conte-en-vers*. Thompson has assigned to it the motif number J 2675, describing it delicately as "Bungling Rescuer Caught by Crab. He tries to rescue woman caught by crab. Is caught himself and found in embarrassing position."

The earliest song text—from the *Percy Folio Manuscript*—is reprinted in Farmer, IV, pp. 14 ff.; and Cray, pp. 42–44.

Arthur Argo sings a variant from Scotland under the title "The Lobster" on *A Wee Thread o' Blue* (Prestige 13048). An American version, with a tune, is in *Songs of Roving and Raking*, p. 2. The Robert W. Gordon Collection of American Folk Song, University of Oregon, has an undated but probably late 1920's text forwarded by J. Barre Toelken which adds this chip-on-the-shoulder tag:

Now my story is done, and I don't know anymore.
There's an apple up my ass-hole, and you can have the core.

The editor's collection contains two versions. That printed here is from John Terrence O'Neil who learned it as a boy from the singing of his father about 1940 in New York City. (See the endnote to "The Foggy Dew," *supra*.) The second version is an almost incoherent text of two stanzas and a narrated recounting of the missing verses.

The melody O'Neil used, and recognized as such, is the first half of "The Limerick Rake," a copy of which is in O Lochlainn, *Irish Street Ballads,* p. 84.

Seven Old Ladies

In the *Oxford Dictionary of Nursery Rhymes,* pp. 248–250, Iona and Peter Opie give a history of the original, a popular song, which was parodied for political and patriotic purposes long before "Seven Old Ladies" went into the lavatory. They date it from a manuscript compiled between 1770 and 1780. Chappell, *Popular Music of the Olden Time,* p. 732, fixes the song's date to 1792, when it first appeared in sheet music. Fuld, p. 331, has a concise survey of its appearances in print.

A text and tune for the popular song fashioned from the older nursery rhyme is in the *Abelard Folksong Book,* "Songs for Saturday Night," pp. 6–7.

Brand sings a version of the bawdy song on Vol. III of his record series (Audio Fidelity 1824); that version is reprinted in *Songs of Roving and Raking,* p. 62. William and Ceil Baring-Gould, *The Annotated Mother Goose* (New York, 1962), p. 118, mention "Three Old Ladies" as a "raucous college song," but give only two inoffensive and uninformative lines. Lynn, p. 37, has a close variant of the version here.

The Opies, *Lore and Language of School Children,* p. 364, deem "Seven Old Ladies" a "hoary scatological song concerning the Bishop of Winchester's daughter." They, sad to say, do not elaborate.

The melody, known from the nursery rhyme, "Oh, Dear, What Can the Matter Be," was fitted to the shape-note hymn "Send Us a Blessing," according to G. P. Jackson, *Spiritual Folk-Songs of Early America,* 2nd ed. (Locust Valley, N. Y., 1952), p. 209. Always serviceable, it pops up again in a 1967 popular song, "Round, Round," as recorded by Jonathan King.

Three variants of this have been gathered in Southern California. That used here was noted by the editor from the singing of a secretary who had volunteered her services as a political campaign worker in Los Angeles in 1964. It has been patched in a few torn spots in the fourth and fifth stanzas from the text contributed by Burson as sung at UCLA four years earlier.

The Sewing Machine

This was sung by Burson's Carnegie Tech informant who had served in Germany during the postwar occupation at the end of World War II. Apparently it has had only a limited currency, confined to a relative handful of men who served in Europe at that time.

The song seems to have been influenced—in the first stanza, at any rate—by "Charlotte the Harlot." Some versions of "Charlotte" are sung to the same tune, "Down in the Valley," and the tune may have suggested the textual borrowing.

Other military songs to the same tune are in Wallrich, pp. 25–6; 79.

The Sexual Life of the Camel

This sophisticated ditty is one of the more popular songs in the urban singing tradition, judging from the editor's collecting experiences. It is a good example, too, of the sort of song most likely to be retained by educated urban singers. Although they do not eschew the bawdy by any means, they appreciate it more if it is clever, literate, and, like the limerick, dependent upon some specialized information for its full impact.

Songs of Roving and Raking, p. 101, has these two stanzas embedded in a longer song set to the traditional Irish street ballad tune, "Mush Mush Mush Toura-liady." The same is in *Songs of Raunch and Ill-Repute*, p. 3. Reuss, pp. 273–74, prints a variant from Michigan State University credited ultimately to military currency. He also has a two-stanza variant from Indiana University, collected in 1964, with no tune indicated. Reuss cites no less than 46 variants from three midwestern institutions, those variants now housed in the Indiana University Folklore Archives, and gives references to occurrences of the song in ephemeral collections.

Robert Reisner, *Graffiti* (New York, 1967), p. 58, prints two versions without music, garnered from lavatory walls. He adds: "Quite common in England and has been set to music."

The version here, one of four nearly identical texts in the editor's files, was contributed by Robert Easton who collected it in Los Angeles in 1960. The poem is also sung to "My Bonnie Lies Over the Ocean."

She Was Poor But She Was Honest

This seemingly began life in the English music halls, circa 1875, and must have acquired bawdy verses early in life. At one time, extended versions were not uncommon, probably because it was widely sung by British troops during the

War to Save the World for Democracy, 1914–18. Five years after the armistice, Robert W. Gordon gathered this ten-stanza text, numbered 246 in the Gordon Collection of American Folk Song at the University of Oregon.

She was poor but she was honest,
Victim of a village crime,
Of the squire's guilty passion
And she lost her own good nyme.

Then she went right up to Lunnon
For to hide her ghastly shyme,
And she met another squire,
And she lost her nyme agyne.

She was poor but she was foolish,
Victim of a rich man's whim,
He seduced here, then he left her,
She'd a little child by him.

You'll find her in the theayter.
See her sitting in the stalls,
And at home an hour lyter
Plying with some strynger's balls.

You'll see her in her limoosin
In the park, and people say
All the squires and nobby people
Stop to pass the time of day.

In a quiet country cottage,
There her aged parents live,
Drink the champagne that she sends them
But they never can forgive.

You will find her in the gutter
Selling matches by the box.
For a tanner you can up her.
Ten to one you get the pox.

See him passing in his carriage
With his fyce all wreathed in smiles.
See her sitting on the pyvement
Which is bloody bad for pyles.

See him passing to the Commons,
Making laws for rich and pore.
See her walking of [sic] the pyvements,
Nothing but a bloody whore.

240

It's the syme the whole world over.
It's the poor they always blyme,
And the rich, they takes their pleasures.
Isn't it a bloody shyme?

Count Vicarion, i.e., Christopher Logue, has a ten-stanza text also and an imperfectly notated tune, No. III. Logue may have doctored his text, however. A full and probably expurgated version of the original is in Sandburg, pp. 200–01. Wallrich, p. 114, has another song to the same tune.

The variant printed here was collected by the former student of Mrs. Hawes from the same informant who sang "The Monk of Great Renown."

The English import was parodied in the United States sometime about 1948 to serve as a lampoon of a former governor of a Southern state who was accused of fathering a child on the wrong side of the blanket. The melody for the lampoon is a cross between the original tune and "Red River Valley."

She was poor but she was honest,
The victim of a rich man's whim,
With that Southern Christian gentleman, Big --- ------,
And she had a child by him.

Now he sits in the legislature
Making laws for all mankind,
While she walks the streets of Cullman, Alabama,
Selling grapes from her grapevine.

Now the moral of this story
Is to never take a ride
With that Southern Christian gentleman, --- ------,
And you'll be a virgin bride.

It's the rich what gets the glory.
It's the poor what gets the blame.
It's the same the whole world over, over, over.
It's a lowdown, dirty shame.

One of three variants of the song in the editor's files, this was forwarded by Roger D. Abrahams from Austin, Texas, where it is apparently enjoying a currency among college students. A second variant from the Lone Star State lays the child on the doorstep of a former governor of Texas, suggesting that the song might persevere in oral tradition by the expedient of attaching itself to, and slandering local politicians.

The Western Kentucky Folklore Archives at UCLA contain six texts of the song collected at Murray State College between 1955 and 1958. Curator D. K. Wilgus adds that it was sometimes tagged to local basketball players.

A recorded text is included on *The Unexpurgated Folk Songs of Men.*

Snapoo

The origin of "Snapoo" and its more widely celebrated relatives seems to be one of the more contentious of folkloristic subjects. The first proposal has it that the song was modeled upon the German Romantic poet Uhland's "Der Wirtin Töchterlein," which Minnie Sears' *Song Index* notes is sung to an eighteenth-century melody. But Robert W. Gordon has suggested instead that "Snapoo" was probably derived from "Drei Reiter am Thor," a German folk song dating from the sixteenth century. Joanna Colcord instead prefers the French folk song, "Le Retour du Marin."

Any of these will do to explain the origin of the words; the source of the melody is just as unsettled. Nettel, *Sing a Song of England,* p. 265, says that the English tune for "Snapoo" is "well known in America, in the minor key" as "When Johnny Comes Marching Home." But how reconcile Union Army bandmaster Patrick S. Gilmore's "authorship" of "When Johnny Comes Marching Home" in New Orleans in 1864?

In spite of the "Irish" sound of the tune, in spite of the fact that Gilmore was born in Ireland, and in spite of the opinions of most authorities who identify the air as derived from a traditional Irish melody (the usual nominee for honors is "Johnny, I Hardly Knew Ye"), Gilmore himself said that he learned the *traditional Negro* melody from an unidentified Negro singer. Gilmore's willingness to credit the tune to someone else—even though his own pseudonym of "Louis Lambert" is on the sheet music—can be accepted at face value. Gilmore's assertion that the melody is a Negro traditional air can be discounted.

The easiest, and most logical, explanation is that Gilmore did indeed learn the melody from a New Orleans Negro, but the Negro in turn had learned it either at sea himself or while working on the docks.

Hypothetically, the song the Negro was singing was "Snapoo," a sea chanty before the Civil War. The tune for "Snapoo" was indeed similar to "When Johnny Comes Marching Home," set in the major; that melody, sung by a

242

traditional Negro singer who flatted the third and seventh of the scale in char-
.acteristic blues fashion, would sound *minor* to the unwary Gilmore.

The original major melody of "Snapoo" having given birth by Gilmore's mid-
wifery to the minor tune which Gilmore called "When Johnny Comes Marching
Home," "Snapoo" has now gone full circle, discarded its own tune and picked up
"When Johnny."

The full extent of the tune family has not been explored. The specter of attempt-
ing to account for melodies as varied as "Mademoiselle from Armentieres,"
"Balm of Gilead," and "Son of a Gambolier" is apparently too much to sur-
mount.

Historical notes on "Snapoo" may be found in Nettel, pp. 263 ff.; Dolph, p. 82;
Colcord, pp. 110–112; and Hugill, pp. 95–97, which also has other chanties
using the same lines. (It may be that "Barnacle Bill" or "Bollochy Bill the Sailor"
borrowed its first verses from "Snapoo.") See also Legman, pp. 399–400; and
Harlow, pp. 98–99. Silber, pp. 174 ff.; and Willard A. and Porter W. Heaps,
The Singing Sixties (Norman, Okla., 1960), p. 348, have historical notes on
the Civil War marching song. Bronson, I, p. 310, has three versions of "The
Crow Song" set to "When Johnny Comes Marching Home."

The version here is a conflation of two in the editor's files. The first two stanzas
are from a variant collected by a former student of Mrs. Hawes from a British
veteran of World War II. The balance of the song and the melody are from the
editor's collection, given by an attorney who learned the song in the early 1930's
in New York City.

The song is also set to "She'll Be Coming 'Round the Mountain When She
Comes," a simple-minded off-spring of the same "Snapoo" tune family.

Sound Off

This is a patchwork of stanzas collected between 1955 and 1964 by the editor,
plus those which he remembered from his own basic training at Camp Chaffee,
Arkansas, in 1952. The informants were Mark Hayworth, Sheldon Horlick,
Ed Schweri, Jacques Vidicam, and Gerry Olsen, all of whom now live in Southern
California, but who served at various military posts.

Other versions may be found in Lomax, p. 595; *Hoosier Folklore,* VI (1947),
p. 78; VI (1947), pp. 109–10; and VII (1948), p. 54. It is dated in these notes
to the First World War. Contemporary stanzas are in George C. Carey, "A Collection of Airborne Cadence Chants," *Journal of American Folklore,* LXXVIII
(1965), pp. 52–61.

Abrahams, p. 170, has "Jody the Grinder," one title of the mosaic of verses and
songs celebrating the cocksmith who takes advantage of the husband's absence.

See also Bruce Jackson, "What Happened to Jody," *Journal of American Folklore,* LXXX (1967), pp. 387–396.

The 15-stanza "I've Got a Gal" in *Songs of Raunch and Ill-Repute,* p. 13, is "Sound Off" using the "Honey Babe"—sometimes called "Swing Cadence" or "Airborne Chant"—framework:

> I've got a gal in South Souix Falls,
> Honey, honey.
> I've got a gal in South Souix Falls,
> Babe, babe.
> I've got a gal in South Souix Falls,
> She's got tits like basketballs.
> Honey, oh baby mine.

James J. Fuld, *American Popular Music* (Philadelphia, 1955), p. 69, credits one Willie Duckworth with the copyright version, dated to 1951. Fuld adds "the first regular edition" was in Colonel Bernard Lentz, *The Cadence System of Teaching Close Order Drill,* 4th rev. ed. (Harrisburg, Pa.: Military Service Publishing Co., 1950), p. 67.

Stackolee

This Negro ballad is widespread throughout the South, the core of the story told in tale, legend, song, and toast. Strangely enough, it has appeared in comparatively few collections, undoubtedly because most versions contain verses thought to be beyond the pale.

Abrahams, pp. 78–83, and 123–136, offers a perceptive analysis in socio-psychological terms to accompany three texts collected from Philadelphia Negroes. His notes include a comprehensive bibliography and discography of the song, to which may be added the versions sung by Dave Van Ronk (Prestige 13056); Tom Paley on *The New Lost City Ramblers,* Vol. IV (Folkways FA 2399); and Clarence Edwards, *Country Negro Jam Sessions* (Folk-Lyric 111). The Edwards version is only faintly related to the ballad. One Archibald—identified as Speckled Red by Neil Rosenberg—recorded the song commercially in the early 1950's on Imperial X5358.

Stackolee apparently was a real person, the local bully who ran things about 1870 in the Negro section of Memphis, Tennessee. His flouting of the white man's law—no doubt tacitly assisted by a police force traditionally willing to overlook intra-racial crime—coupled with his high-handed manner gave to him a reputation far beyond his just deserts. His seeming ability to avoid the clutches of the law and the vengeance of rivals became encrusted with a superstitious aura: he had, some legends say, sold his soul to the Devil in exchange for very mortal powers, sexual and physical. The Devil's end of the bargain lay in a magic John B. Stetson hat which Stackolee's rival, Billy Lyon, tries to steal. This occasions Billy's death and the ballad.

Bruce Jackson, "Stagolee Stories: A Badman Goes Gentle," *Southern Folklore Quarterly,* XXIX (1965), pp. 228–33, recounts tales of Stack's considerable talents aside from devil-dealings.

The editor collected this version in Los Angeles from a white informant who, in turn, had it from another white singer. That "prime" source, a knowledgeable afficionado of folk song, used a melodic variant of the tune Paley sings; the phonograph record may have "contaminated" the informant's version. According to Roger D. Abrahams, Paley's melody comes ultimately from a recording made by Mississippi John Hurt (Okeh 8654) in 1928 under the title "Stack O'Lee Blues." The text here has no such ties with recordings; the "prime" source pasted it together from print and oral sources. At least one of the oral sources was a Negro semi-professional guitarist who performed on weekends in Los Angeles under the name of "Travelin' Man." The editor has been told that "Travelin' Man" disappeared from his haunts about 1960; rumor had it he died from an overdose of heroin.

The white informants are both school teachers and preferred anonymity to the dubious publicity they might receive were their names printed here.

The Sterilized Heiress

A fragment of this song was forwarded to the editor after a broadcast appeal for bawdy songs. Appended was this note:

> This bawdy song was chanted to me by my college classmate _____
> _____ in Connecticut in 1941. The subject is the case in which the
> heiress sued her mother (or guardian) for a large sum of money because
> she had been left an inheritance provided she produced an heir—and the
> mother apparently undertook to prevent the girl from producing this heir.
> (I won't even sing this one to my husband—so I guess it's either very
> bawdy or crude.)

A fuller text, credited to the collection of Gershon Legman, is in *Songs of Roving and Raking,* p. 82; the same is in Legman's own *The Limerick,* pp. 241–42, where he names the heiress and ascribes the song to the late Gene Fowler, p. 441.

There are two variants of this in the editor's collection, both from Southern California. Abrahams has forwarded a virtually identical copy from Texas in a manuscript collection dated April 17, 1959, and that copy served to straighten out a confused line in the third stanza.

The melody here is borrowed from the English music-hall song, "Botany Bay." The editor has been informed that it is also sung to the tune of "Rosin the Beau" in some New York state schools of higher education, and the version in the

Western Kentucky Folklore Archives housed at UCLA is to be sung to "My Bonnie Lies Over the Ocean."

Teasing Songs

A number of these have been reported from oral tradition. The Opies have three from English school children, pp. 94, 97. Nancy Leventhal collected a similar rhyme from Hawthorne, California, children. See *Western Folklore*, XXII (1963), p. 245, and the references there. Brand sings another on *Bawdy Western Songs* (Audio Fidelity 1920) under the title of "Pinto Pony" and prints one in his book, p. 36, as "The Clean Song." The latter he also has recorded on *Bawdy Sea Chanties* (Audio Fidelity 1884). Lynn's *Housemothers*, p. 28, has one, the Gordon collection another. Francis Very reported yet another in "Parody and Nicknames Among American Youth," *Journal of American Folklore*, LXXV (1962), p. 262. Reuss, pp. 269–72, has two, as well as ephemeral references. The tune he prints is close to that used here. Finally, Logue, aka Vicarion, has "A Clean Story," No. VII.

The form itself has a respectable antiquity. The *Percy Folio Manuscript,* dating to perhaps 1615, contains a poem entitled "A Friend of Mine" with three introductory stanzas tacked on to what would appear to be an even older folk song. (The first two of these stanzas are omitted here.)

It was my chance, not long ago,
By a pleasant wood to walk,
Where I unseen of any one
Did hear two lovers talk.

And as these lovers forth did pass
Hard by a pleasant shade,
Hard by a mighty pine tree there,
Their resting place they made.

"In sooth," then did this young man say,
"I think this fragrant place
Was only made for lovers true
Each other to embrace."

He took her by the middle small—
Good sooth I do not mock—
Not meaning to do any thing
But to pull up her   (smock)

Block whereon she sat, poor silly soul,
To rest her weary bones.
This maid she was no whit afraid,
But she caught him fast by the   (stones)

246

Thumbs, whereat he vexed and grieved was,
So that his flesh did wrinkle.
The maid she was no whit afraid,
But caught him fast hold by the   (pintle)

Pimple which he had on his chin likewise.
(But let the pimple pass.)
There is no man here but he may suppose
She were a merry lass.

He boldly ventured, being tall,
Yet in his speech but blunt
He never ceased, but took up all
And catch'd her by the   (cunt)

Plump and red rose lips he kissed full sweet.
Quoth she, "I crave no succor."
Which made him to have a mighty mind
To clip, kiss, and to   (fuck her)

Pluck her into his arms. "Nay, soft," quoth she,
"What needeth all this doing?
For if you will be ruled by me,
You shall use small time in wooing.

"For I will lay me down," quoth she,
"Upon the slippery seggs,*
And all my clothes I'll truss up round,
And spread abroad my   (legs)

"Eggs which I have in my apron here
Under my girdle tucked;
So shall I be most fine and brave,
Most ready to be   (fucked)

"Ducked unto some pleasant springing well,
For now it's time of the year
To deck, and bathe, and trim ourselves,
Both head, hands, feet, and gear."

"Suzanne Was a Lady" is from the singing of Donald Naftulin, M.D., in Los Angeles in 1964. He learned the song some twenty years before as a boy in Toledo, Ohio. "The Ship's in the Harbor" is one of two versions in the editor's collection and was sung in 1958 by Virginia Newbold, eight, of Santa Monica. The last two are from the editor's boyhood and are similar to texts forwarded by Roger D. Abrahams as sung in Texas.

---

* A seat or stool, but here probably in reference to an outhouse.

247

Thais

The correct text of Newman Levy's satirical setting of the story of the whore of Alexandria may be found in his *Opera Guyed* (New York: Alfred A. Knopf, c. 1928).

The story was first set down by a tenth-century German nun, Hrotsvitha, and that version ultimately led to Anatole France's novel and Jules Massenet's opera of the same name. Levy has managed to boil down the opera's three hours to one five-minute ballad.

The passage of writer-attorney Levy's poem into oral tradition is not so easily traced. The tune, if any, to which Levy intended his poem to be sung is nowhere indicated.

This unique version of the song, with some small changes wrought in Levy's original text, was first sung to the editor by Phyllis Zasloff in Los Angeles, about 1955. Her melody is a variant of "Son of a Gambolier."

The editor wishes to acknowledge the courtesy of Alfred A. Knopf, publishers of Levy's poems, who permitted this folk redaction to be printed here.

The Tinker I

This song, also known as "The Highland Tinker," has had a long and involved history in oral tradition. It is a descendant of a bawdy parody of "The Jolly Beggar" (Child 276) crossed with an older broadside, "Room for a Jovial Tinker: Old Brass to Mend." Legman, *The Horn Book*, pp. 226–27, sketches this history, adding that Burns collected another version of the bawdy parody, calling it "The Jolly Gauger." That song is in *The Merry Muses*, p. 78. A mosaic of marginalia in James C. Dick, *The Songs of Robert Burns*, reprint edition (Hatboro, Pa., 1962), and especially in the "Appendix," p. 119, of the added *Notes on Scottish Songs* point out that both bawdy and non-obscene versions of "The Jolly Tinker" coexisted in Scots oral tradition.

Child handled two distinct versions of "The Jolly Beggar" collected by the indefatigable William Macmath from his aunt in Kirkcudbrightshire in 1893. As printed in Child, V, p. 113, the first verse and chorus of the first of Macmath's pieces run:

There was a jolly beggar, as mony a ane has been,
And he's taen up his lodging in a house near Aberdeen.
    Wi his yi yi yanti, his eerie eerie an
    Wi his fine tan taraira, the jolly beggarman.

Macmath's second version, which Child felt constrained to bespatter with asterisks to indicate the expurgation of offensive lines, has a chorus rhythmically

248

similar to that of "The Tinker" and one which shares the same rhyme:

> Wi his long staff, and ragged coat, and breeches to his knee,
> And he was the bauldest beggar-man that eer my eyes did see.

The second Macmath text is still clearly a version of the Child ballad, but within it are obviously the seeds of the modern bawdy song, "The Tinker." Contrary to Legman, the present editor suspects that Burns' bawdy song, "The Jolly Gauger," is an earlier offshoot of the ribald versions of the Child ballad, but otherwise unrelated to the modern-day song.

This bawdy variant of the Child ballad, from which "The Tinker" directly devolves, was later influenced by the older broadside, dated to 1616 in *The Roxburghe Ballads,* III, pp. 230 ff. (A more accessible text is in Eberhard and Phyllis Kronhausen, *Pornography and the Law,* rev. ed. [New York, 1964], pp. 33 ff.) The analogous stanzas of "Room for a Jovial Tinker" are:

1. It was a lady of the North she loved a Gentleman,
   And knew not well what course to take, to use him now and then.
   Wherefore she writ a Letter, and sealed it with her hand,
   And bid him be a Tinker, to mend both pot and pan,
   With a hey ho, hey, derry derry down; with hey trey, down down,
   derry.

2. And when the merry Gentleman the Letter he did read,
   He got a budget on his back, and Apron with all speed,
   His pretty shears and pincers, so well they did agree,
   With a long pike staff upon his back, came tripping o'er the Lee,
   With a hey ho, hey, derry derry down; with hey trey, down down,
   derry.

7. But when the Lady knew his face, she then began to wink,
   "Haste, lusty Butler!" then quoth she, "To fetch the man some drink.
   Give him such meat as we do eat, and drink as we do use,
   It is not for a Tinker's Trade good liquor to refuse."
   With a hey ho, hey, derry derry down; with hey trey, down down,
   derry.

10. At last being come into the Room, where he the work should do,
    The Lady lay down on the bed, so did the Tinker too:
    Although the Tinker knocked amain, the Lady was not offended,
    But before that she rose from the bed, her Coldron was well mended,
    With a hey ho, hey, derry derry down; with hey trey, down down,
    derry.

The matter of the gypsy's *glamour,* mentioned by Brand, p. 69, is also of some interest. The gypsy appears not infrequently in balladry in a stereotyped role, that of the super-sexed wanderer alternately mending pots and rupturing hymens.

The *glamour* of the oldest ballads involving gypsies, Child 200 A–F and Gb, for example, has been rationalized into something more comprehensible to the more or less sophisticated singers of recent years. In Child 200, it is romantic love; in "The Tinker," it is sheer good-natured lust. Both are more understandable than the business of spells and charms to singers who no longer pay credence to the lore of the witches.

In any event, "The Tinker" does not seem to be old. Peter Fryer's *Mrs. Grundy*, p. 41; and Eric Partridge, *A Dictionary of Slang and Unconventional English*, 5th ed. (New York, 1961), identify "kidney wiper as a twentieth-century dysphemism for the male organ. Partridge cryptically adds: "Ex a ribald song."

Five versions of the modern bawdy song have been reported. Brand, pp. 69–70; *Songs of Raunch and Ill-Repute*, p. 29; and *Songs of Roving and Raking*, p. 57, have American versions; that in Pinto and Rodway, p. 438, is from the British Isles. The text in Logue, *Count Vicarion's Book*, No. LIV, has been retouched— to no great advantage. The tune there is a pastiche of borrowed melodic phrases, partially reminiscent of "Solomon Levi."

The editor's files contain five variants of "The Tinker" gathered from Pennsylvania, Texas, and California. At least one of the California texts comes directly from the singing of British troops during World War II, when the song was wide-famed and widely sung. That version, as do many of the British texts, adds this tag to the chorus:

Hanging down, swinging free,
Hanging down, swinging free,
With a yard and a half of foreskin
Hanging down below his knee.

The first version printed here was collected by the editor in Los Angeles in 1964 from a psychiatric social worker who, with straight face, said he learned it from a patient.

The Tinker II

This version of "The Tinker" is a conflation of two variants. A text forwarded by Abrahams from Texas served to fill in lacunae in that given by a housewife and semi-retired school teacher, age 36, who learned it, she thinks, from an older brother about 1945.

250

For references to the tune which she used, "Rosin the Beau," see Margaret Dean-Smith, *A Guide to English Folk Song Collections;* Belden, pp. 255 ff.; Brown, III, p. 61, and V, pp. 32–35; Spaeth, pp. 40–44; and see Samuel Bayard's note to "Heavenly Welcome," in George Pullen Jackson's *Another Sheaf of White Spirituals* (Gainesville, Florida, 1952), p. 164.

To Thee, Hershey Hall

Until the editor obtained, through the courtesy of Roger D. Abrahams, a copy of Richard Reuss' dissertation, the traditional currency of this song was thought doubtful. Only one version had been gathered in Southern California, that by Miss Anne Smith at UCLA in 1960, as sung by a 22-year-old male.

Reuss, however, made it clear that this was no local song. Reporting "a remarkable currency among students in recent years, particularly among coeds," Reuss, p. 150, cited 54 texts collected at Michigan State University between 1947 and 1956, 19 more from Indiana University, and a scattering from high schools and universities from Ohio to Texas. D. K. Wilgus also reported another text, from Murray State College, collected in 1948, contained in the Western Kentucky Folklore Archives at UCLA.

The song, obviously, sported traditional credentials.

Peter Seeger reported in an open letter dated September 16, 1945, from Saipan an analogous parody to the tune of "Pretty Baby" supposedly composed by "state-side WAVES" during World War II. Though perhaps sung by women, it, too, has an emphatically masculine viewpoint:

> If you're nervous in the service and you don't know what to do,
> Have a baby, have a baby.
> If you're hurried and you're worried and you're feeling kind of blue,
> Have a baby, have a baby.
> If you're tired of regimentation and you don't like your chow,
> And you'd go back to civilization if you only knew how,
> I can help you, pretty Wavie, if you'd like to leave the Navy.
> Just have a pretty baby on me.
> I really mean it!
> Just have a pretty baby on me.

Again the masculine attitudes of sexuality are reflected in a parody given to the editor in 1967 by Miss Debbie Bonetti as sung at a California State College, Los Angeles, sorority to the tune of "Hey, Look Me Over." The traditional currency of this is questionable, but for purposes here, it is a fair enough example of the adaptive sexual behavior and response of women in the United States:

> Hey, roll me over,
> Pull up my dress.

Now that I'm an A O Pi
I always will say "yes."

Down with virginity,
Up with the vice.
I figure whenever he's got you down,
You oughta give him a slice.

So I'll be up in just a minute,
Feelin' satisfied.
Then down upon the bed again
With my legs spread wide.

My reputation will be shot,
But I'll look 'em in the eye,
For I'm an Alpha Omicron Pi,
Yes sir, I'm an Alpha Omicron Pi.

Finally, the Western Kentucky Folklore Archives at UCLA contain "We Are the Dirty Bitches," a one-stanza brag collected by Daphne A. McCord at Sullins College, Bristol, Tennessee, in 1957. The name used in the song has been edited to avoid problems of libel.

We are the dirty bitches
Of - - - - - - - C.,
Born in a whorehouse,
Knocked down, dragged out, scraped across the universe.
Of all the dirty bitches,
We are the worst.
We hail from - - - - - - - C.,
The biggest whorehouse on earth.

Reuss's tune, and that used here for "To Thee, Hershey Hall," unrecognized by Miss Smith or her informant, is "My Wonderful One," the perpetual favorite of weddings and receptions, written by Dorothy Terris, Paul Whiteman and Ferde Grofe in 1922.

Too Rally

"Too Rally" is sung to the tune of the English music-hall song, "Botany Bay." That fact, plus the whaleboat-gig-barge status ranking suggests that the song began its career in the British fleet. The last six stanzas here appear to be more recent additions by American sailors.

Songs of Roving and Raking, p. 101, has one stanza of "Too Rally" in a quatrain ballad to the melody of "Mush, Mush, Mush Touraliady":

> The crew they all ride in the dory.
> The captain he rides in the gig.
> It don't go a goddamn bit faster,
> But it makes the old bastard feel big.

Songs of Raunch and Ill-Repute, p. 3, has this verse, the two-stanza "Sexual Life of the Camel" (*supra.*, p. 49), and these localized quatrains:

> Exhaustive experimentation
> By Darwin, Huxley and Hall
> Has proved that the ass of the hedgehog
> Can hardly be buggered at all.

> Here's to the girls of P.C.C.
> And here's to the streets that they roam,
> And here's to their dirty faced bastards,
> God bless them, they may be our own.

> Here's to old Occidental,
> And here's to the old Scripps Trail,
> And here's to those sorority maidens,
> Who gave us our first piece of tail.

According to the Caltech graduate who loaned a copy of the scarce songbook, "P.C.C." is Pasadena City College; "Occidental," spelled as "Oxidental" in the collection, is a nearby liberal arts college. "Few Techmen date there," he adds. On the other hand, Scripps College for Women in Claremont, California, "is one of the most popular date sources for Caltech undergrads. 'Scrippsies' are often bright and intellectual or 'artsy-craftsy.' The girls are not noted for sexual conservatism."

The original song from whence the melody was appropriated is in Long and Jenkin, pp. 5–6; and Hugh Anderson, *Colonial Ballads* (Victoria, 1955), pp. 18–19.

Logue-Vicarion has "The Hedgehog Song," No. VI, with a nonsense chorus and poetic meter which suggests it, too, fits "Botany Bay." The verses are dissimilar.

The version of "Too Rally" here was learned by Pete Seeger during World War II, and passed on to Bess Lomax Hawes. It is used with their permission. See, too, the version in Brand, pp. 18–19.

Uncle Joe and Aunty Mabel

Parodies of scripture and religious texts are not infrequent, though this is the only bawdy parody of a Christmas carol in the editor's collection. Richard Reuss' dissertation, pp. 144–46, has another, offering four texts of "The Twelve Days of Christmas [Finals]," including this from fraternity members at Ohio Wesleyan in May, 1964:

> On the first day of Christmas,
> My true love gave to me
> A hum job in a pear tree.
>
> (Similarly and cumulatively)
> Two sweaty nads [i.e., gonads?]
> Three French breasts [another text has it: "Three French ticklers"]
> Four inches wet
> Five dripping safes
> Six shooting hard-ons
> Seven shriveled testes
> Eight maidens bleeding
> Nine sixty-nine's
> Ten twats a-twitching
> Eleven empty scrotums
> Twelve fairies fucking.

For a survey of "Parodies of Scripture, Prayer, and Hymn," see George Monteiro's article in the *Journal of American Folklore*, LXXVII (1964), pp. 45–52, the references there; and Reuss, pp. 276–279.

Generally, these religious parodies are not malicious nor anti-clerical. The songs and prayers are borrowed simply because of the humorous shock effect of unfamiliar words in a familiar setting. Some of the parodies, indeed, are quite moralistic, such as this "Hail Mary" collected in 1960 in Los Angeles by Mrs. Jacqueline Brunke from her 10-year-old daughter, Anne:

> Hail Mary, full of grace,
> Bless my boy friend's hands and face.
> Bless his head, full of curls,
> And help him stay away from other girls.
> Bless his arms so big and strong,
> And keep his hands where they belong.
>   Amen.

254

Religious satire or comic reinterpretation of the Bible is not a uniquely American phenomenon. The Opie's *Lore and Language of Schoolchildren*, pp. 6, 21, 87–89, has a representative sampling from England. Robin Hall and Jimmie Mac-Gregor sing a Glasgow children's street song, "Johnny Lad," on *Two Heids Are Better Than One* (Monitor 365) containing these biblical observations:

> Solomon and David led very wicked lives,
> Lunchin' every evenin' with other people's wives.

> But sometimes in the evenings when their conscience gave them qualms,
> Solomon wrote the proverbs and David wrote the psalms.

In the interest of a complete record, the editor calls attention to one further parody of "Hark, the Herald Angels Sing" which has seemingly slipped the notice of folklorists. This was recited in the House of Representatives by Rep. Emanuel Celler on Feb. 27, 1964, during a debate on proposed legislation which would have prevented the Federal Communications Commission from limiting radio and television commercials. Said the New York representative: "Some ads are just plain humbug. I am reminded of the doggerel of my boyhood [ca. 1900] . . .

> "Hark the herald angels sing,
> Beecham's pills are just the thing.
> Peace on earth and mercy mild,
> Two for man and one for child."

The editor has four identical versions of the "Uncle Joe" parody in his files, all from college students, three of them living in Los Angeles, the other in New York. According to Abrahams, the text here is actually part of a longer song, but neither he nor the editor has gathered it.

The Wayward Boy

Ditties set to the familiar "The Girl I Left Behind Me" abound. James Barke, in his essay "Pornography and Bawdry in Literature and Society" in *The Merry Muses of Caledonia*, p. 20, gives this Scots children's song:

> O Mary Ann had a leg like a man
> And a great big hole in her stockin';
> A chest like a drum and a big fat bum
> And a hole to shove your cock in.

Two others are included as "Ditties," *supra*.

As popular as the tune may be, "The Wayward Boy" has been infrequently collected. Legman, *The Limerick*, p. 454, quotes one stanza from a full text from Michigan dated to 1935. Brand sings another on Vol. IV of his *Bawdy Songs and*

Backroom Ballads (Audio Fidelity 1847). That version is similar to this which the editor gathered in 1964 in Los Angeles from an informant in his mid-thirties. Another recorded version is on *Unexpurgated Folk Songs of Men*.

Songs of Raunch and Ill-Repute, p. 21, styles its version "She Stood Right There," and includes this unusual verse:

> Two weeks went by, I heaved a sigh,
> A sigh of pain and sorrow.
> The pimples thick upon my dick,
> But there'll be more tomorrow.

A fragment of "The Wayward Boy" in the Robert W. Gordon Collection of American Folk Song, University of Oregon (No. 3900), can be dated to the late 1920's, the earliest the editor has seen. That fragment, too, contains the venereal intrusion.

Abrahams has garnered a brisk variant from a Philadelphia informant, "Kid" Mike, including it in the unpublished portion of his doctoral thesis, "Negro Folklore from South Philadelphia, A Collection and Analysis" (University of Pennsylvania, 1962), p. 252:

> Last night I slept in a sycamore tree
> The wind blowing all around me.
> Tonight I'll sleep in a nice warm bed,
> All the girls beside me.
>
> Well, she jumped in bed and covered her head
> And swore I couldn't find her.
> She knew damn well she was lying like hell,
> So I jumped on in behind her.
>
> She rolled her gut against my nut
> And told me not to mind her,
> And like a damn fool, I took my tool,
> And in her sausage grinder.
>
> Nine months rolled by and I heard a cry.
> She rolled with pain and horror.
> Three little grunts jumped out of her cunt,
> I'm booting ass tomorrow.

The first stanza, Abrahams adds in a letter to the editor, indicates some relation to "The Gypsy Laddie" tradition. That ballad and this at least share the notion of the wandering hero and the charmed or sexually-hungry girl.

Texts and tunes for "The Girl I Left Behind Me" may be found in Shay, pp. 202 ff.; and in Dolph, pp. 507 ff.; the latter also has other (inoffensive) parodies

256

on pp. 194 ff., and p. 392. The brisk tune has served for other texts, too. Silber has a mock military song from the Civil War, "I Goes to Fight mit Siegel," pp. 325 ff.; and credits the original words to Samuel Lover, p. 327.

Chappell's *Old English Popular Music,* II, pp. 187–89, or his *Popular Music of the Olden Times,* p. 708, has a history of the song, dating it to 1758.

Another song with the same title and using the familiar tune is in O Lochlainn, pp. 36–37. There, too, is "The Real Old Mountain Dew," p. 128, using a set of the melody. O'Neill's *Music of Ireland* has the melody as a dance tune under the title of "The Rambling Laborer," p. 52; and as "The Spalpeen March" in his *Dance Music.*

In the United States, too, the melody has been put to good service. Hudson, pp. 229–30, has a localized version of the song. Jackson has sniffed out the tune's influence on two hymns in *Another Sheaf,* p. 85, and *Spiritual Folk-Songs of Early America,* p. 111. Finally, worn-down versions of the ballad, fragments really, double as play-parties. See Leah Jackson Wolford, *The Play-Party in Indiana* (Indianapolis, 1959), p. 277; B. A. Botkin, *The American Play-Party Song* (New York, 1963), pp. 188–92; and P. J. Wyatt, ed., "Play Party Games from Kansas," *Heritage from Kansas,* V (1961), pp. 16–17.

We Go to College

This is well-known throughout the country, variously attached to schools, living groups or sororities. Reuss, pp. 70–75, reports texts from Ohio State and Arkansas Universities dated to the 1930's, and cites references to underground song collections. In the midwest, he reports, it is sung either to the gospel song, "We Shall Not Be Moved," or to "the familiar college tune known under many names, for example, 'Cheer, Cincinnati' . . ." As he gives it, that tune runs:

Reuss' fifth version of the song contains stanzas the editor has not found on the West Coast. (Block's is a Bloomington, Indiana, department store.)

257

And after school when we go to Block's,
We pick up bags of big woolly socks (oh, horse shit)
We like the way they tickle our box.
We are the Pi Phi girls.[1]
   Balls, Balls. Balls.

And on the days when we go to school,
We watch the teacher play pocket pool (oh, horse shit)
We like the way he handles his tool.
We are the Pi Phi girls.
   Balls. Balls!

Students at Caltech, according to *Songs of Raunch and Ill-Repute*, p. 9, had these. (P.C.C. is "Pasadena City College, two blocks away from Caltech, with plenty of WASP ingenues," according to the computer scientist who loaned the editor a copy of the collection.)

We go to collage [sic], t' collage go we,
We never lost our virginity,
We might have lost it, only they forced it.
We are from P.C.C.

We go to collage, don't we have pluck,
We never work, and we allways [sic] fuck.
Come on over, boys, you may be in luck.
We are from P.C.C.

The Caltech collection has a variant, "The Girls from Sidney," p. 29, in couplets. The first two run:

We are from Sidney, from Sidney are we.
We never lose our virginity. (Oh, bullshit)

We use the very best candles you see,
We are from Sidney we. (Balls, balls)

Jacques Vidicam, a Los Angeles hairdresser, learned another version from an English friend while serving at Fort Sam Houston, Texas, in 1964. Two stanzas he remembered:

We have a new girl; her name is Jane.
She only does it now and again,
And again and again and again and again.
We are from Rodeen School.

We have a new girl; her name is Flo.
We never thought that she'd ever go,
But she surprised the master by jacking him off faster
Than any other girl in school.

Another variant in the editor's collection contains these additional stanzas:

> And every evening at one o'clock,
> We watch the watchman piss off the dock.
> We like the way he handles his cock.
> We go to N.Y.U.

> If we go riding in a canoe,
> We like to take on more than one or two.
> Sometimes we take on the whole goddam crew.
> We go to N.Y.U.

Still another, lampooning the college sorority, has these:

> We are the Pi Phis, happy are we,
> Happy go lucky, bare-ass and free.
> We'd like to share our virginity.
> We are the Pi Phi girls.

> And every month when our time is due,
> We save the rags for you boys to chew.
> We like to save the flavor for you.
> We are the Pi Phi girls.

A handful of other versions of the song have been located. The Opies, *Lore and Language of School Children,* p. 355, have one from English school girls. Oscar Brand sings a variant on Volume III of his recorded collection (Audio Fidelity 1824) and on *Bawdy Songs Goes to College* (Audio Fidelity 1952). *Songs of Roving and Raking,* p. 116, has another.

The text and tune for the version used here were collected by a former UCLA student as sung at that school about 1961.

When I Was Young

D. K. Wilgus, a graduate of Ohio State University, noted this extended version of "When I Was Young" at his alma mater in the late 1930's:

> 'Twas at a dance I met him.
> He asked me for a dance.
> I knew he was a Lambda Chi
> By the way he wore his pants.

> His shoes were brightly polished,
> His hair was neatly combed,
> And when the dance was over,
> He asked to see me home.

As we were strolling homeward
I heard somebody say,
"There goes another Alpha Phi
Being led astray."

'Twas in my father's hallway
That I was led astray.
'Twas in my mother's bedroom
That I was made to lay.

Now listen all my children,
Listen to my plea,
Don't ever let a Lambda Chi
Get an inch above your knee.

For if you do he'll hold you
And promise to be true,
And when he's got your cherry,
He'll say, "To hell with you."

Wilgus' college variant is close to a seven-stanza version from naval currency collected in 1926 and numbered 482 in the Robert W. Gordon Collection of American Folk Songs, University of Oregon. The Gordon text, forwarded by J. Barre Toelken, probably dates from the First World War; how much older this redaction of "Bell Bottom Trousers" may be is debatable.

The version used here was collected by Dale Koby in Northern California and is used with his permission.

Sandburg, p. 219, has a three-stanza fragment to a set of the "Goodnight Irene" tune family. His melody is probably more familiar now as the vehicle for James Stevens' "The Frozen Logger." Reuss, pp. 46 ff., has an extended discussion of the frequent appearance of the fateful warning in ribald songlore.

The melody here is that usually associated with the American folk song known variously as "Johnson's Old Gray Mule" or "Simon Slick."

The Winnipeg Whore

This version is conflated from texts in the Burson collection (the first stanza only) and one as sung to the editor in Los Angeles in 1964 by bookseller and friend Ray Fisher.

The melody, "Reuben, Reuben," was probably first borrowed by woodsmen from East Coast fishermen who themselves used it for other bawdy songs. (See the endnote for "Caviar Comes from Virgin Sturgeon," *supra.*)

Brand, pp. 60–61; *Songs of Raunch and Ill-Repute,* p. 21; and *Songs of Roving and Raking,* p. 115, have variants of "The Winnipeg Whore" in which the girl lifts the narrator's watch and wallet. They conclude:

> She was fiddling; I was diddling,
> Didn't know what 'twas all about,
> Till I missed my watch and wallet,
> Christ almighty, I found out.
>
> Up jumped the whores and sons of bitches,
> Must have been a score or more.
> You'd have laughed to cream your britches
> To see my ass fly out the door.

While this version is more satisfying as a narrative, apparently a stanza is missing —one which would more fully explain why the singer-narrator is flying out the door. One may surmise that in a missing (?) stanza, he protested his losses and was threatened by the company assembled. Such jackrolling was not infrequent in the less-reputable whorehouses serving frontier and logging clienteles.

The Woodpecker's Hole

The record of this song is certainly incomplete. Hugill, p. 424, gives a sailors' version; Reuss, pp. 258–260, has a text, like that used here, from Carnegie Tech ultimately. Reuss also notes that Randolph had the song from the Ozarks, and cites various manuscript appearances.

After that, there is seemingly nothing in print, yet the song is widely sung in children's summer camps in the Los Angeles area with "ear" substituting for "hole."

Why a woodpecker? In Randolph, the subject is a "peckerwood," a local name for what is known elsewhere as "white trash" or "redneck." But it may be that this inane effort is descended from a rhyme culled by Reuss from a *circa* 1890 ephemeral publication called *The Stag Party:*

> A woodpecker flew to the school-house yard,
> And he pecked and he pecked for his pecker was hard.
> Then the woodpecker flew to the school-house door,
> And he pecked and he pecked till his pecker was sore.
> After which he flew back to the yard again,
> And the woodpecker's pecker got over its pain.

In this version, the woodpecker's apparatus provides a play-on-words, lacking in "The Woodpecker's Hole."

The variant used here was gathered by Burson from his Carnegie Tech informant in Los Angeles in 1960.

"The Woodpecker's Hole" echoes in the World War I mock sung to the bugle call, "Reveille," as included in the Robert W. Gordon Collection of American Folk Song, University of Oregon (No. 150) and sent to the editor by J. Barre Toelken:

> There's a sailor in the grass with a soldier on his ass.
> Take it out, take it out, take it out, take it out.

The Yellow Rose of Taegu

The editor obtained a mimeographed copy of this song in Sendai, Japan, in 1953 while serving in the U.S. Army there.

A version sung by troops in the China-Burma-India theater during World War II, probably expurgated, is in William R. Peers and Dean Brelis, *Behind the Burma Road* (New York, c. 1963), p. 152.

The original song was published by Firth, Pond and Co., credited vaguely to "J.K." in the late 1850's, according to Spaeth, *A History of Popular Music in America* (New York, 1948), p. 135.

Notes

1. 237 F. 2d 796. This case was eventually to be appealed to the United States Supreme Court which used it as a vehicle to formulate a new test of obscenity —one which the justices expected would lead to a more mature evaluation of sex in the arts.

2. Bronson, II, p. 15, in the headnote to "The Carnal and the Crane" (Child 55). Like Bronson, the present editor has been unable to locate anything particularly obscene in the music itself, but others might. After all, Emile Laurent and Paul Nagour could assure their readers: "Indeed lovers of Wagnerian music confess to a sexual exaltation which appears but rarely in the works of other composers. . . . [I]t would require too technical a description here in explanation of its manifold eroticism. The reader is advised to closely analyze his sensations at the next Wagnerian recital he attends and to examine for himself the sexual fundament of the associations aroused in him by the music." *Magica Sexualis,* reprint edition (North Hollywood, Calif., 1966), p. 205. Their necromancy is no worse than that of the medieval clerics who considered the major scale the *modus lascivus,* one capable of arousing lustful inspiration, and therefore one to be avoided.

3. It is this same humor which removes the bawdy song from the prurient. The immodest ballad has only one overt function, that of entertainment. Titillation is incompatible with humor; the man doubled over in belly-aching laughter is not one intent upon copulation.

4. These are numbers LXXVI, CXLVI, and CCLII in *A Collection of Epigrams* (London: J. Walthoe, 1735), a copy of which is in the William Andrews Clark Memorial Library, Los Angeles. They are reprinted with other epigrams in the editor's anthology, *The Fifteen Plagues of Maidenhead* (North Hollywood, Calif., 1966), pp. 50 ff.

5. The statutes are collected in *Roth* v. *U.S.*, 354 U.S. 483–84, n. 12, 13. Most states have considerably expanded the coverage of these laws. California's Penal Code, Section 311.6, even goes so far as to proscribe songs such as those in this collection: "Every person who knowingly sings or speaks any obscene song, ballad, or other words in any public place is guilty of a misdemeanor."

6. Stanzas 12 through 16 from "Little Mathy Groves" as given by H. M. Belden, *Ballads and Songs Collected by the Missouri Folklore Society* (Columbia, Mo., 1940), p. 58. David J. Winslow reports a seven-year-old Pennsylvania girl thought "there was some impropriety in saying the word 'girdle'" in this rhyme: "In nineteen-forty-four/My mother went to war;/Her girdle snapped/And killed the Japs,/And that was the end of the war." "An Annotated Collection of Children's Lore," *Keystone Folklore Quarterly*, XI (1966), p. 160.

7. Stan Hugill, *Shanties from the Seven Seas* (London, 1961), p. 508.

8. *More Traditional Ballads of Virginia* (Chapel Hill, North Carolina, 1960), p. 301. Davis adds: "Perhaps the indelicacy or obscenity of many versions has reduced the number of texts that reach collectors, certainly the number of published texts. Since some of these more free-spoken texts and their tunes may be among the best ballad versions, there is need of a serious scholarly project which will reduce such squeamishness to a minimum." Thirty-two years earlier, Davis had made the same observation, calling the ballad "one of the last strongholds of ribaldry." Davis' earlier remarks are cited in D. K. Wilgus, *Anglo-American Folksong Scholarship Since 1898* (New Brunswick, N.J., 1959), p. 238.

9. *Index Librorum Prohibitorum* (London: Privately printed, 1877; New York, 1962), pp. xix-xxv. The ambivalent Ashbee published this first of three bibliographies under the bawdy pun-name, Pisanus Fraxi.

10. See Roger D. Abrahams, *Deep Down in the Jungle* (Hatboro, Pa., 1964). In a letter to the editor, Abrahams has called attention to the collecting activities of "students of Scottish songs including those at work at the School of Scottish Study," Kenneth S. Goldstein, Arthur Argo, and "too many others to count." The fact remains that little has been published and only Abrahams' own work is a systematic survey. From the first, Continental folklorists have been far more open in dealing with erotic materials, though no less ethnocentric. See, for examples, *Anthropophyteia* and *Kryptadia*, journals devoted to the erotic, but very scarce, copies of which are in UCLA's Department of Special Collections; and Aleksandr N. Afanasyev's *Stories from the Folk-lore of Russia* (Paris: Charles Carrington, 1897) reprinted as *Ribald Russian Classics* (Los Angeles, 1966).

11. Kenneth S. Goldstein pointed this out in a conversation with the editor in 1960. Goldstein specifically included children's lore in his typing of the "pure" oral tradition, a conclusion which the editor's experience does not wholly support. See Nancy C. Leventhal and Ed Cray, "Depth Collecting from a Sixth Grade Class," *Western Folklore*, XXII (1963), pp. 231 ff.; and see Marilyn Eisenberg Herzog's collecting reported in "The Absurd Elephant: a Recent Riddle Fad," *ibid.*, XXVI (1967), pp. 27 ff.

12. See Farmer's five-volume *Merry Songs and Ballads* (1895–1897), issued

263

in some editions with the binder's title on the spine as *National Ballads and Songs*. Probably the most intellectually honest of all was F. J. Furnival, co-editor with J. W. Hales and others of the *Percy Folio Manuscript*. Furnival insisted upon publishing all the songs in the manuscript; his co-editors were unsympathetic. Only Furnival's name appeared on the addendum volume, Percy Folio M.S., *Supplement: Loose and Humorous Songs* (The Ballad Society, 1867). Legman, *The Horn Book*, p. 367, lists similar Scots publications. Sigurd V. Hustvedt, *Ballad Books and Ballad Men* (Cambridge, Mass., 1930) tells something of the history and rivalries of the various ballad editors.

13. After working through "three or four thousand texts of several hundred songs in the Indiana University Folklore Archives and elsewhere," Richard A. Reuss concluded that between 40 and 60 percent of traditional college songlore might be classified as bawdy. "An Annotated Field Collection of Songs from the American College Student Oral Tradition," unpublished M.A. thesis, Indiana University, 1965, p. 5, n. 8.

14. *Motif-Index of Folk-Literature,* Revised and Enlarged Edition (Bloomington, Indiana, 1955), pp. 16–17. Thompson's reluctance to include the ribald is particularly curious in that his motif-index, of course, does not reprint the tales themselves, but simply catalogues the component elements.

15. Donal O'Sullivan notes that "the pitiful theme of girls led astray and betrayed, being unhappily a commonplace of rural life everywhere, is naturally represented in folk song. So far as Ireland is concerned, such songs are found more frequently in manuscripts than in printed books, for reasons that may be readily understood; but it would be wrong to conclude from this (as has sometimes been done) that the subject is avoided by folk singers. . . . Anyone who has noted Irish Gaelic folk songs from oral tradition must be aware that this statement is hardly borne out by experience." *Songs of the Irish* (Dublin, 1960), p. 162.

16. Kenneth S. Goldstein, *A Guide for Field Workers in Folklore* (Hatboro, Pa., 1964), pp. 150–1.

17. As collected by Mrs. Nancy Leventhal from a 12-year-old boy in Hawthorne, California, in 1959.

18. *Deep Down in the Jungle,* p. 239. Martha Wolfenstein discusses the story in *Children's Humor* (Glencoe, Ill., 1954), pp. 63–91.

19. *Ribald Russian Classics,* p. 57. See also Legman, *The Horn Book,* pp. 182–83.

20. In commenting on the function of children's lore, the editor is subsuming certain observations of Roger D. Abrahams who took the manuscript here to heavy task.

21. In a little-noted, provocative article, William Hugh Jansen has termed this "esoteric" folklore. See "The Esoteric–Exoteric Factor in Folklore," *Fabula,* II (1959), pp. 205 ff. Women who learn bawdy songs use them in closed circles also—college sororities and living groups are great trading grounds, but here, too, there is the protection of the secure group. In mixed groups, the songs are sung when the women have been accepted, on the male's terms, as "broadminded," or "modern," or "sophisicated." Steven Marcus, *The Other Victorians* (New York, 1966), p. 113, notes "that women's idea of their own sexuality (at least in a majority of cultures) is historically a response to what men want and demand that sexuality to be, and that in general women are content to accept whatever model of their own sexuality men offer to and demand of them." Bawdy songs, reflecting a strongly masculine viewpoint, can be said to serve as reinforcement for the role women are expected to play sexually.

22. *Beyond Laughter* (New York, 1957), p. 110. See also Sigmund Freud, *Wit and Its Relation to the Unconscious,* as translated by A. A. Brill, and printed in *The Basic Writings of Sigmund Freud,* A. A. Brill, ed. (New York, 1938), pp. 728–42.

23. *Neurotica,* No. 9 (1951), pp. 49 ff.

24. Grotjahn, *op. cit.,* p. 60, sums this: "Where the man discovered love through sex, the woman discovered sex through love."

25. As collected by Dale Koby in Northern California in 1961. The tune is "The Chandler's Wife."

26. See A. S. Limouze, "The Hump Song," *Journal of American Folklore,* LXIII (1950), p. 463; Edward Ives, *Larry Gorman, the Man Who Made the Songs* (Bloomington, Ind., 1964), *passim.* Gorman, like Robert Burns before him, carefully fashioned new lyrics to traditional folk tunes, but these melodies were so widely known in their communities that they served the same function as do today's popular songs.

27. "Songs of the Western Miners," *California Folklore Quarterly,* I (1942), pp. 216 ff.; Hugh Anderson, *Colonial Ballads* (Victoria, 1955), p. 147; Guy and Candie Carawan, *We Shall Overcome* (New York, 1963), *passim.*

28. This Gresham's Law of oral tradition is demonstrated in the editor's study of the texts of "Barbara Allen in America: Cheap Print and Reprint," in *Folklore International,* D. K. Wilgus, ed. (Hatboro, Pa., 1967), pp. 41 ff. Reuss, *op. cit.;* independently has made similar observations, pp. 11 ff.

29. David M. Pendergast and Clement W. Meighan amply demonstrate that present day Piaute Indians retain in their myths considerable historical fact about the culture of long-vanished Puebloid peoples who lived in Southern Utah between 800 and 1150 A.D. See their article, "Folk Traditions as Historical Fact: A Piaute Example," in the *Journal of American Folklore,* LXXII (1959), pp. 128 ff.; Lord Raglan's rejoinder in the following volume, pp. 58–59; and Meighan's rebuttal, *ibid.,* pp. 59–60. Raglan's theory, most succinctly stated in *The Hero,* is "firstly that the alleged historical facts embodied in local tradition are not facts at all, and secondly that the real facts of history are never

preserved by local tradition."

30. See his "Prescriptive and Descriptive Music Writing," *The Musical Quarterly,* XLIV (1958), pp. 184–195.

31. In traditional ballad-singing, even though the narration is seemingly all-important, singers are, or were, conscious of their vocal performance. Neighbors did judge to some degree a ballad singer's singing style—his ability to project the story—if not his vocal quality. Moreover, with the introduction of musical instruments and the parallel diminution of *a capella* singing, the words lost some of their significance. Ultimately, this trend led to a reversal of values: With the creation of the string band in the so-called "hillbilly" or "Nashville" tradition, occasional verses were used only to break up virtuoso instrumental performances. Ballad singing, that is, verbally-oriented music, has waned at the same time. The popular music of the mid-1960's exhibits a similar lack of verbal orientation. It is not infrequently difficult, even impossible, to discern the recorded texts of songs sung by popular music performers who are, seemingly, more interested in a total "sound"; their audiences apparently tune out the words, or rely upon fragments of the poem for whatever *textual* satisfaction they will derive. The ultimate comes with the performances of such phenomenally popular groups as the Beatles; it is impossible for a person of normal acuity to pick out the music in the flood of ecstatic female exhultations. For the screaming girls, it is doubtful if such performances have any *musical* value whatsoever, no matter how worthy they may be as cathartic exercises.

32. These brief notes on the description of bawdy song as a music form were shaped largely by conversations with Charles Seeger and three of his crucial articles: "On the Moods of a Music-Logic," *Journal of the American Musicological Society,* XIII (1960), pp. 224 ff.; "Systematic Musicology—Viewpoints, Orientations and Methods," *ibid.,* IV (1951), pp. 204 ff.; and "Preface to the Description of a Music," a report read to the International Society for Musical Research, Fifth Congress, Utrecht, July, 1952.

Bibliography of Frequently Cited Works

Roger D. Abrahams, *Deep Down in the Jungle* (Hatboro, Pa., 1964).

Hugh Anderson, *Colonial Ballads* (Victoria, 1955).

H. M. Belden, *Ballads and Songs Collected by the Missouri Folk-Lore Society*, 2nd ed. (Columbia, Mo., 1955).

Oscar Brand, *Bawdy Songs and Backroom Ballads* (New York, 1960).

Bertrand Harris Bronson, *The Traditional Tunes of the Child Ballads*, Vols. I, II, III (Princeton, N.J., 1959, 1962, 1966).

The Frank C. Brown Collection of North Carolina Folklore, Vols. II and III, edited by H. M. Belden and A. P. Hudson (Durham, No. Car., 1952); Vols. IV and V, edited by Jan P. Schinhan (Durham, 1962).

Robert Burns, *The Merry Muses of Caledonia* (The Auk Society, Edinburgh, 1959).

Norman Cazden, *The Abelard Folk Song Book* (New York, c. 1958).

William Chappell, *Old English Popular Music*, reprint edition (New York, 1961).

———, *Popular Music of the Olden Time*, reprint edition (New York, 1965).

F. J. Child, *The English and Scottish Popular Ballads*, reprint edition (New York, 1965).

Joanna C. Colcord, *Songs of American Sailormen* (New York, 1938).

Ed Cray, *The Anthology of Restoration Erotic Poetry* (North Hollywood, Calif., 1965).

Margaret Dean-Smith, *A Guide to English Folk Song Collections* (Liverpool, 1954).

Edward Arthur Dolph, *Sound Off*, rev. ed. (New York, 1942).

Thomas D'Urfey, *Wit and Mirth: or Pills to Purge Melancholy*, 6 vols. in 3, reprint edition (New York, 1959).

Henry S. Farmer, *Merry Songs and Ballads*, 5 vols. (London [?], 1895–97).

Edith Fowke, *Traditional Singers and Songs from Ontario* (Hatboro, Pa., 1965).

James J. Fuld, *The Book of World-Famous Music* (New York, 1966).

Frederick J. Furnivall, *Bishop Percy's Folio Manuscript, Supplement: Loose and Humorous Songs* (London, 1867).

Patrick Galvin, *Irish Songs of Resistance* (New York, n.d.).

John Greenway, *American Folksongs of Protest* (Philadelphia, 1953).

Gavin Grieg, *Folk-Song in Buchan and Folk-Song of the North-East*, reprint edition (Hatboro, Pa., 1963).

Frederick Pease Harlow, *Chanteying Aboard American Ships* (Barre, Mass., 1962).

Lester Hubbard, *Ballads and Songs from Utah* (Salt Lake City, 1961).

Arthur Palmer Hudson, *Folk Songs of Mississippi* (Chapel Hill, No. Car., 1936).

Stan Hugill, *Shanties from the Seven Seas* (London and New York, 1961).

G. Malcolm Laws, Jr., *American Balladry from British Broadsides* (Philadelphia, 1957).

———, *Native American Balladry* (Philadelphia, 1951).

Clifford Leach, ed., *Bottoms Up!* (New York, 1933).

Gershon Legman, *The Horn Book* (New York, 1964).

———, *The Limerick* (Paris, 1953); also reprint edition (San Diego, 1967).

[Logue, Christopher], *Count Palmiro Vicarion's Book of Bawdy Ballads* (Paris, 1956).

Alan Lomax, *Folk Songs of North America* (New York, 1960).

Lionel Long and Graham Jenkin, *Favorite Australian Bush Songs* (Adelaide, 1964).

Frank Lynn, *Songs for Singing* (San Francisco, 1961).

———, *Songs for Swingin' Housemothers*, new enlarged edition (San Francisco, 1963).

George Milburn, *The Hobo's Hornbook* (New York, 1930).

Colm O Lochlainn, *Irish Street Ballads* (Dublin, 1939).

Francis O'Neill, *The Dance Music of Ireland* (Chicago, 1907).

———, *The Music of Ireland* (Chicago, 1903).

Iona and Peter Opie, *The Lore and Language of Schoolchildren* (London, 1959).

Vivian de Sola Pinto and Allan Rodway, *The Common Muse* (London, 1957).

Vance Randolph, *Ozark Folksongs,* 4 vols. (Columbia, Mo., 1946–50).

Richard A. Reuss, "An Annotated Field Collection of Songs from the American College Student Oral Tradition," unpublished M.A. thesis, Indiana University, 1965.

Carl Sandburg, *The American Songbag* (New York, 1927).

Frank Shay, *American Sea Songs and Chanteys* (New York, 1948).

Irwin Silber, *Songs of the Civil War* (New York, 1960).

Claude M. Simpson, *The British Broadside Ballad and Its Music* (New Brunswick, N.J., 1966).

"Songs of Raunch and Ill-Repute," mimeographed and privately circulated at Ricketts House, California Institute of Technology, Pasadena, Calif., circa 1960.

Songs of Roving and Raking, dittographed and privately circulated at the University of Illinois, circa 1961, and credited by Reuss, *supra.*, p. 345, to John Walsh.

Sigmund Spaeth, *Read 'Em and Weep* (New York, 1926).

Stories from the Folk-lore of Russia, edited by Aleksandr Afanasyev (Paris, 1897); reprinted with a new introduction by Milton Van Sickle as *Ribald Russian Classics* (Los Angeles, 1966).

The Unexpurgated Folk Songs of Men, edited by Mack McCormick (International Blues Record Club, Berkeley, Calif., 1964).

William Wallrich, *Air Force Airs* (New York, 1957).

267

Index

Titles placed within quotation marks are those which the editor has assigned. Italicized entries indicate texts and/or tunes.

272